LA METTRIE'S
L'HOMME MACHINE
A STUDY IN THE ORIGINS OF AN IDEA

LA METTRIE'S
L'HOMME MACHINE

A STUDY IN THE ORIGINS
OF AN IDEA

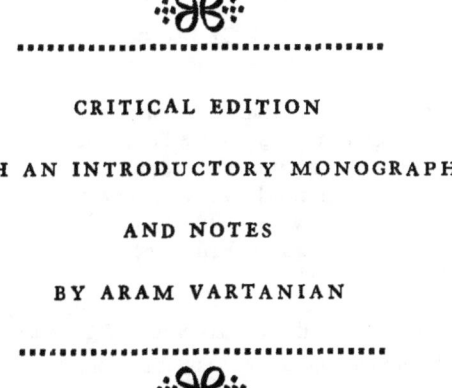

CRITICAL EDITION

WITH AN INTRODUCTORY MONOGRAPH

AND NOTES

BY ARAM VARTANIAN

PRINCETON, NEW JERSEY
PRINCETON UNIVERSITY PRESS

1960

Copyright © 1960 by Princeton University Press

All Rights Reserved

L.C. Card 60-5759

Publication of this book
has been aided by the Ford Foundation
program to support publication,
through university presses,
of works in the humanities
and social sciences.

Printed in the United States of America by
Princeton University Press, Princeton, New Jersey

CONTENTS

I.	Biographical Sketch of La Mettrie	1
II.	Interpretation of *l'Homme machine*	13
III.	The Development of La Mettrie's Thought	40
IV.	The Historical Background of *l'Homme machine*	57
V.	The Critical Reaction of La Mettrie's Contemporaries	95
VI.	*L'Homme machine* since 1748	114
	A Note on the Text	137

L'Homme machine	139
Notes	199
Bibliography	251
Index	259

LA METTRIE'S

L'HOMME MACHINE

A STUDY IN THE ORIGINS OF AN IDEA

CHAPTER I

BIOGRAPHICAL SKETCH OF LA METTRIE

THE publication late in 1747 of *l'Homme machine* marked the climax not only of La Mettrie's thought but of his fortunes as well, for it was not unusual that the pattern of a philosophe's life should reflect intimately the history of his mind. Compelled to leave Holland, where he was then residing, because of the outspoken materialism of the book, and unable to return to France owing to prior offenses against the censorship there, La Mettrie found refuge in a desperate hour at the court of Frederick the Great of Prussia. Having at last won, through the Philosopher-King's favor, both security from his many enemies and ample leisure to think and write, he had the bad luck to perish only a few years later as the result of what might be called a gastronomic accident.

For someone who on the appearance of *l'Homme machine* was to achieve an intellectual notoriety second to none in Europe, almost the whole of La Mettrie's previous existence had been so strangely inconspicuous that the main source of information about it remains the brief *Eloge* composed on the occasion of his death by Frederick II. The biographical account given therein has in recent years been rectified and augmented at various points by the painstaking researches of M. Pierre Lemée.[1] But despite all the available facts, our knowledge of La Mettrie's life and personality continues to be elusive and full of gaps, particularly since his correspondence has apparently been lost.

Julien Offray de La Mettrie was born at Saint-Malo, in Brittany, on December 19, 1709, the son of a well-to-do merchant in the textile trade. His schooling in the humanities took place at the provincial *collèges* of Coutances and Caen, where he gave early proof of certain tastes and abilities about which Frederick remarks: "Il aimait passionnément la Poésie et les Belles-Lettres . . . [et]

[1] *J. O. de La Mettrie, médecin, philosophe, polémiste; sa vie, son oeuvre*, 1954.

remporta tous les prix de l'éloquence. Il était né orateur." This special talent of his was still in evidence, long afterward, in *l'Homme machine.*

Having gone next to the Collège du Plessis in Paris, La Mettrie's vocational interests appear to have turned for a time toward the Church, and, according to Frederick again, "il devint 'janséniste,' et composa un livre qui eut vogue dans le parti." Since all trace of it has vanished, no one will ever have the pleasure of knowing how a Jansenistic treatise by La Mettrie reads. This is a pity, for it is strongly to be suspected that this phase of his youth had an important influence on the course of his subsequent development. In the "physiologic predestination" of the human machine, there is an echo, however much transformed, of the sense of inner compulsion that typifies Jansenist thought. La Mettrie eventually surmounted that state of mind, in part at least, by a process of intellectual objectification, which culminated both logically and psychologically in the *homme machine* doctrine. Similarly, in his defiant glorification of the sensual, as in his revolt against the tyranny of remorse, it seems natural enough to perceive a "reaction formation" on the part of the middle-aged philosopher against the adolescent tendencies that had led him to Jansenism. It is unfortunate, however, that these comments, based on the meager information in the *Eloge*, can be offered as no more than plausible conjectures.

In 1725 La Mettrie entered the famous Collège d'Harcourt to study philosophy and natural science. He must have graduated as a *bachelier* around 1727—at about the time, incidentally, when Diderot, whose ideas were one day closely to parallel his own, was entering the same establishment. In view of La Mettrie's later admission of indebtedness to Cartesian thought for the man-machine thesis, it is worth mentioning that the Collège d'Harcourt, during the years he studied there, was pioneering the introduction of Descartes, banned until then from the schools, into its curriculum.

In the final choice of a career, the young man was greatly influenced by the advice and example of François-Joseph Hunauld, a native of Saint-Malo and friend of the La Mettrie family, who had already made a name for himself in medicine, and was soon to occupy the chair of anatomy at the Jardin du Roi. For about five years La Mettrie was a student at the Faculté de médecine of Paris, and enjoyed in addition the mentorship of Hunauld. At the beginning of 1733, however, he betook himself to the Medical Faculty of Rheims for the purpose of obtaining the doctor's degree, a practice then common for those desiring to avoid the expensive formalities that were customary in Paris. La Mettrie was received as a *bachelier en médecine* at Rheims on March 2, 1733, and, with a dispatch that explains the popularity of its Medical School, was raised to the dignity of doctor on May 29 of the same year.

All too conscious of the shortcomings of medical education in France, La Mettrie went next to study under the renowned Boerhaave, at what was considered to be the finest Faculty of Medicine in Europe—that of Leyden. The time spent there, although brief, was to shape his destiny. In the years immediately following, La Mettrie settled down to professional practice in the Saint-Malo region. The nature of his daily activities can be pieced together in some detail from his *Observations de médecine pratique* (1743), a work that shows to advantage the clinical perspicacity and experimental leanings of the ambitious country doctor. On November 14, 1739, La Mettrie married the widow Marie-Louise Droneau. His domestic life, owing to incompatibilities of temperament, soon proved to be unhappy, and this no doubt contributed to his decision before long to embark on a course of lonely and restless wanderings. Two children were born of the marriage: a daughter in 1741, and in 1745 a son who died in infancy.

Despite the burden of his routine duties at Saint-Malo, La Mettrie undertook the huge and laudable task of disseminating in France the works and theories of Boerhaave. The principal writings of the latter which were translated or adapted by him during this period appeared under the titles: *Système de M. Boerhaave sur les maladies vénériennes* (1735); *Aphorismes sur la connaissance et la cure des maladies* (1738); *Traité de la matière médicale* (1739); *Les Institutions de Médecine* (1739-40); and *Abrégé de la Théorie chimique* (1741). Aside from these labors, La Mettrie also published two original works, the *Traité du Vertige* (1737), which was not without merit, and a *Nouveau Traité des maladies vénéri-*

ennes (1739), which added little to either the subject or the author's reputation.

Toward the end of 1742, having left his family behind, La Mettrie went to Paris, doubtless with the aim of seeking out fortune.[2] The somewhat cryptic remark by Frederick II that La Mettrie, in taking this step, was "attiré par la mort de Hunauld" has been understood to mean that he had hopes of inheriting a fair portion of his mentor's choice clientele. If this was indeed his plan, it could not have succeeded very well, for we next find him installed in the post of personal physician to the Duc de Grammont (a by no means humiliating substitute!), and shortly thereafter he became the medical officer of the Gardes Françaises regiment, of which his patron was the colonel. In this capacity, La Mettrie had the opportunity to broaden and diversify his professional experience during the War of the Austrian Succession. He took part in the battle of Dettingen (June 27, 1743), the siege of Freiburg (Autumn 1744), and in the slaughterous contest at Fontenoy (May 11, 1745). The death of Grammont on the last-named occasion came as a keen loss to La Mettrie, who commented in his ingenuous way: "Chez ce Seigneur, je voyois familièrement ce qu'il y avoit de plus grand à la Cour & à la Ville; & sans doute la plus belle fortune m'attendait à Paris, pour ne rien dire du plaisir d'être attaché à un homme poli, doux, affable."[3] But what he had seen in the course of the war was to leave its imprint in the form not only of a deep aversion to human bloodshed but also of numerous observations of medical interest in *l'Homme machine* and in his other writings.

During a large part of the war years La Mettrie was actually in Paris—probably from the summer of 1743 until the following spring, and again in the early months of 1745. It is regrettable that very little is known about his frequentations there. We may reasonably suppose with M. Lemée that he became acquainted with Fontenelle through the latter's friend and future biographer, abbé Trublet, who was a fellow *malouin*. He was unquestionably in

---

[2] This must have been soon after Hunauld's death in Saint-Malo on the 15th of December, 1742. It can be inferred from a remark by La Mettrie (*l'Ouvrage de Pénélope; ou Machiavel en médecine*, Berlin, 1748-50, III, 254) that he was still in Saint-Malo during the early part of that month.

[3] *ibid.*, III, 271.

close touch with Maupertuis, another native of Saint-Malo, whom he favored in 1745 with an "épître dédicatoire" at the head of his *Histoire naturelle de l'âme*. Through Maupertuis La Mettrie met the Marquise du Châtelet, with whom he soon adopted the familiar tone of the "Lettre critique" addressed to her in the 1747 edition of the same work. His relations with "la belle Emilie" might, moreover, have proved no less ardent for having been somewhat transitory, if, as it seems likely, she was the mysterious "Madame la Marquise de ***" to whom La Mettrie gratefully dedicated *La Volupté* (1745), for what he tells us was that lady's personal contribution to the subject matter of the book. There is an additional reason for placing him in the honorable ranks of Mme du Châtelet's lovers: in the "Lettre critique" that he wrote to her, La Mettrie allowed himself to make what is obviously an intimate allusion veiled by an amusing word-play: "Et quel rapport y a-t-il entre la faculté de sentir, qui est purement passible, & le mouvement toujours actif? Je vous avoue, Madame, que je saisirois avec plaisir l'occasion d'avoir avec vous des Entretiens Métaphysiques sur ce sujet."

It was at the siege of Freiburg, as Frederick relates, that La Mettrie succumbed to the oft-cited "fièvre chaude," in the course of which, thanks to a gift for self-observation, he seized upon the crucial idea that was developed soon afterward in the *Histoire naturelle de l'âme*: "Il crut s'apercevoir que la faculté de penser n'était qu'une suite de l'organisation de la machine, et que le dérangement des ressorts influait considérablement sur cette partie de nous-même, que les métaphysiciens appellent l'âme." This work, his first venture in philosophy, brought immediate reprisals from the orthodox-minded, which cost him his position with the Gardes Françaises. Eventually a decree of the Parlement of Paris, dated July 9, 1746, condemned it to the flames. But it may be taken as a proof of La Mettrie's professional competence that, the zeal of his enemies turning to his profit, he was next appointed to the more important post of "Médecin-Inspecteur des Hôpitaux des Armées en campagne," which put him in charge of the military hospitals of Lille, Ghent, Brussels, Antwerp, and Worms.

As if scandalizing the pious were not serious enough, La Mettrie now gave vent to his indignant feelings about the self-seeking ineptitude which, in the medical world of the eighteenth century, seemed to typify the French practitioners in particular. The *Politique du Médecin de Machiavel*, appearing in 1746, aptly ridiculed many of the bigwigs of medicine in France, with the expected result that the combined animosity of the two powerful groups of clerics and doctors soon obliged its author to look to his safety. In August or September of the same year, La Mettrie fled across the border into Holland. It was his own opinion that this step had been necessitated more by the enmity of the doctors than by that of the Church.[4] There seems to have been no official decree of arrest or exile made out formally against him; but La Mettrie, no doubt well aware of the devious methods of French justice at the time, was unwilling to take any chances: "Je me suis expatrié, quand j'ai vu que je courrois risque d'être arrêté." Once in Holland, he was drawn irresistibly to Leyden, so rich in memories of student days: "Je m'exilai par goût au lieu qui me forma."[5] But La Mettrie was not a man who could long cower under persecution, or let a challenge go unanswered. With a boldness of spirit which was surely foolhardy under the circumstances, and which was rarely to find its equal among his fellow philosophes, he struck back zestfully against both the charlatans and the bigots who had driven him from his native land. During 1747 La Mettrie composed against the former the ironic comedy, *La Faculté vengée*, and against the latter, *l'Homme machine*.

It has been conjectured that the writing of *l'Homme machine* was completed sometime in August 1747,[6] and this date, while not ascertainable, is probable enough. The book itself must have started to circulate by November or early December. That La Mettrie had written it hastily in a surge of enthusiasm can be inferred as much from its impulsive style and rambling structure as from the many inaccurate references for which he had trusted to memory despite the closeness of the Leyden library. The work was brought out by Elie Luzac, a young Leyden publisher of French

[4] "Pouvoient-ils ne pas réussir à venger leur Amour propre irrité, en intéressant dans la dispute un Dieu de Paix?" and: "La fureur des Médecins démasqués me mit dans la triste nécessité d'abandonner les hopitaux militaires que le Ministère m'avoit confiés" (*ibid.*, III, 204, 371).

[5] *ibid.*, I, ii.

[6] Ernst Bergmann, *Die Satiren des Herrn Maschine*, Leipzig, 1913, p. 14.

Protestant background, who, while he did not personally share its materialist point of view, was staunchly devoted to the ideals of intellectual liberty and a free press. This time La Mettrie had made an earnest attempt to preserve his anonymity, so that it is not impossible that Luzac was telling the truth when, in the "Avertissement de l'Imprimeur" appended to the text, he professed ignorance of the author's name.

The appearance of *l'Homme machine* met with angry protests from all classes of "right-thinking" people. The thousands of pages of debate and abuse that were to be printed as a result, will be dealt with in another chapter. In the meanwhile, the watch dogs of orthodoxy lost no time in baring their teeth, and on this grave occasion (as Frederick puts it), "... calvinistes, catholiques et luthériens oublièrent ... que la consubstantiation, le libre arbitre, la messe des morts et l'infaillibilité du pape les divisaient." Luzac was summoned on December 18 before the Consistory of the Eglise Wallonne de Leyde and ordered (1) to deliver up all available copies of *l'Homme machine*, in order that these might be destroyed; (2) to reveal the identity of the author; and (3) to make apologies for having published the book, together with a solemn promise not to commit such an offense again.[7] Although Luzac complied with the first and third demands, he apparently refused to satisfy the second one; but whether he acted from a desire to protect the author or was actually unable to furnish his name cannot be said. His partial compliance, obtained by extralegal pressure, would not appear in any case to have bound him morally; for during 1748 Luzac surreptitiously placed in circulation enough copies of *l'Homme machine* to gratify the increasing curiosity of the reading public, until finally he deemed it wise to go abroad for a time. But when, probably sometime in January, the author of the book had been found out, La Mettrie was compelled to leave Holland immediately. He arrived in Berlin on February 7, 1748, in response to an invitation from Frederick the Great which, through the good offices of Maupertuis, he had received in time to escape the storm unleashed against him.

The nature of the negotiations that brought La Mettrie to Berlin has never been made clear, although the available documents per-

---

[7] Cf., P. Valkhoff, "Elie Luzac," *Neophilologus*, IV (1918), p. 13.

mit a reconstruction of the story in its main lines. Several months before the publication of *l'Homme machine*, La Mettrie's anxiety over the risk he was about to take must have led him to think seriously of preparing a sure refuge against possible disaster. What could have been more normal, in the event, than to turn for aid to Prussia, where his friend Maupertuis had just been given broad recruiting powers as President of the Berlin Academy by a monarch who made it a point of personal honor to rescue philosophers from theological persecution? It was no doubt with a full knowledge of these facts that La Mettrie instructed Luzac (as the latter states in his "Avertissement") to forward six copies of *l'Homme machine* to the Berlin address of the Marquis d'Argens, in order presumably that Frederick might judge for himself how worthy its author was, should the need arise, of being rescued. We know definitely from a letter of Frederick's dated November 19, 1747—in other words, long before the outbreak of the trouble in Holland—that Maupertuis had already broached to him the plan of bringing La Mettrie to Berlin, and that the King was very favorable to it, regarding the philosophe not only as a man of wit but also, because of the malevolence recently shown toward the *Histoire naturelle de l'âme*, as "la victime des théologiens et des sots."[8] Maupertuis was authorized in the same letter to make to La Mettrie whatever proposal he thought fit, which he apparently did without much delay. Finally, on January 7, 1748, Maupertuis writes to inform Frederick that he has received La Mettrie's grateful acceptance of the offer to come to Berlin.[9] The royal hand had reached out none too soon.

In Prussia La Mettrie's bold and irreverent tongue delighted the anticlerical taste of Frederick II, who came soon to feel a genuine affection, not common with him, for his new "acquisition." Before long, La Mettrie was on a footing of actual familiarity with the King, to the mixed reactions of surprise and envy of the group of French courtiers at Potsdam. Besides being elected to membership in the Royal Academy of Sciences, he was given the two posts of *lecteur* and *médecin ordinaire* to His Majesty. He naturally had his place in that brilliant circle of *beaux-esprits*, made up of Vol-

[8] L. A. de La Beaumelle, *Vie de Maupertuis*, Paris, 1865, p. 368.
[9] *ibid.*, p. 370.

taire, D'Argens, Maupertuis, Algarotti, and others, in whose company Frederick liked to charm away the cares of state during the dinner parties at Sans-Souci. It was in this setting that there gradually took form the image, passed down to posterity, of a "joyeux La Mettrie, le maître des jeux, des ris et des bons mots." But though he could be amusing, his habitual effrontery and tactlessness did not fail to excite, on occasion, a secret hostility even in those who remained outwardly his friends, such as Voltaire and D'Argens. This circumstance, while it caused him no special annoyance during his lifetime, proved later to be decidedly harmful to his historical position. For after his death La Mettrie was to have no loyal supporter, save Frederick alone, to challenge the gross misrepresentation of him by his many enemies as a wholly debauched and vicious immoralist.

Actually La Mettrie's was a far more complex, not to say enigmatic, personality than his contemporaries realized. What they mistook for his true physiognomy was in large part a caricature of his own making. In his life, as often enough in his writings, he showed a strong predilection for the well-elaborated hoax. La Mettrie took, in fact, considerable pains to confirm his detractors in the worst opinions they were disposed to hold of his character, with the perverse intention, it would seem, of justifying all the more fully his own feelings of contempt for their gullibility. He triumphed in the end by a private sense of superiority over all those who were so naïve or uncharitable as to take his posturings at face value. This was La Mettrie's preferred means of reprisal against a society that did its best to ostracize him because it did not agree with his ideas.

Behind the gaily impudent, sensual, irresponsible visage that La Mettrie turned like a Harlequin-mask toward the world, there were concealed impulses and feelings of a quite different nature. We suspect that he laughed so loudly and incessantly, not merely to disconcert his critics and to mock them, but also to check the melancholy that he felt welling up within himself. Being an astute psychologist, La Mettrie has left a good enough description of his own delicate manic-depressive equilibrium to enable us to interpret much of his behavior. The passage in question, amounting almost to an *apologia pro vita sua*, is sufficiently important to be quoted at length: "Qu'on ne me reproche donc plus d'avoir toujours vu belle & bonne compagnie, d'avoir été galant, homme de plaisir, de spectacles, car c'est à ces Ecoles que je me suis formé le goût. D'ailleurs souffrez cette réflexion. Entre la gaieté & la tristesse, qui n'a pas éprouvé combien est mince la barrière que la Nature y a mise? Elle n'a pas mieux séparé l'instinct & la raison. La bonne humeur peut donc déserter au moment qu'on s'y attend le moins; la raison même, qui a plus de poids, nous joue tous les jours ces tours-là; & tel qui a bien servi son Maître à diner, avant souper s'est allé jetter par la fenêtre, de peur d'être pris par les voleurs & pendu, comme je l'ai vu dans un chef d'office de Mr. le Vicomte du Chayla. Tout gay que je suis, même en exil, dans une solitude & un ennui mortel pour tout autre, je puis donc devenir triste, mélancolique, hypocondriaque. Autre conséquence, tandis que je suis en train d'en tirer, c'est que j'ai toujours eu la même facheuse faculté. Bref, j'ai craint qu'on ne dît un jour, *quantum mutatus ab illo!* Voilà la raison pour laquelle j'ai pris ma Medecine Prophylactique à l'Opéra, aux Concerts, à la Comédie, à table, au bal, & jusqu'aux Marionettes.... Ainsi on ne me dira point encore: *Medicè, cura te ipsum.* Peut-on mieux se guérir, que de s'empêcher d'être malade?"[10]

One wonders about the cause of the sadness in himself that La Mettrie tried so energetically and, on the whole, successfully to suppress by his somewhat forced pursuit of pleasure. Unfortunately too little is known of his early years to justify any positive answer. It may be imagined at most that as an adolescent he had been possessed of some sort of idealistic intransigence—the Jansenist episode being one of its manifestations—which, having yielded in time to the shabby reality of life, had left him with a deep sense of disillusionment and, no doubt, a secret remorse. This youthful rigorism remained, in fact, a pronounced trait of his adult personality despite all the affability and buffoonery that served to conceal or temper it. For a man supposedly given to ease and self-indulgence, La Mettrie displayed a puzzling wilfulness, not merely to say what he thought in the face of opposition, but to exasperate his enemies by a repeated defiance which brought him more than once to the brink of "martyrdom." This intransigent attitude is per-

[10] *L'Ouvrage de Pénélope*, II, 124-26.

haps best observed in his relationship to the medical profession. La Mettrie's persistent satirizing of the doctors (a literary genre in which he was unexcelled at the time) owed its impetus to such exacting standards of professional integrity and competence that he could not avoid excoriating, for one reason or another, almost every major figure in French medicine. Throughout these works, the accent of the embittered idealist is unmistakable. And although his contemporaries were content to see in them nothing but the outpourings of a slanderous delirium, the reader today who is informed about the general quality of medical practice in the eighteenth century, particularly in France, will not be likely to find fault with the author's candor.

Knowing La Mettrie's indocility of character, we are not amazed to learn that he soon tired of the rewards and entertainments of Frederick's court. "L'honneur d'approcher d'un Grand Roi," he explains, "n'empêche pas la triste idée que c'est avec son Maître qu'on est, quelque aimable qu'il soit; enfin une telle Dignité est semée de trop de pièges, dont mon Tempérament Anti-Courtisan ne me garantiroit peut-être pas. Nous autres Bretons, nous sommes véridiques, un peu durs pour la plupart.... A la Cour, il faut plus de complaisance & de flatterie, que de Philosophie; jusqu'ici je ne me suis appliqué qu'à cette dernière, qui a tiré mon âme de sa fange naturelle; & ce n'est point à 39 ans, qu'il faut commencer à apprendre à ramper."[11] It turned out, too, that after several years of exile La Mettrie felt the pangs of homesickness. He begged Voltaire to try to secure through influential friends permission for his return to France. The latter remarks about this: "Cet homme si gai, et qui passe pour rire de tout, pleure quelquefois comme un enfant d'être ici. . . . En vérité, il ne faut jurer de rien sur l'apparence."[12]

But amid the public pleasures and private sorrows of Potsdam, La Mettrie was as active intellectually as ever. During this brief interval he produced a number of philosophical works, among them: *l'Homme plante* (1748); *Discours sur le bonheur* (1748); *Les Animaux plus que machines* (1750); and *Le système d'Epicure* (1750). In the medical domain, he published a *Traité sur la Dys-*

[11] *ibid.*, III, 276-77.
[12] Voltaire, *Oeuvres complètes*, éd. Moland, Paris, 1877-83, XXXVII, 320.

senterie and a *Traité de l'Asthme* (both in 1750), and the best and longest of his satires on the sad state of French medicine: *l'Ouvrage de Pénélope, ou Machiavel en médecine* (1748-50). He dashed off, besides, a series of ironic pamphlets against some German critics of his ideas, with whom he had become embroiled in polemics mainly because of *l'Homme machine*.

On November 11, 1751, La Mettrie died unexpectedly in a manner that was to be no less a cause for scandal than his other doings. At the home of the French ambassador to Prussia, Lord Tyrconnel, whom he had recently cured of a troublesome ailment, La Mettrie consumed a prodigious amount of "pâté de faisan aux truffes," fell gravely ill, and died a few days later. He could hardly have gratified his enemies more handsomely than by this tragicomic finish, so curiously in keeping with the whole tenor of his life. Ascribed to the effects of gluttony, it was triumphantly hailed by the religious party as an act of divine vengeance, and cited as a practical refutation of the materialist philosophy. Today it is far from certain that La Mettrie, although an incautious eater, was actually destroyed by that vice. Judging by the few known symptoms of the case, the probability is either that the *pâté* was spoiled, or, according to Dr. Boissier's diagnosis, that the fatal complaint was something in the order of enteritis, peritonitis, or volvolus.[18] Aside from the providential explanation of its cause, La Mettrie's death also gave rise to rumors that the famous atheist, finally repentant at the moment of agony, had died in the lap of the Church. But these must surely be dismissed as pious fabrications, for Frederick II made a point of finding out just how the philosophe had fared *in extremis*, and only on being assured that he had met with an honorable end did His Majesty deign to compose personally the *Eloge de La Mettrie* and have it read before the Berlin Academy. La Mettrie's remains were buried in the French Catholic Church of Friedrichstadt, far from the land to which he had longed to return. One of his own remarks, which perhaps came closest to summing up the meaning of his harried existence, would have made a fitting epitaph: "Heureux pour qui la fortune n'est rien; la liberté de penser, tout; & la vraye Patrie, où l'on en jouit."

[18] Raymond Boissier, *La Mettrie, médecin, pamphlétaire et philosophe*, Paris, 1931, p. 24.

CHAPTER II

INTERPRETATION OF *L'HOMME MACHINE*

THE THESIS of La Mettrie's principal work springs from the persuasion that all prior efforts to clarify metaphysically the nature of mind have failed. The dualism of Descartes and Malebranche, the Leibnizian monadology, and even Locke's conjecture that God might have superadded thought to matter, all seem to him to be mere verbalizings rather than rational explanations of the mystery of mental phenomena. As for the various theological dogmas about the nature of the soul (which have always unduly influenced metaphysical loyalties), La Mettrie sets them aside as indifferent to the issue, since whatever God might be presumed to have revealed scripturally on the subject must be interpreted, if it is to make sense at all, in the light of human reason and experience. Nevertheless, La Mettrie rightly anticipated that the Christian religion, with its spiritualist creeds and oppressive policies, would pose the most serious threat to his intellectual enterprise. The strong polemical animus that permeates the argument of *l'Homme machine* is therefore directed mainly against the theologians.

La Mettrie breaks with the whole of theological and metaphysical tradition by his proposal to restate the general problem of mind as a problem of physics—that is, to regard man as a mechanical entity in which psychic events are regularly produced by organic causes. This radical step was perhaps an inevitable outgrowth of the seventeenth-century scientific attitude. Once science was held capable of understanding things, ideally, only in terms of more or less exactly measurable quantities and motions, there remained hardly any choice for psychology, insofar as it too wished to be scientific, but to model its method of investigation on that of mathematical physics, and to assume finally that man, like the cosmos, was a machine.

Although La Mettrie was the first to draw this conclusion in its full force, the materials with which he was able to support it were in large part already given. That the organism at least—if not the whole man—ought to be considered a machine was the physiological doctrine, long since established, of the iatromechanist school, to which La Mettrie adhered faithfully. In order to illustrate the dependence of mental life on bodily processes, he adduces a great many well-known facts taken from the spheres both of medical and of everyday experience. These experiences, which occupy a sizeable portion of *l'Homme machine*, have to do with the psychological effects of such factors as organic disease, fatigue, drugs and stimulants, hunger, diet, pregnancy, sexual desire, age, climate, and so on. La Mettrie adds corroborative data of a more technical sort, drawn from the eighteenth century's modest store of knowledge about neuropathology and comparative brain anatomy, which tend to show that general differences of behavior, among the various species as among the individual members of each species, are due to the specific structure and condition of the central nervous system. But the principle which these observations are meant to bear out—namely: "Les divers Etats de l'Ame sont toujours corrélatifs à ceux du corps"—does not amount in itself, despite its value for La Mettrie, to a demonstration of the materialist standpoint. For the mind-body parallelism, recognized long before him, had already been diversely resolved into nonmaterialist systems of philosophy by Descartes, Malebranche, Spinoza, and Leibniz.

La Mettrie's originality lies in his offering the correlation between mental and physiological states as empirically sufficient to validate the *homme machine* as a comprehensive psychological theory. Unlike the exponents of the metaphysical tradition which he rejects, he is content to give to his psychology a plausibly relative, in contrast to an elusively absolute, basis. La Mettrie's materialism thus represents, not a metaphysical position in any proper sense, but simply a philosophy of the special branch of science that concerns him. The degree of truth claimed for the man-machine concept turns out on examination to be hypothetical. It expresses a *modus cognoscendi* designed to promote scientific inquiry, rather than any ultimate knowledge about the nature of things. In this regard, La Mettrie not only denies that the *homme machine* idea gives an a priori definition of man but concedes that its heuristic value as a theory can hardly be expected ever to exhaust its object and to encompass the human essence. He states: "L'Homme est une Machine si composée, qu'il est impossible de s'en faire d'abord une idée claire, & conséquemment de la définir. ... Ainsi ce n'est qu'*à posteriori*, ou en cherchant à démêler l'Ame, comme au travers des Organes du corps, qu'on peut, je ne dis pas, découvrir avec évidence la nature même de l'Homme, mais atteindre le plus grand degré de probabilité possible sur ce sujet."

La Mettrie himself neglects, it is true, to discuss directly or to fix with care the scope and meaning of the materialism present in *l'Homme machine*—a fact that has helped many of his critics to go astray. Nevertheless, he has scattered in the text a sufficient number of clues to reveal to a circumspect reader the spirit of his thought. Perhaps the most telling of these is the assertion that "la Nature du mouvement nous est aussi inconnue que celle de la matière." If such is the case, then the nature of the "machine" with which man is hypothetically equated would likewise be unknown, and there could be no question of raising the correspondence between organic and psychic phenomena to the level of identity—an opinion which, in fact, La Mettrie nowhere attempts to establish. Although he does assume that mental events are caused by their physical counterparts, this fails to lead him to any critical discussion of the problem of causality, for it is obvious enough that what he means by a "cause" is merely an invariable (or unusually frequent) sequence observed between physical and mental states. The inner connection of this sequence is admitted to be unknowable, and, insofar as the scientific utility of the man-machine idea is concerned, it need not be known. For example, at the same time that he attributes differences of behavior among the animal species to their different organizations, La Mettrie does not hesitate to confess that "notre faible entendement, borné aux observations les plus grossières, ne puisse voir les liens qui règnent entre la cause & les effets. C'est une espèce d'*harmonie* que les Philosophes ne connoîtront jamais." The unknowability of things in themselves is regarded, not as the stumbling block, but rather as a precondition of science, for it prompts and justifies "la Méthode de ceux qui voudroient suivre la voie que je leur ouvre, d'interpréter les choses surnaturelles, incompréhensibles en soi, par les lumières que chacun a reçues de la Nature." The carrying out of this method in psychology rests, in turn, on the assumption that all psychic phenomena are *without exception* dependent on physical factors. Again, La Mettrie offers no proof that such a perfect mind-body parallelism actually exists (however much the evidence cited might point in that direction), nor does his materialism require him strictly to do so. If he asserts that "tout dépend de la manière dont notre Machine est montée," this is said, not because the case is necessarily so, but because such a supposition, whether or not it is entirely true, provides the theoretical context in which his scientific goal may be pursued with the least hindrance.

The *homme machine* idea gives us, therefore, no more than a mechanical model, or a picturable analogy, of the mind—not its essence. The sophistication which La Mettrie shows in this respect concerning the limits of natural science was, for that pre-Kantian age, not unimpressive. It was very likely due, not so much to any direct preoccupation on his part with the problem of knowledge, as to the restraining influence of Pyrrhonism, which, as he himself remarks, persisted as an underlying trait of his intellect. But if the man-machine remains basically a hypothesis, it must be said to enjoy as such a special status, for it is patently not a mere conjecture put forth to be tested and, if found wanting, to be exchanged conveniently for a better one. Rather, it imposes itself with a practical finality; it is, so to speak, a necessary hypothesis. The *homme machine* idea, as formulated by La Mettrie, coincides in general with the possibility of a strictly scientific explanation of psychological events. Seen in this light, its value has remained classic, even if, as sometimes happens in such cases, its eventual success as a truism served to obscure its historical importance. Yet the validity within its appropriate sphere of La Mettrie's hypothesis has, since 1748, really been called into question, not by the proposal of any superior conception with which to replace it, but simply as a result of the progressive refinements that have been made in the concrete application of the term "machine" to the organism.

The reader of *l'Homme machine* will probably wonder why its author did not make the hypothetical and relativist meaning of his materialism as plain as it has been made here, and why he often appears instead to claim a more radical truth for it than the close analysis of his ideas will support. There is no doubt that his mode of presentation is often overly assertive and rigid for what he actually has to say. The causes lie, however, far less in confused thinking on La Mettrie's part than in the requirements put upon him by the milieu in which he had to express himself. His vehement tone and blunt style were largely due to the fact that *l'Homme machine* was not only an exposition of materialist science but a powerful piece of philosophic propaganda as well—for these two aims were not easily separable in the Enlightenment. Moreover, La Mettrie was prevented from offering the man-machine as the hypothesis it was for a rather special reason. His contemporaries, as it happened, were still too painfully aware of the many abuses of conjecturing that had only recently typified French science, particularly in the Cartesian school; and they were at the same time deeply grateful to Newton and his disciples for having, as it was imagined, banished hypotheses forever from the sphere of natural science. For La Mettrie to have suggested that what he advanced was hypothetical in character would have been, under the circumstances, almost equivalent to admitting that it was arbitrary and worthless. This can be inferred readily enough, for instance, from Luzac's "Avertissement," in which the publisher sought to avoid possible reproaches against himself for having printed *l'Homme machine* by remarking about the philosophical argument of the book: "Si les conséquences que l'Auteur en tire sont dangereuses, qu'on se souvienne qu'elles n'ont qu'une Hypothèse pour fondement. En faut-il davantage pour les détruire?" Nor should it be forgotten that in the eighteenth century the presumed demonstrability of the spiritualist position in metaphysics could not have been challenged effectively, at least in the opinion of most people, by a mere hypothetical objection. This is attested by one of the many critics of La Mettrie's work, who voiced a typically negative judgment: "Non content d'attaquer, par les argumens les plus frivoles, des vérités revêtues de toute l'evidence dont elles sont susceptibles, il veut encore leur substituer une hypothèse, où tout est & ne peut être que vague & sans preuves, où lui-même est embarrassé à chaque pas."[1] Doubtless foreseeing such disparagement of the type of truth he wished to pursue, what La Mettrie did was to affirm the man-machine idea for the benefit of the average reader with the apparent force of a foregone conclusion, while on a deeper level it was made to convey to a more astute reader no more than a general scientific hypothesis, although that word was carefully avoided in describing it. Actually, there was at the time no suitable term available for La Mettrie to use.

Besides the mind-body correlation, another essential feature of *l'Homme machine* is its attempt to prove that the organism as such possesses inherent powers of purposive motion. In the pages that deal with this question, La Mettrie infers such a motile property of matter from the phenomenon of muscular irritability, the significance of which in physiological theory he was among the first to grasp. He thereby succeeds in providing a foundation in empirical fact for the broad conception which may be said, in the following words, to sum up his philosophy: "Posé le moindre principe de mouvement, les corps animés auront tout ce qu'il leur faut pour se mouvoir, sentir, penser, se repentir, & se conduire en un mot dans le Physique, & dans le Moral qui en dépend."

The problem of the relationship of motion to matter, which La Mettrie thus decides in a manner favorable to his scientific aims, was one of the gravest obstacles that materialism, in the intellectual setting of the period, was called upon to surmount. For it was repeatedly claimed by antimaterialist writers that the idea of matter could not be shown in itself to imply movement of any kind, much less movement that was to all appearances regular, creative, and almost intelligent. In biology this line of reasoning lent support to the common belief that there must be present in the organism an immaterial substance of some sort—that is, a soul —which alone could account for its vital activity and, a fortiori, for its instrumentality in the higher psychic functions. The leading exponent of such a view at the time was Georg Ernst Stahl, who, together with his followers, earned the honor of being La Mettrie's philosophic bête noire. The Stahlian animism had sprung

[1] Jacques François de Luc, *Observations sur les savans incrédules, et sur quelques-uns de leurs écrits*, Genève, 1762, pp. 384-85.

up early in the century as an understandable reaction to the inadequacies of the Cartesian mechanistic ideal as it was applied to the sciences of life. Descartes's biology, which served more or less to circumscribe the doctrines of the iatromechanist school, had made no real differentiation between the active organism and the operations of an ordinary machine. To this extent it had failed to do justice to the specific nature of the vital process, which may be said, among other things, to consist in the ability of the living—as distinct from the artificial—machine to move itself immediately and autonomously from within. To uphold the status of mechanistic biology, it therefore became necessary in the end to show that the organism was not only a machine, but a genuinely self-sustaining system. If this could not be done, its ultimate source of motion, placed by default outside the material realm, will have altogether eluded quantitative determination, and will thereby have rendered meaningless in physiology the law of the conservation of energy. This, in turn, could only have abrogated the hope of building a scientific psychology on a physical basis, and left the door open instead to animistic explanations. Such were the terms of the challenge that the man-machine idea was called upon historically to satisfy. La Mettrie tells rather modestly how, as a materialist, he simply extended to the human species Descartes's animal-automaton theory. Actually, he proposed and achieved much more than that, for his primary task was to *vitalize* the Cartesian "dead mechanism" approach to biology. In order to lift the *homme machine* beyond the reach of animistic criticism, La Mettrie had first to show that purposive motion could be a property of organized matter as such, or, put differently, that the man-machine was automatic in a manner that no man-made machine, requiring direction from without, could truly duplicate.

This theoretical need is met in *l'Homme machine* by the principle of irritability, which is based on data furnished in part by common observation and in part by experiments reported in the works of Harvey, Cowper, Steno, and Boyle. The persistence of functional movement in isolated muscle fibers, no less than in whole organs severed from the central nervous apparatus, is taken by La Mettrie as conclusive proof of his contention that organic activity is not caused by any kind of "soul." Since the influence of such a soul, presumably situated in the brain, would have to act by way of the nerves, the fact of autonomous muscle contraction makes it plain that the irritable force inheres in the physical structure of the moving parts themselves. But having thus made motion a property of matter on the strength of an induction from decisive physiological data, La Mettrie, resisting the temptation to generalize about matter as such, attributes this property only to the organic systems which actually display it. There is, then, a scientific justification for the notion of organic automaticity at which he arrives: "Le corps humain est une Machine qui monte elle-même ses ressorts: vivante image du mouvement perpétuel." It is the "oscillation naturelle dont est douée chaque fibre" that makes the organism such a unique type of machine. In the *homme machine*, moreover, which exhibits a closed self-feeding system quite different from that of conventional machines, its circular causality prevents us from assigning a beginning or an end to its operations: "l'Homme n'est qu'un Assemblage de ressorts, qui tous se montent les uns par les autres, sans qu'on puisse dire par quel point du cercle humain la Nature a commencé." The biological philosophy implicit in this view of things cannot, properly speaking, be classed as either mechanistic or vitalistic in a restrictive sense, for it really represents an attempt to combine those two traditionally opposed attitudes into a unified standpoint. La Mettrie has by no means neglected the specifically vital characteristics of the organism; but at the same time he remains entirely convinced that these are knowable to science only insofar as they are seen *sub specie machinae*. His idea of the "living machine," defined hypothetically by its purposive self-motion, may thus be said to express a "vitalo-mécanisme à base dynamique."

Although La Mettrie's contribution to the history of the irritability concept will be evaluated in a later chapter, it may be said here in passing that his treatment of the subject is one of the most original and impressive features of *l'Homme machine*. To be correctly understood, however, it must be seen in relation to eighteenth-century physiology. The concrete phenomena with which La Mettrie illustrates irritability have to do with only one of its many forms, namely, with the uniform response of muscle cells to stimulation. Contractility was, in his time, the only experimentally known phase of the irritable process. In this connection, the behavior of cardiac muscle was of particular value in establishing the doctrine of irritability, as, indeed, La Mettrie's list of examples makes sufficiently clear. The reason for this was not merely that the heart seemed unusually excitable, but also that the separation of cardiac fibers from the nerve impulse was technically far more feasible than in the case of other muscles. Moreover, in contrast to skeletal and smooth muscle, the heart offered a much more dramatic proof of autonomous energy because, when resected and divided, it could contract even without the benefit of artificial stimulation—a fact that made it possible to derive the automaticity of the organism as a whole from that of the heart, which became the mainspring in the network of internal stimuli that maintained the body in a continuous state of vital activity.

It is of special significance that, while La Mettrie's data were limited to the subject of muscular contraction, he nevertheless had enough scientific imagination to conceive of irritability as a general property of living substance. In this respect, his conception came close to the standpoint of modern physiology, which of course regards irritability as the specific response to stimuli manifested by practically all organic systems, from bacteria and protozoa, through plants, to such complex animal structures as the brain itself. Anticipating such an approach to the problem, La Mettrie affirms that "chaque petite fibre, ou partie des corps organisés, se meut par un principe qui lui est propre, & dont l'action ne dépend point des nerfs."[2] With respect to the functional mode of the irritable reaction, he observes further: "Tel est ce principe moteur des Corps entiers, ou des parties coupées en morceaux, qu'il produit des mouvemens non déréglés, comme on l'a cru, mais très réguliers." The "siège de cette force innée" is placed by him in the living tissues themselves: "dans la substance propre des parties, abstraction faite des Veines, des Artères, des Nerfs, en un mot de l'Organisation de tout le corps." La Mettrie thereupon proceeds to describe

[2] In *Les animaux plus que machines*, he refers to the same property as "ce ressort inné, si universellement répandu par-tout, qu'il est difficile de dire où il n'est pas, & même où il ne se manifeste pas par des effets sensibles, même après la mort, même en des parties détachées du corps, & coupées par morceaux"; *Oeuvres philosophiques*, Amsterdam, 1774, II, 68. (All references to La Mettrie, unless otherwise indicated, will be given in this edition.)

the role of this general property in the performance of a number of reflex actions. However unobjectionable such a step might seem to present-day physiology, it must be said that here he remains unaware of the specific differences that would now be recognized between reflex excitation and the kind of nerveless muscular irritability that he has already accepted as the *principe moteur* of the organism. He also attempts to use the irritability principle as a basis of explanation for various sympathetic and even psychosomatic reactions; but in this area the eighteenth century's ignorance about the autonomic nervous system causes his remarks, despite their promise, to be rather vague and speculative. In the final analysis, the chief merit of La Mettrie's discussion is that it views the phenomenon of irritability as the key to the mystery of life itself, and proposes to erect the mechanistic theory of mind on this firm biological foundation.

According to La Mettrie, it is the irritable nature of the brain that permits it to fulfill the special task of coordinating and directing the motions of the machine as a whole. Serving as the basis of mental energy ("car le cerveau a ses muscles pour penser, comme les jambes pour marcher"), irritability supplies the material impetus in the play of psychodynamics proper: "Il est la source de tous nos sentimens, de tous nos plaisirs, de toutes nos passions, de toutes nos pensées." Psychosomatic phenomena, which are among the far-reaching effects of this cerebral irritability to which La Mettrie affixes the Hippocratic label of *enormon*, would prove nothing against the man-machine theory, for these are simply somatopsychic phenomena seen subjectively in reverse. Finding the origins of psychic life where he does, La Mettrie is inclined to view the rational mind in refraction, as it were, through the primary level of the instincts, and to speak rather summarily of "ce merveilleux Instinct, dont l'Education fait de l'Esprit." The subrational perspective of his psychology produces, now and then, a flash of psychiatric insight, as when he remarks about the role of the instinctual forces: "Par là s'explique tout ce qui peut s'expliquer, jusqu'aux effets surprenants des maladies de l'Imagination." The materialism of *l'Homme machine* may be said, in this regard, to have come as a needed corrective for the somewhat ingenuous faith in reason held by the Enlightenment. It enabled

La Mettrie to judge realistically the extent to which the nonrational and the irrational enter into almost all forms of human thought and conduct, and to rise as a psychologist above the rank and file of his contemporaries with, for example, the following words of the *Système d'Epicure*: "La raison pour laquelle rien n'étonne un philosophe, c'est qu'il sait que la folie & la sagesse, l'instinct & la raison, la grandeur & la petitesse, la puérilité & le bon sens, le vice & la vertu, se touchent d'aussi près dans l'homme, que l'adolescence & l'enfance."[3]

The twofold dynamism—physical and mental—that derives from the irritability principle still leaves unsolved, however, the question of how the self-moving organism "par cela même qu'il est originairement doué d'un soufle de Vie, se trouve en conséquence orné de la faculté de sentir, & enfin par celle-ci de la Pensée." Concerning this progression, La Mettrie states that "il est constant que le mouvement & le sentiment s'excitent tour à tour," and further, relying on the authority of Locke, that "la pensée n'est qu'une faculté de sentir." This, of course, explains nothing about the inner link between organic process and the rise of consciousness: it merely takes cognizance of an empirically given connection between the two. The truth is that the growth of subjective reality from matter in motion remains, in La Mettrie's opinion, a metaphysical riddle lying beyond the competence of psychological investigation; and since for him the nature of matter is as unknowable as that of motion, it ensues that "pour ce qui est de ce développement, c'est une folie de perdre le tems à en rechercher le mécanisme." We must interpret in the light of these qualifications the somewhat bolder assertion that he later allows himself: "Je crois la pensée si peu incompatible avec la matière organisée, qu'elle semble en être une propriété, telle que l'Electricité, la Faculté motrice ... etc." Actually, the term "property" is used here simply to denote the observed correlation between physiological and psychic events: "C'est par cette file d'observations & de vérités qu'on parvient à lier à la matière l'admirable propriété de penser, sans qu'on en puisse voir les liens, parce que le sujet de cet attribut nous est essentiellement inconnu." The latter part of this sentence obviously rules out the possibility of demonstrating that mind and

[3] *ibid.*, III, 238.

mechanism are the same thing; and it is evident, once more, that no greater validity is claimed for the *homme machine* than that of a general scientific hypothesis. This point of view accounts, by the way, for La Mettrie's strange hesitation—so inexplicable in an arch-unbeliever—to decide the issue of personal survival after death. Prudent as his indecision was, it was really more than that. For if matter and motion remain unknown in essence, the demands of logical consistency do not permit it to be said—however much common sense might urge an answer in the negative—whether or not a "machine" perishes utterly.

A number of subsidiary themes take their place in *l'Homme machine* around the central thesis described in the preceding pages. One of the most conspicuous of these is the question of atheism. In the eighteenth century, to deny the soul's immateriality meant more or less to doubt God's existence, because the divine presence in the world was presumably discernible only to the spiritual man. La Mettrie was unable, as a result, to ignore the theological problem raised by his philosophy; but he dealt differently with it on each of the two levels of argument in *l'Homme machine*. On the propagandist plane, his tendency is frankly atheistic ("l'Univers ne sera jamais heureux, à moins qu'il ne soit Athée," etc.), although what this really expresses is little else besides a general hostility to the established religion. But on the philosophical plane, atheism is presented neither as a premise nor a consequence of the man-machine theory. La Mettrie recognizes that God, strictly speaking, might or might not exist entirely apart from the question whether man is or is not to be viewed as a machine, and he is ready enough to avoid useless controversy over an irrelevant point: "Ce n'est pas que je révoque en doute l'existence d'un Etre suprême; il me semble au contraire que le plus grand degré de Probabilité est pour elle." But since the notion of God, lying as it does beyond our analytical powers, can be of no service—and has often been of much disservice—to natural science: "Ne nous perdons point dans l'infini, nous ne sommes pas faits pour en avoir la moindre idée." The interests of scientific inquiry, which alone claim La Mettrie's attention and loyalty, are best served by a naturalistic view of things, and within such a context—which is that of *l'Homme machine*—the destiny of man has existentially no meaning other than that of all organic beings: "Qui sait d'ailleurs si la raison de l'Existence de l'Homme, ne seroit pas dans son existence même? Peut-être a-t-il été jetté au hazard sur un point de la surface de la Terre, sans qu'on puisse savoir ni comment, ni pourquoi; mais seulement qu'il doit vivre et mourir, semblable à ces champignons, qui paroissent d'un jour à l'autre."

At the time, this transparent naturalism clashed with the popular theologizing of nature which, typifying the outlook of deists no less than of Christians, had long sought to subordinate the order of nature to the order of Divine Providence. In his elimination of finalist reasoning from the domain of science, La Mettrie does not doubt that a great many structures, particularly in biology, show a remarkable adaptation to specific functions (e.g. the eye is "constructed to see"). He is not persuaded, however, that such purposeful design in nature forces one logically to choose, as almost all his contemporaries insist, between God or Blind Chance as its generating cause. Instead, he replaces the entire conceptual framework of natural theology with the original idea of a "creative nature," which, by avoiding the old and sterile dichotomy of God *versus* Chance, transcends both the teleological and the fatalistic traditions, that is, it arrives at a synthesis of the orthodox and the Epicurean physics. Just as the self-determining powers of the organism were inferred from the phenomenon of irritability, La Mettrie now turns to another biological discovery of decisive theoretical value, namely, Trembley's polyp—which had already exercised a deep influence on the scientific imagination of the 1740's —in order to support empirically his new and challenging conception. The polyp's amazing ability to regenerate into new zoophytes from each of its severed pieces becomes, in his eyes, a sort of revelation of the self-ordering creativity of Nature: "Nous ne connoissons point la Nature: des causes cachées dans son sein pourroient avoir tout produit. Voiez . . . le Polype de Trembley! Ne contient-il pas en soi les causes qui donnent lieu à sa régénération? Quelle absurdité y auroit-il donc à penser qu'il est des causes physiques pour lesquelles tout a été fait, & auxquelles toute la chaine de ce vaste Univers est si nécessairement liée & assujetie, que rien de ce qui arrive, ne pouvoit ne pas arriver; des causes dont l'ignorance absolument invincible nous a fait recourir à un Dieu.

... Ainsi détruire le Hazard, ce n'est pas prouver l'existence d'un Etre suprême, puisqu'il peut y avoir autre chose qui ne seroit ni Hazard, ni Dieu; je veux dire la Nature, dont l'étude par conséquent ne peut faire que des incrédules."[4] The cosmic machine resembles the organism in that its moving and directing principle is to be found inside, not outside, its own structure. The immanent finality which La Mettrie perceives in the natural world has the effect of transforming its *être* into its *raison d'être*. But such a viewpoint is once again put forth, as the conditional phrasing of the passage just quoted makes quite clear, not as metaphysical or demonstrable truth, but simply as an assumption indispensable to science.

Another important theme related to the man-machine idea may be stated in La Mettrie's own words: "Dès Animaux à l'Homme, la transition n'est pas violente." The behavior of human beings, when traced to its instinctual sources, seems to him to differ merely in degree, not in kind, from that of the higher animals. He rejects on this ground the age-old opinion which sees man's uniqueness as a creature in his possession of a moral sense, a conscience, and feelings of remorse. Without doubting the reality or importance of these psychic traits, La Mettrie regards them simply as the effects of particular neural mechanisms, and has little trouble in showing that animals also display, within the sphere of activity proper to them, more or less similar responses under comparable circumstances. Besides the rich promise for experimental psychology of this line of thought, one of its immediate advantages is that La Mettrie, having taken for granted the dependence of the moral instinct on a healthy organic equilibrium, proceeds to adopt toward crimes committed under morbid influence an attitude which is strikingly more humane and enlightened than that typified by the penology of the times.

His belief in a gradual transition from animal to human intelligence suggested to La Mettrie, moreover, his curious project of instructing the anthropoid ape to speak. Ill-advised as this expectation was, and notwithstanding the mockery with which it

[4] On this question, consult my "Trembley's Polyp, La Mettrie, and 18th-century French Materialism," *Journal of the History of Ideas*, XI, 3 (June 1950), pp. 259-86.

was promptly greeted, it indicates an experimental approach to animal psychology, which, though historically premature, was not without value for the future. More exactly, it was the structural analogy between the brain of man and that of the ape which led La Mettrie to wonder if their considerable difference of behavior might not be due less to any organic dissimilarity than to the educative merit of the environment in which each of the species had lived and developed. This in turn entails the assumption that natural—i.e. prehistoric—man must have been very much like present-day anthropoids. With such a notion we are brought of course to the threshold of evolutionist theory without, however, quite crossing it. What is involved in *l'Homme machine* is still the problem of cultural, not of organic, evolution, inasmuch as the fateful event on which the whole of man's subsequent superiority to the ape is made to hang is, not any fact of physical adaptation, but the invention of language.

This brings up the epistemological question, which occupies a significant, if somewhat secondary, place in *l'Homme machine*. It is claimed that the use of language has created man's aptitude for science and the arts by gradually transforming, in the course of centuries, the operations of his brain into those of what might be described as a coding and decoding machine—although La Mettrie chooses the more familiar *clavecin* as his mechanical model. In keeping with the musical analogy, the cerebral instrument is said to translate into consciousness the countless perceptions stored within it when the corresponding set of notes has, so to speak, been struck on the keyboard of memory. Once these combinations have been assigned suitable signs—i.e. when a method of notation or language has been devised—thinking proper arises with the act of variously comparing, relating, and combining the sense impressions stocked in the brain by means of their given symbols. Then the mind, like a self-performing piano which listens to itself play, can simultaneously order the signs in a great diversity of patterns and keep present to consciousness the sensations that these evoke; that is, it can stand aside from its own sensory content and examine the arrangements it imposes on them—in a word, it can reflect. La Mettrie therefore considers all thinking to be essentially symbolic in nature, and, as the system of coding grows in complexity and precision, thought becomes clearer and more comprehensive, or simply truer. It is possible at this juncture to glimpse the underlying nexus in *l'Homme machine* between the theory of science and the theory of knowledge. Just as the symbol does no more than point toward the real, science is nothing but an *approach* to reality, so that the description of thinking as a symbolic process remains fundamentally in agreement with the presentation of the man-machine as a general heuristic hypothesis.

La Mettrie's standpoint in epistemology, which obviously owes a great deal to Lockean empiricism, fails to come to grips, however, with the crux of the problem of knowledge. It uncritically equates the symbolized idea with the sensation from which it arises, as if the idea were contained in the sensation exactly as it exists in the understanding. Perhaps the most flagrant abuse of this sort occurs with La Mettrie's ingenuous remarks about the origin of numerical notions, where the strong presumption of a purely intellectual factor in the shaping of sense experience ought to have made him more circumspect. But treating the symbolic representation of sensations simply as a mechanical problem, he neglects the entire question of the formal relation of ideas to the sensory impressions which link them to the objective world. Here too we reach the limits of his psychological method. La Mettrie's attention is confined necessarily to a more or less peripheral aspect of the theory of knowledge—an aspect which, by lending itself to mechanical picturization, can be annexed to the *homme machine* hypothesis.

La Mettrie's description of thinking as the effective manipulation of symbols results in his assigning, contrariwise to his age, the predominant role among the mental faculties to the imagination, which is regarded as subsuming the functions of judgment, reasoning, and memory: "Toujours est-il vrai que l'imagination seule aperçoit; que c'est elle qui se représente tous les objets, avec les mots & les figures qui les caractérisent; & qu'ainsi c'est elle encore une fois qui est l'Ame, puisqu'elle en fait tous les Rôles." An important corollary of this is La Mettrie's opinion that science and art are mutually rooted in the imaginative process, inasmuch as both activities, regardless of their specific differences, are concerned with the symbolization of experience. Scientific as well as artistic genius may be defined, therefore, as the ability to represent, by means of at once the most precise and most intricate symbolism, a given segment or phase of human experience: "La plus belle, la plus grande, ou la plus forte imagination, est donc la plus propre aux Sciences, comme aux Arts. Je ne décide point... si la Nature s'est mise en plus grands frais, pour faire Newton, que pour former Corneille (ce dont je doute fort;) mais il est certain que c'est la seule imagination diversement appliquée, qui a fait leur différent triomphe & leur gloire immortelle." Aside from their general interest, these words help to clarify the meaning of the *homme machine* idea, which was itself an example of that pictorial-symbolic representation of reality for which science and art were equally indebted to the imagination. The hypothesis of La Mettrie's book may be said, in this respect, to parallel the esthetics of the eighteenth century, which was dominated by the ideal of imitation. The man-machine was, like the artistic creation, a formal approximation of what existed objectively in the natural world, for science too aimed here at achieving an "imitation of nature." Such an affinity between science and art was possible, in turn, because the latter had already assimilated to itself the concept of nature. The *homme machine* could fall in with the esthetic aim of faithfully reproducing nature, because nature itself had for some time been felt to be above all a consummate, transcendent work of art. This characteristic attitude is often present in La Mettrie's writings, as for instance in the following lines (where it is combined logically enough with the relativist basis of his philosophy): "Nous voyons tous les objets, tout ce qui se passe dans l'Univers, comme une belle Decoration d'Opera, dont nous n'apercevons ni les cordes, ni les contrepoids. Dans tous les corps, comme dans le nôtre, les premiers ressorts nous sont cachés, & le seront vraisemblablement toujours."[5]

The psychology of imagination outlined in *l'Homme machine*

[5] *Oeuvres*, II, 215. In *Les animaux plus que machines*, La Mettrie remarked further about the soul: "je ne vous la définirois pas, je vous la dessinerois d'après nature. Mais hélas! mon ame ne se connoît pas plus elle-même, qu'elle ne connoîtroit l'organe qui lui procure le plaisir du spectacle enchanteur de l'univers, s'il n'y avoit aucun miroir naturel ou artificiel. Car quelle idée se forger de ce qu'on ne peut se représenter, faute d'image sensible! Pour imaginer il faut colorer un fond, & détacher de ce fond par abstraction des points d'une couleur qui en soit différente" (*ibid.*, II, 80-81).

has important implications also for the history of literature and the arts. In La Mettrie's view the imagination, which like a "magic lantern" translates the real world onto the *toile médullaire* of the mind, does not function in a merely cinematographic fashion; by its synthesizing powers of comparison and selection, it recomposes the stream of phenomenal impressions and individual impulses into forms that reason and judgment can use effectively. At the same time, La Mettrie attributes to imagination the inner mobility that permits the mind to find its way speedily and dexterously amid the maze of sense perceptions and memory traces that constantly clutter it—a process without which the formal organization of ideas, or thinking, would be impossible. And since thought is held to consist in this ability to assemble an instantaneous succession of tableaux from the ever increasing welter of mental data, the sense of temporal reality is itself a product of "l'imagination, véritable Image du tems, qui se détruit & se renouvelle sans cesse." La Mettrie, who elsewhere describes man as an "animal imaginatif," shows a perfect awareness of the originality of his point of view when he writes about the imagination: "Sotement décriée par les uns, vainement distinguée par les autres, qui l'ont tous mal connue, elle ne marche pas seulement à la suite des Graces & des beaux Arts, elle ne peint pas seulement la Nature, elle peut aussi la mesurer. Elle raisonne, juge, pénètre, compare, approfondit." In short, it would not be too much to say that La Mettrie attempted the first radical rehabilitation of the imaginative faculty in his epoch, anticipating in that regard the efforts of Diderot and the pre-Romantics. And although he did not work out its consequences for esthetics, he did open the way to a revision of the eighteenth century's tendency to define art too narrowly in terms of what is "decorative" and "agreeable." For there is implicit in La Mettrie's treatment of imagination a new evaluation of the nature of art, thanks to which literature eventually escaped from the inhibiting control of an exaggerated rationalism, and rediscovered its true sources in the elemental forms of consciousness produced by the interplay of sensation and instinct.

It is necessary to omit from the present discussion several other themes in *l'Homme machine* which are of lesser importance. However, it would be worthwhile to consider briefly certain features of the work which, although unrelated logically to its thesis, are nevertheless inseparable from its distinctive physiognomy. The critical appraisal of *l'Homme machine* has in the past suffered generally from the resolve to find in its pages, to the exclusion of nearly all else, a system of materialism. This has often resulted in a tendency to dismiss as irrelevant, trivial, frivolous (or even worse) many of its extraphilosophical traits, which are both pronounced and curious. While the man-machine idea (but not for that reason a "materialist system") is surely what dominates it, La Mettrie's book is in fact a multifaceted mirror which reflects not only the background of *lumières* and science, but also various aspects of eighteenth-century taste and *moeurs*. It is impossible, without taking into account these pervasively qualifying factors, to discern the true character of the work.

One is perhaps surprised that in La Mettrie's presentation of the man-machine thesis there is little enough of the intellectual drabness or austerity that such a subject is likely to suggest to the technology-ridden consciousness of our own day. Instead, it is enveloped in an atmosphere that may be described as one of sensual exuberance. This doubtless reflects the author's temperament, but it also reflects more than that, for La Mettrie's personality was an intensified expression of the social and ideological milieu which produced *l'Homme machine*. To understand the special filiation of mood and idea in that work, we must first recall that at the time what was really felt to be deadening was the metaphysics of dualism, which, with the theology it supported, had ossified into a series of platitudes. By contrast, materialism came as a quickening and liberating current. Because it was possible to see in matter a source of spontaneous energy, the man-machine became associated in the moral sphere, somewhat paradoxically, with attitudes of freedom from restraint and *joie de vivre*. In this respect La Mettrie's thought proved to be the culmination—and, by its excesses, all but the parody—of the Epicurean tradition, which had habitually combined naturalism in philosophy with the ethical ideal of *volupté*. This explains what might otherwise impress us in *l'Homme machine* as a bizarre contradiction between content and form, between the abstract, rather depressing doctrine and the extremely lively, playful tone in which it is conveyed. It also discloses a connection between the Dionysian strains of the "Dédicace à Haller" and the sobering thesis of the book, which at first glance would seem mutually unrelated.

La Mettrie's style and mode of composition likewise appealed to that sensuously impressionable and mentally vivacious mood of eighteenth-century France, which he himself personified perhaps to an immoderate degree. The text of *l'Homme machine* pours itself out with the garrulous ease of an improvised monologue, unconstrained by any plan of exposition. The nervous, restless impulse that drives La Mettrie from one topic nimbly to the next has, it is true, the merit of forestalling philosophic tedium, but it also has the disadvantage of precluding all thoroughness of method. Moreover, he strives to persuade, not merely by fact and logic, but also by a witty (if sometimes boorish) self-assurance of expression, a show of arresting (but often belabored) epigrams, and by overtones of raillery and defiance that tend to enlist on his side our agonistic sympathies. La Mettrie presses his memory into service to enrich the text with a rather piquant display of erudition. By seeking, all in all, to enlighten the intellect by means of first titillating the imagination and the senses, *l'Homme machine* gratified so well the tastes of its contemporaries that it succeeded in winning for its ideas, almost overnight, a wide and lasting dissemination.

A more special feature of the work—shared by most of La Mettrie's writings—is the erotic note that plays lightly but persistently over its pages. This is something the critics have in general been inclined to ignore, or at best to regard as a regrettable lapse of decorum in an otherwise serious thinker. Yet the sexual allusiveness of La Mettrie's style has an important meaning for the historian of culture. It ought not to be viewed merely as a passive, somewhat inane survival from the Epicurean past, nor even simply as a device for enhancing the popularity of the author's doctrine. Rather, there is evident in La Mettrie's entire method of thought an underlying interaction between *volupté* and materialism, with the result that scientific and erotic curiosity seem for him to function together in a sort of alliance, each serving to strengthen and stimulate the other. A key to the understanding of this reciprocity is given, in fact, in the "Dédicace à Haller," which plainly eulogizes the aim of scientific investigation as the satisfaction of an intellectual "instinct" that bears the hallmarks of erotic pleasure ("Enfin l'Etude a ses Extases, comme l'Amour!") About the philosophical life La Mettrie confesses characteristically: "Pour le bien goûter, j'ai quelquefois été forcé de me livrer à l'amour. L'amour ne fait point de peur à un sage: il sait tout allier & tout faire valoir l'un par l'autre." The significance, and indeed the psychic possibility of such a close cooperation between Eros and Philosophy is to be sought, not only in La Mettrie's temperament, but also, and perhaps primarily, in the specific nature of his intellectual task. The man-machine theory, in denying the spirituality of the soul, found itself irreversibly at odds with the principal religious dogma by means of which Christianity had long sought to justify its general repression of the sexual impulse in favor of a more or less ascetic ideal of life. More than that, the mechanistic method in psychology stressed the importance of the instinctual basis of the higher spiritual activities. It was perhaps to be expected, then, that such a scientific enterprise would from the start enter into association with some portion of the erotic energy which it served to liberate, and would utilize it to break down the common system of barriers that had been erected by the same religious authority against both intellectual and sexual curiosity.

No less unusual than the erotic overtones of his mode of expression is the frivolous and facetious manner that La Mettrie often adopts in the exposition of his ideas. This idiosyncrasy soon gave him, among his contemporaries, the reputation of being, as Voltaire put it, the opposite of Don Quixote: "sage dans l'exercice de sa profession, et un peu fou dans tout le reste."[6] Although critics have seen this trait as an unhappy side effect of La Mettrie's irrepressible high spirits, it may be said actually to point to a special harmony between form and content in *l'Homme machine*. For it is true enough that a *grain de folie* was by no means an extraneous quality in the first person destined to proclaim that "man is a machine." Such an opinion, on the face of it, struck the eighteenth century as being quite absurd; and it doubtless still impresses us so today, even though we now realize better that the paradoxical figure cut by an idea before the tribunal of common-sense experi-

[6] Voltaire, *Oeuvres*, XXXVII, 319.

ence does not, in itself, necessarily argue anything in particular against its scientific value. Yet it might not always be easy in practice to publicize an idea of that sort with, as it were, a completely straight face; consequently there is often enough an initial stage in the history of such ideas, when they can be presented most effectively in the guise of intellectual extravagances. La Mettrie was certainly well qualified by his sense of humor no less than by his outspokenness to perpetrate the man-machine doctrine, in a style curiously compact of earnestness and levity, on a puzzled but —despite itself—fascinated world. Moreover, his own awareness of what the situation demanded was revealed more directly by the ironic fictions with which, in several of his polemical pamphlets, he came to the defense of the *homme machine* against its solemn critics.

Although the main purpose of this chapter has been to interpret the meaning and importance of *l'Homme machine* in relation to the eighteenth-century background from which it sprang, a few concluding remarks about the status of the work from the critical standpoint of our own time might prove not out of place.

What strikes readers today as a general weakness of La Mettrie's man-machine theory is not only the inadequacy of concrete detail supporting it, but also his almost complete neglect of chemistry. Yet, if he does not present the organism as the specifically *biochemical* machine we know it to be, this is owing not to any basic separation in his mind between physics proper and chemistry, but rather to the relatively meager fund of knowledge available in his period concerning the latter subject. La Mettrie simply prefers to conceive of the man-machine in terms of what is known to him with the highest degree of scientific certainty—that is, in terms of mechanics. This is not meant, however, to exclude from future study the relationship of mental phenomena to chemical processes, once the latter will have been brought within the purlieu of exact investigation. The same may be said about the absence of mathematics from the actual formulation of the *homme machine* hypothesis, which, while it tacitly assumes the possibility of a quantitative system of psychophysical correlations, is unable as yet to draw on any dependable data to corroborate such an assumption. Moreover, the type of mechanism to which La Mettrie, inspired by the analogy of Vaucanson's famous automata, would like to compare the living organism impresses us nowadays as singularly primitive. The ideal form of the machine, for him as for his age, was the *horloge*, with the limitations peculiar to it. For if on the one hand the clock is able to tell time, it remains on the other totally oblivious to time; and this very resistance to an inner shaping by virtue of duration is, in fact, what permits it to perform its task so admirably. But in this respect what is true of horology is not true of biology. And La Mettrie's *homme machine* may be blamed for exhibiting too rigidly the character of a clock, moving in an ever regular, linear fashion, and hardly modified structurally or functionally by the cumulative effect of the sequence of motions in which it engages. But if La Mettrie fails, in this sense, to define the organism properly as a self-adapting biochemical machine, this implies once again no opposition on his part to such a conception, which, indeed, his own less comprehensive idea of the self-moving machine would seem already to point to. His failure here merely reflects the narrow range of mechanical possibilities encompassed by the scientific imagination of the eighteenth century.

It will perhaps appear that La Mettrie's philosophy does not always succeed in freeing itself from those very traits of earlier metaphysical systems against which he inveighs so strongly. Although he conceives of matter and motion, not aprioristically, but simply as secondary qualities, still he is not sufficiently aware that even as "mere appearances" their nature and properties are by no means uniformly determinable, but admit of a great many phenomenological variants. In brief, his empiricism itself retains uncritically a vestigial form of the universal postulate that he finds so abhorrent in the method of rationalist metaphysics. Along with this, it would seem that La Mettrie continues to think in terms of the old Scholastic notion of substance, as for example when he states: "Concluons donc hardiment que l'Homme est une Machine; & qu'il n'y a dans tout l'Univers qu'une seule substance diversement modifiée." However, it ought not to be inferred from this that his thought maintains any genuine link with traditional philosophy. What La Mettrie expresses is really little more than a shadow of the substance idea, preserved for the sake of terminological ease; but the substance of the concept has, so to speak, gone out of the concept of substance. Inasmuch as La Mettrie regards the essence of matter as undefinable, it is evident that his materialism can have no metaphysical roots in the ground of substance. More than that, he remains habitually indifferent even to the universality of matter, with the result that in his thinking—unlike that of various materialists before and after him—man escapes the fate of being more or less swallowed up as an insignificant particle in an inhuman universe. La Mettrie's medical outlook has the effect of keeping his gaze firmly fixed on the flesh-and-blood entity, detached for all practical purposes from the cosmic setting. In this respect the *homme machine* philosophy, for all its declared resolve to deflate the conceits of mankind, retains an unmistakably humanistic, or more correctly perhaps, an anthropocentric emphasis, which is concerned, moreover, with affirming and describing the irreducible reality of each individual as given in his physical constitution. All in all, the intent of La Mettrie's materialism is not only to circumvent the concept of substance, but to direct scientific attention to the concrete variability of what, in the eighteenth century, was too abstractly and uniformly assumed to be "human nature."

As regards the controversy between vitalism and mechanism, it has already been suggested that La Mettrie deserves credit for having shown the way out of a dilemma which even today is far from being generally outgrown. If the vitalist position springs rightly enough from an intuitive grasp of the quality of living things as distinct from the nonliving, it remains nonetheless very difficult to base a body of scientific biology directly on such an intuition. It is the idea of mechanism that realizes the possibility of a *science* of vital phenomena; the biologist must in actual practice be both a vitalist and a mechanist—the first in order to apprehend the specific reality of the object with which he deals, and the second in order to be able to explain it. What has been described in this chapter as La Mettrie's vitalo-mechanist orientation in biology, with its tendency to merge the two historically contrary viewpoints, represents an attempt on his part to discard altogether the vitalism *versus* mechanism issue by indicating that it rests, in the last analysis, on a problem falsely posed.

Insofar as he is a mechanist, La Mettrie holds to the belief that each pair of related organic and psychic events (which constitute a single event seen from different sides) has its determining cause; so that man is for him but a special instance of the absolute reign of law in nature. He does not, however, trouble to put this opinion beyond dispute by demonstrating that no phenomenon, be it viewed objectively or subjectively, could possibly elude the chain of causal necessity. The truth is that the reign-of-law notion, far from being a consequence of his materialism, is itself a presupposition, empirically quite unverifiable, on which the latter is founded. And since, if there do actually exist physical or psychic facts that are causally indeterminable, these would for that very reason lie outside the range of scientific inquiry, the man-machine theory need not show any further concern about them. It is obvious, then, why La Mettrie nowhere feels obliged to discuss earnestly the question of moral freedom—an omission for which, incidentally, he has been unjustly taken to task by some critics who have overconstrued the meaning of his materialism. Because science is able to deal, by its nature, only with what is determinable, the aim of building a scientific psychology must necessarily take no notice of whatever remains basically unpredictable about the mind, even if this unpredictability should turn out in the end to be its most constant and authentic trait. But here the inadequacy of the *homme machine* idea simply epitomizes the limits inherent to any "science of man." For the assumption made by science that things—mental no less than physical—are determined has nothing to do with whether they are *really* so. It merely expresses the inability of science to deal with phenomena except to the extent of their determinable properties and relations, and its indifference to facts that must finally remain indeterminate and unrelated in their mode of being. La Mettrie does not, on the whole, claim for the man-machine hypothesis a broader scope of validity than is warranted, nor the power to account for what seems from the start to lie beyond its reach. Nevertheless, one of the principal vices of his philosophy is the implication, always present in it, that beyond its utmost limits there can be no further hope of apprehending, by a method other than the mechanistic, the real nature of things.

Although La Mettrie's helplessness before the problem of freedom leaves him no choice but to ignore it altogether, one may suggest that he contributed historically, in an indirect way, to setting that problem in a clearer and more fruitful perspective than it had known before him. This resulted from the dissolving influence of *l'Homme machine* on dualist metaphysics. Within the framework of the psychophysical correspondence adopted in one form or another by the exponents of dualism, it had proved impossible to make any truly meaningful distinction between mind and matter. For if the modifications of matter were believed to be governed by a chain of necessary causes, and if at the same time mental events were seen as regularly paralleling those modifications, it ensued that the realm of mind was no less deterministic in character than that of matter. Dualism thus ended by conceding, willy-nilly, the most significant claim advanced by materialist science—namely, that all phenomena are ruled by necessity; and thereafter it made little difference to keep insisting that mind and matter were nevertheless not the same qualitatively. Coming at this stage in the history of philosophy, the man-machine doctrine did the valuable service of stripping down what had become largely a useless metaphysical construct. By bringing together under a common designation all events, whether physical or mental, which could be interpreted from the standpoint of determinism, it helped in the long run to extricate the problem of freedom—that is, of an inner creativity in both the psychic and material worlds—from the dualist formula, which had proved unfit to do it proper justice. Though La Mettrie is far from intending or foreseeing the outcome, what was to develop finally from the critique implicit in *l'Homme machine* was the dichotomizing of reality into the categories of the determinable and the indeterminable, or, put differently, into the face of things that lies within the field of scientific vision, and the face that is inexorably turned away from it.

But the main goal and achievement of the man-machine idea was, of course, to bring the established method of science into a more intimate and radical union with the specific reality of human nature. For the point is, and has always been, that man in his essence is neither a mind, nor a body; nor is he a mind accompanied by a body, and still less a body accompanied by a mind. He is simultaneously the one and the other, indistinctly and uninterruptedly; that is, he intuitively apprehends his being as a "mind-body." It is for this intuition to provide, so far as possible, the vantage point from which psychology as a science must survey and order its materials, if, that is, it pretends to deal with the real, and not with a theoretically fragmented, man. The dualist assumption, by viewing man basically as a composite of two incompatible substances, could only lead inquiry away from the essential unity of his nature given immediately in experience, and hence away from its possible elucidation. Seen against this background, the merit of *l'Homme machine* lay not so much in its having substituted materialism for spiritualism (for each of these is in itself a more or less neutral abstraction), as in its new and effective orientation of curiosity toward the permanent nucleus of the human mystery. Compared to the smug obfuscations of dualist metaphysics, La Mettrie's proposal to explain how in men and animals alike the phenomena of life, consciousness, thought, and will depend on organic functions gave promise of a more concrete and better focused attack on the mind-body nexus. To be sure, with less inquisitive followers it also risked becoming in its turn as rigid and unimaginative a doctrine as the one it had done well to replace; and indeed this was to be its fate in the varieties of dogmatic materialism devised since the eighteenth century. However, so long as the *homme machine* was understood and applied in the spirit of its author as an inclusive heuristic hypothesis, it may be said to have defined, up to the present time, the rational basis of the type of psychophysiological investigation to which psychology indisputably owes its status as a science of man.

CHAPTER III

THE DEVELOPMENT OF LA METTRIE'S THOUGHT

IT IS STRANGE that, despite many studies on La Mettrie, hardly any mention has yet been made of the evolution of his materialism, or, more particularly, of the man-machine idea that is central to it. The truth is, however, that there took place a crucial change in his philosophical outlook between the *Histoire naturelle de l'âme* of 1745 and *l'Homme machine* of 1747, and that also from 1748 on his interests continued, although less dramatically, to mature and expand in new directions.

Notwithstanding the story of La Mettrie's conversion to materialism by his *fièvre chaude* of 1744, there is evidence before that date of his predilection for such a mode of thought, which would seem, indeed, to have sprung almost irresistibly from the interaction of his temperament and his medical training. From the description he has left of the psychic states accompanying his attack of cholera in 1741, it may be inferred that La Mettrie was already well aware of how vividly the mind-body dependence reveals itself to self-observation during illness.[1] And as early as the *Traité du vertige* of 1737, he had drawn a suggestive conclusion about the nature of mind from certain facts concerning the mental disturbances caused by depression of the cerebral cortex: "On ne doit pas douter que cette petite paralysie, donnant lieu à quelque dérangement dans la distribution des esprits animaux, n'entraîne nécessairement celui de l'esprit; tant il y a d'analogie, & pour ainsi dire, de sympathie entre l'esprit & ce fluide subtil qui circule dans tous les petits filamens nerveux, qu'il paroît par toutes sortes d'observations sûres *que l'un dépend presque essentiellement*, non seulement de la circulation, mais de la quantité & de la qualité de l'autre."[2] Similarly, in the comments he added to his translation of

---

[1] La Mettrie, *Observations de médecine pratique*, Paris, 1743, pp. 9-10.
[2] La Mettrie, *Abrégé de la théorie Chymique. . . . Auquel on a joint le Traité du Vertige*, Paris, 1741, p. 212. (Italics are mine.)

Boerhaave's *Institutiones rei medicae*, we have occasional glimpses of a materialist interpretation of scientific data, which was prompted by La Mettrie's grappling with the major problems of medical theory in his epoch.

But it was not until the *Histoire naturelle de l'âme*, his first venture in philosophy,[3] that La Mettrie gave systematic expression to the intellectual attitudes that he had gradually acquired as a result of his professional experience. This he sought to do, surprisingly enough, by setting up a mechanistic physiology within the conceptual framework of Aristotle's metaphysics. Consequently, the *Histoire de l'âme* remains something of a tour de force. It attempts to reconcile a materialist view of the soul so unorthodox as to have deceived no one, with the Aristotelian-Scholastic complex of ideas (of which various exponents are briskly cited) that had long since been, so to speak, the official property of La Mettrie's chief adversary, the Catholic Church. Although this work, recalling in certain respects the Aristotelianism of a Renaissance figure such as Pomponazzi, deserves to be studied as a philosophical curiosity in its own right, it must be evaluated here mainly from the standpoint of the evolution of *l'Homme machine*.

The *Histoire de l'âme* exhibits, in contrast to the unordered flow of thought in *l'Homme machine*, the conventional architecture of a metaphysical treatise. Starting out from prior definitions of matter and its properties, La Mettrie takes up in deductive fashion first the general principles governing the behavior of living things, and next the specific natures of the different faculties peculiar to the animal as well as the human soul. This characteristic structure, which is in keeping with the special aims of the book, was discarded totally in *l'Homme machine*. The seemingly haphazard composition of the latter reflects the new spirit of La Mettrie's materialism—that of an experimental ideal ranging restlessly within the wide compass of an exploratory hypothesis. That is probably why in 1751 he altered the title of the earlier work to *Traité de l'âme*. From the author's later standpoint, its method

[3] I am leaving out of account the anonymous *Essais sur le raisonnement* (1744), which has been ascribed in turn to Le Mercier and to La Mettrie. In my opinion, internal evidence renders doubtful its attribution to the latter, though the pamphlet is plainly from the hand of a "médecin matérialiste."

would no longer seem empirical enough to merit the designation of "histoire naturelle"; and, when placed beside *l'Homme machine* in the *Oeuvres philosophiques*, it would resemble a veritable *tractatus*—which is in fact precisely how it impresses the reader today.

For our present purpose, it will suffice to sum up in its main lines the metaphysical reasoning on which the *Histoire de l'âme* rests. Matter, considered to be a passive principle when viewed abstractly, is said to acquire by virtue of *form* the "force motrice" which it otherwise possesses only "en puissance."[4] Two types of form are recognized: the passive and the active. The first kind refers to the "propriétés mécaniques-passives de la matière"—that is, to extension and its correlatives of size, shape, and situation[5]—which, when they are unaccompanied by the active forms that bestow force, La Mettrie regards as insufficient for describing the essence of matter. Although the extensibility of matter enables it to take on an infinity of passive forms, it does not actually do so without the aid of the active forms (or motion).[6] But since these latter, in order to confer motive force, must in turn depend on certain passive mechanical properties of matter,[7] La Mettrie soon finds himself involved in a circular argument. Hardly daunted, he goes on to affirm that the "substance des corps" does possess *force motrice* in an "union essentielle & primitive," inasmuch as all existing bodies, being capable of motion, represent in effect combinations of matter and the appropriate active forms.[8]

Another and higher potentiality is realized when, by virtue of the "formes substantielles," matter manifests in organized beings the ability to *feel*. The substantial forms are of two sorts: those that correspond to the structure of the organism, and those that constitute its "principe de vie."[9] The second category comprises the "vegetative soul" and the "sensitive soul." La Mettrie takes pains, thereupon, to prove that the so-called rational soul is nothing but a modification of the *faculté sensitive*; in other words, he follows Locke in maintaining that all our ideas result from sensation. He concludes that there is only one substance—matter—in man and beast alike, and that "l'Ame dépend essentiellement des organes du corps, avec lesquels elle se forme, croît, décroît."[10]

[4] *Oeuvres*, I, 68-69, 73. [5] *ibid.*, p. 75. [6] *ibid.*, p. 76.
[7] *ibid.*, pp. 79, 81. [8] *ibid.*, pp. 77-78, 79-80. [9] *ibid.*, p. 89.
[10] *ibid.*, p. 232.

This outline, however brief, is enough to make it clear that if in the *Histoire de l'âme* La Mettrie arrives at some of the same conclusions as those of *l'Homme machine*, he does so by a very different route. The entire metaphysical basis of the earlier work was, in fact, abandoned in 1747. One reason for this must doubtless have been La Mettrie's awareness that he had failed on the whole to establish, in accordance with his aims, a materialist metaphysics. His "doctrine of forms" suffered from a glaring inner ambiguity. On the one hand, he employed the concept of form in the purely physical sense of "de simples modifications de matière." But on the other hand, because it was evident that "les parties de cette substance qui reçoivent des formes me peuvent pas elles-mêmes se les donner,"[11] he was obliged to make of form also the cause of the modifications. The materiality of the cause, however, was far from being as apparent as that of the effect. Thus form became, as the occasion demanded, either passive or active, the modified or the modifier, material or nonmaterial; and La Mettrie was unable in the end to resolve these contradictory aspects of natural process into a single coherent explanation. If the problem of a materialist metaphysics is to show how, by logical necessity, matter engenders from itself the world of forms by which life, sensibility, and thought are sustained, it must be admitted that in the *Histoire de l'âme* the solution of this problem remained largely verbal.

In *l'Homme machine* such questions were dropped altogether, and La Mettrie instead asked ironically how anyone, "à moins que de ressusciter avec l'Auteur de l'Histoire de l'Ame l'ancienne & inintelligible Doctrine des *formes substantielles*," could hope to explain by what means matter, "d'inerte & simple, devient active & composée d'organes." But the best evidence of his dissatisfaction with the "pseudometaphysics" of the *Histoire de l'âme* and of the changed outlook that followed it is to be found in the "Lettre critique à Mme du Chattelet" which he affixed to the 1747 edition of the work, and which may thus be said almost to coincide in time with the writing of *l'Homme machine*. The importance of the "Lettre critique" for plotting the development of La Mettrie's thought has apparently escaped scholarly attention. It is admittedly

[11] *ibid.*, p. 81.

not an easy piece to interpret, for, together with sincere autocriticism, it contains (in the manner dear to its author) a large share of tongue-in-cheek humor. However, if we bear in mind the general differences already noted between the *Histoire de l'âme* and *l'Homme machine*, the import of much of the "Lettre critique" will become fairly clear, and will serve in turn to clarify more fully those same differences. In 1747, then, La Mettrie complained as follows about his own mode of reasoning in the *Histoire de l'âme*: "Cet Auteur entreprend d'abord de nous persuader que la matière n'est pas seulement susceptible d'activité, ou même dépositaire du mouvement; mais de plus il paroît soutenir qu'elle a la force motrice, ou la puissance de se mouvoir par elle-même. Or, si on lui demande comment cette puissance parvient à l'ACTE? comment une matière qui est en repos, vient à se mouvoir? il répond sans balancer, que cela vient de je ne sai quelle FORME SUBSTANTIELLE ACTIVE, par laquelle la matière acquiert l'exercice actuel de sa faculté motrice. D'où vient encore cette forme substantielle? d'une autre matière déjà revêtue de cette forme, & qui par conséquent a déjà reçu le mouvement d'une autre substance également active. N'est-ce pas là, Madame, visiblement expliquer le mouvement par le mouvement . . . ? Car voit-on autre chose, dans tout ce vieux jargon inintelligible, qu'une communication successive de mouvemens, qu'une puissance motrice, laquelle n'est jamais dans la matière qui reçoit le mouvement, mais toujours dans celle qui le lui communique, & qu'elle l'a encore elle-même emprunté d'une autre; de sorte qu'en remontant à la première substance matérielle qui a mis les autres en mouvement, il s'ensuit qu'elle tient d'ailleurs son principe d'activité, je veux dire de cette Intelligence suprême, universelle, qui se manifeste si clairement dans toute la Nature. . . . Jusques-là, Madame, le choix que fait notre Ecrivain des Maîtres qui le guident, n'est pas heureux; il veut nous éclairer sur les propriétés de la matière, & il affecte de marcher dans les ténèbres de l'Antiquité, & de nous offrir par-tout les frivolités des Scholastiques. . . . Les Scholastiques ont cru devoir attribuer à la matière une faculté sensitive, périssable comme les autres formes, afin de ne point confondre l'Ame matérielle des Animaux, avec l'Ame spirituelle de l'Homme. C'est pourquoi, depuis Descartes même, ils ont introduit en Philosophie ce phantôme antique des FORMES SUBSTANTIELLES. Notre Auteur, séduit peut-être par des autorités respectables, a rappellé ces chimères qu'on croioit à jamais bannies; il a voulu ranimer des ETRES DE RAISON, qui ne peuvent que semer le doute dans l'esprit des Hommes qui pensent."[12]

These lines, which are at first puzzling because of their self-deprecating tendency, make good sense when they are viewed as preparing the ground for *l'Homme machine*, where La Mettrie, after the loss of his metaphysical pretensions, was to confine his thinking scrupulously to the domain of physiological psychology and to refrain completely, as we have seen, from asserting anything about the general properties of matter or from setting up "motive force" as a regular attribute of bodies. What is retained in *l'Homme machine* of the original concept of *force motrice* is, in fact, merely its biological counterpart—the idea of organic automaticity. Since La Mettrie's new concern is to show concretely how the organism moves itself independently of any immaterial cause, he now establishes its "specific energy," not by deduction from a definition of matter, but by inference from the data of muscular irritability. Along with this, he gives up the hope of expounding rationalistically the development of organic forms. Instead, the self-procreating behavior of the polyp is cited in proof of the claim that matter contains within itself, without the benefit of any soul whatever, the causes necessary for generation; and that biology, ignorant as it still is of these, must at least assume their existence and efficacy. It is therefore not accidental that La Mettrie made no reference to the polyp in the *Histoire de l'âme*, and that the principle of irritability, destined soon to play so decisive a role in his biological philosophy, was mentioned there only in passing and with a somewhat different intention. In contrast to the *Histoire de l'âme*, what *l'Homme machine* plainly accomplishes is the thoroughgoing divorce of biology from both metaphysics and theology. And if, on the one hand, the method of biological explanation is thereby restricted and made to coincide with the scope of a hypothetical materialism, on the other, it is assured absolute freedom and indefinite possibilities within its special limits. Concurrently with

[12] La Mettrie, *Histoire naturelle de l'âme, nouvelle édition augmentée de La Lettre Critique à Madame La Marquise du Chattelet*, Oxford, 1747, pp. 3-5, 7.

this, the elimination from psychophysical inquiry of obsolete Aristotelian notions—such as those of substantial form, sensitive soul, and the rest—reflects La Mettrie's renunciation of the desire to explain the inner connection between consciousness and organic process. Instead, he is left in *l'Homme machine* simply with the factual evidence of a constant correlation between those two orders of phenomena, and is resigned to accept such a correlation as the practical equivalent of a causal link.

Apart from the dissimilarities already noted, the *Histoire de l'âme* cannot even be said properly to contain the man-machine idea. The mechanistic conception which is present in its pages has, when compared to that of *l'Homme machine*, a subordinate position and a different meaning. While it is true that in 1745 La Mettrie subscribes in a general way to the iatrophysical doctrine "puisée à la source boerhavienne," and proceeds to treat in detail the various mechanisms of sight, hearing, smell, and so forth, it does not follow from this that he already thinks of *man* as a machine. The reason is that he still believes, in a quite conventional manner, that mechanism as such can apply only to the unconscious and instinctual acts of the organism. Thus, a separation is made regularly in the *Histoire de l'âme* between the organic machine itself, and the vegetative and sensitive souls, both of which are regarded, not without some vagueness, as alternately receptive and presiding principles—nonmechanical, though material and extended, in nature. About the vegetative soul, for example, La Mettrie states: "Les anciens entendoient par l'âme végétative la cause qui dirige toutes les opérations de la génération, de la nutrition & de l'accroissement de tous les corps vivans. Les modernes, peu attentifs à l'idée que ces premiers maîtres avoient de cette espèce d'âme, l'ont confondue avec l'organisation même des végétaux & des animaux, tandis qu'elle est la cause qui conduit & dirige cette organisation."[13] The same kind of distinction is made between the merely mechanical, as opposed to the truly conscious, aspect of sensation: "Les philosophes ont rapporté à l'âme sensitive toutes les facultés qui servent à lui exciter des sensations. Cependant il faut bien distinguer ces facultés, qui sont purement mécaniques, de celles qui appartiennent véritablement à l'être sensitif."[14] In the

[13] *Oeuvres*, I, 92. [14] *ibid.*, p. 100; see also pp. 93-94, 98.

first group are included the various apparati of sensation and the organic dispositions that determine instincts, inclinations, appetites —in short, everything over which no conscious control can be exercised. The second class includes the faculties belonging "en propre à l'être sensitif, comme les sensations, les perceptions, le discernement, les connoissances, &c."[15] From this it would seem that in the *Histoire de l'âme* a remnant of animistic thought, however materialized it might be, is still present; and consequently the soul is viewed as a special physical substance, rather obscure in nature, which inhabits the body and remains at the same time distinct from, but under the influence of, the organic functions. It is for this reason that, on occasion, La Mettrie can speak about the sensitive soul independently of the organism which it animates: "Nous ignorons quelles qualités doit acquérir le principe matériel sensitif, pour avoir la faculté immédiate de sentir; nous ne savons pas si ce principe possède cette puissance dans toute sa perfection, dès le premier instant qu'il habite un corps animé."[16] That is also why in the *Histoire de l'âme* the problem of fixing the "siège de l'âme" assumes such an importance that La Mettrie is obliged to take special pains to arrive at a solution, whereas in 1747 this problem is treated, on the whole, indifferently and negligently. It is not until *l'Homme machine* that La Mettrie, in possession of a new idea of mechanism radical enough to embrace both the conscious and unconscious processes, at last equates the soul quite simply with the total product of the innumerable operations of the organic machine.

That in 1745 La Mettrie had not yet thought of the man-machine theory is further borne out by textual evidence. The original edition of the *Histoire de l'âme* contains some remarks which read like a blunt denial of the author's subsequent philosophy, for on that occasion La Mettrie said about the mechanical basis of instinct in animals: "Mais ce même corbeau, ces oiseaux de la grande espèce qui parcourent les airs, ont le sentiment propre à leur instinct; ce ne sont donc point, encore une fois, des automates, comme le veut Descartes, semblables à une pendule ou au fluteur de Vaucanson. Et à plus forte raison Spinosa a-t-il tort de prétendre que l'homme ressemble à une montre plus ou moins parfaite (qui marque les

[15] *ibid.*, p. 101.   [16] *ibid.*, p. 178.

heures, les minutes, les jours du mois, de la Lune, ou seulement quelques-unes de ces choses, selon son mécanisme, ainsi qu'elle les marque plus ou moins régulièrement selon la bonté & la justesse de ses ressorts) ou à un Vaisseau sans pilote au milieu de la mer, qui par sa construction a le pouvoir de voguer, mais est déterminé par les vents & par les courans à aller plutôt d'un côté que de l'autre, en sorte que ce sont toujours les uns qui le poussent ou les autres qui l'entraînent."[17] It is obvious why these lines, which flatly contradicted the standpoint of *l'Homme machine*, were removed from the 1751 version of the *Traité de l'âme*. At the same time another passage, in which La Mettrie had again ascribed to Spinoza what were one day to be his own opinions, was also deleted: "Ne connoissant ni Dieu, ni Ame, Cartésien outré, il fait de l'homme même un véritable automate, une machine assujetie à la plus constante nécessité, entraînée par un impétueux fatalisme, comme un vaisseau par le courant des eaux."[18] In fact, La Mettrie was led by the change in his philosophical outlook to add to the text of 1751 a remark which indicated a complete reversal in his estimate of Spinoza, the erstwhile "monstre d'incrédulité": "Dans le système de Spinosa . . . adieu la Loy naturelle, nos principes naturels ne sont que nos principes accoutumés! . . . Suivant Spinosa encore, l'homme est un véritable Automate, une Machine assujettie à la plus constante nécessité. . . . L'Auteur de *l'Homme machine* semble avoir fait son livre exprès pour défendre cette triste vérité."[19]

In the cases of Descartes and Locke, just as in that of Spinoza, La Mettrie's loyalties were reversed by the evolution of his thought. It would be no exaggeration to say that the *Histoire de l'âme* had been written, above all, against the philosophy of Descartes. La Mettrie had sought in Aristotelian metaphysics—adopted by him "parce qu'elle forme un système solide, bien lié, & comme un corps qui manque à tous ces membres épars de la physique moderne"[20] —the means he needed to refute such key doctrines of Cartesianism as the dual nature of man, the passivity of matter, the *bête ma-*

---

[17] La Mettrie, *Histoire naturelle de l'âme*, La Haye, 1745, pp. 150-51.
[18] *ibid.*, pp. 249-50.
[19] *Oeuvres philosophiques*, Londres [Berlin], 1751, *Abrégé des Systêmes*, pp. 237-38.
[20] *Oeuvres*, I, 86-87.

chine, innate ideas, and so forth. Simultaneously he had revealed himself as a close and ardent follower of Locke, in keeping with whose example the *Histoire de l'âme* had made central to its discussions the problem of demonstrating the identity of the sensitive and rational souls, as if that purely epistemological issue had a decisive bearing on the author's general thesis. In *l'Homme machine*, however, these relationships underwent a neat *volte-face*. Aware now that the crucial problem of his materialism was mechanistic rather than epistemological in character—for it had to do with establishing the true automaticity of the organic machine—La Mettrie demoted the British empiricist to a secondary position among the precursors of the man-machine theory, and went on to upbraid "tous ces petits Philosophes, mauvais plaisans, & mauvais Singes de Locke," who, like himself a few years earlier, had "laughed impudently in Descartes's face." At the same time Descartes was openly honored as the intellectual ancestor of *l'Homme machine*.

Although the impulse toward a coherent philosophy of science was no doubt of primary importance in the development of La Mettrie's ideas, certain biographical factors should also be taken into account. The *Histoire de l'âme* impresses us, in comparison with *l'Homme machine*, as a mitigated defense of materialism, in the course of which the author, proceeding in the footsteps of Aristotle, strives continually to harmonize his views with theological orthodoxy. This traditionalist approach may plausibly be attributed, at least in part, to practical considerations. During the composition of the *Histoire de l'âme*, La Mettrie was still living in France, where both his professional career and his personal safety were at stake. He consequently had every reason to probe the ground carefully and to seek a possible accommodation with the authorities in power. When the failure of this attempt eventually forced him into exile, he imagined (too hastily, it is true) that he had little else to lose, and so it was natural enough that his thinking should grow bolder and more incisive. Moreover, it was not the acquisition of new knowledge that brought about the shift in La Mettrie's orientation, because the biological data which he used to conclusive advantage in 1747 had been, for the most part, available to him in 1745. The maturing of his materialism must be regarded principally as the outcome of a fresh interpretation of the scientific facts that were known to him previously. This, however, does not mean that La Mettrie, already believing privately in 1745 what he was to express publicly in 1747, had simply decided at first to "coat the pill" in order to render it more palatable. His philosophical outlook was sincerely different in the *Histoire de l'âme*, and it is not inconsistent to suppose that the vicissitudes of his life were among the causes that brought about the subsequent change in that outlook.

It remains now to consider briefly how La Mettrie's writings from 1748 on confirmed, extended, or modified the thesis of *l'Homme machine*.

The first of these works, *l'Homme plante*, is concerned with describing the various parallels between the structure and functioning of the human and the vegetable "machines." As expected, the vegetative soul of the *Histoire de l'âme* is here explicitly withdrawn from the domain of plant physiology.[21] However, the chief significance of *l'Homme plante* lies in the fact that it adopts and construes materialistically the Leibnizian chain of Being concept, which later serves as an important ingredient of the evolutionist theorizing in the *Système d'Epicure*. The world of organic beings is said to compose, from the simplest up to the most complex mechanisms, an "échelle imperceptiblement graduée, où l'on voit la nature exactement passer par tous les degrés, sans jamais sauter en quelque sorte un seul échelon dans toutes ses productions diverses."[22]

In the *Discours sur le bonheur*, a work not yet understood as fully as it deserves, La Mettrie unfolded some of the major consequences for moral philosophy that were implicit in the man-machine doctrine. The gist of his remarks appeared to the eighteenth century hardly less outrageous than original. Viewing happiness—the ever-elusive *summum bonum*—through the medium of his medical interests, La Mettrie was inclined to find it mainly in what might be called nowadays a state of emotional well-being, which he divorced in all essential respects from the observance of a given moral code and from any specific pursuits or commit-

[21] *ibid.*, II, 16-17.
[22] *ibid.*, p. 20.

ments of an intellectual or religious sort. Such a conclusion was, in his opinion, urged on us by common experience. For it is no secret that many persons are made happy by some "vice," while the corresponding "virtue" would probably render them unhappy; that some are made anxious and wretched by a belief in God and in eternal punishment, whereas a frank agnosticism would restore their tranquillity of mind; that still others, finally, are blissful in a state of gross ignorance which, if dispelled, would only bring them suffering. Therefore, reasons La Mettrie, such ideal values as virtue, faith, and knowledge cannot be said to have more than an incidental connection, either positive or negative as the case may be, with the problem of individual happiness. The crux of the matter is that the world is actually full of people who are immoral but happy, and of others who, despite all their virtuous qualities, are unhappy; of many who are intelligent, cultured, or pious, but nevertheless miserable, and of others who, although stupid and devoid of faith, are yet favored with self-satisfied good spirits. This embarrassing state of affairs, which moralists and theologians have always done their hypocritical best to ignore or conceal, is clarified easily enough by the man-machine theory. According to La Mettrie, happiness is basically neither an ethical, religious, nor intellectual fact, but a psychological one; and, like all psychological phenomena, it is a product of the organic machine, which is unique in each case and gives to each person the destiny of his particular set of desires and capabilities. Within the framework of this individual endowment, the mind, under the influence of the body, possesses an instinct toward happiness, just as the latter possesses an instinct toward health. But the one will be unhappy, and the other will be sick, in proportion to the inability of a defective constitution to realize the instinct in question. We are "heureusement ou malheureusement né"; the rest is relatively unimportant. This critique by La Mettrie does not, it is true, cast much light on the key problems of ethics, which are those of moral freedom and the nature of obligation. Its upshot is, however, to bring into serious doubt the conventional link, which has perhaps always been too complacently accepted, between the so-called moral (or "higher") life and the attainment of individual happiness.

Having denied one of mankind's most cherished illusions—namely, the hope of discovering a general formula for happiness—La Mettrie goes on to treat, with his usual aplomb, the no less delicate subject of remorse. Whereas in *l'Homme machine* remorse was regarded as the automatic response to a violation of the natural sense of right and wrong, the *Discours sur le bonheur* looks upon it as an unnatural reaction inculcated during the early years of childhood. Since our wishes and conduct, determined as they are by the organism, cannot in any case be chosen freely, there could be no rational justification for remorse. The practical demands of society should be enforced, as La Mettrie sees it, by the sole means of inspiring a healthy objective fear in those who would transgress against the laws—a fear that now becomes, incidentally, his pragmatic equivalent of the moral sense. But the nurturing by education of the morbid inward fear known as remorse (or guilt) is as psychologically harmful as it is socially useless. First, those who are most vulnerable to it are, as a rule, those who need it least; while the really vicious, for whom it is specially intended, manage to be far less affected by it. Thus remorse has the general effect of preventing the relatively virtuous from enjoying life, without, however, spoiling sufficiently the fun of the relatively wicked. Besides, it is more or less ineffectual with everyone because it is ordinarily felt *post facto*; whereas to have a restraining influence on specific actions, it would have to precede them. Given the same circumstances and the same psychophysical factors that have already produced a particular act, these will continue to produce it regardless of the remorse felt on each occasion. In short, while remorse—or the sense of guilt—makes hardly anyone better, it succeeds in making everyone unhappier. La Mettrie sees in the torments of conscience a sort of futile revenge exacted by society for its impotence to obtain perfect submission to its wishes.

Notwithstanding how the eighteenth century saw it, such a new application of the man-machine idea to the moral sphere was motivated by an attitude of psychiatric humaneness rather than by a desire to encourage vice. To be sure, La Mettrie was a rather poor psychologist in supposing that remorse could be altogether avoided by a suitable upbringing, and also in minimizing its inhibitory effects on behavior in general. But these were mainly errors of exaggeration. The core of his reasoning surely makes better sense to us today than it did to his contemporaries. It may be summed up as follows: There is in every human being, apart from his personal traits and life situation, an autonomous instinct toward a state of psychic well-being, which, however, is too often frustrated by the attempts of society to link happiness with specific ethical, religious, or intellectual creeds. This instinct, which normally seeks its goal by means of sensual gratification and by pleasure in all its other forms, should be freed and given a more positive role in the mental economy, for Nature has in fact intended that everyone be happy. But before things can come to that, the individual must acquire by a desensitization of conscience the requisite degree of resistance to remorse, without which he will be unable, in the face of social pressures, to satisfy his unique desires in the confident and cheerful frame of mind that is more or less identical with happiness. It is made plain by these attitudes that La Mettrie was among the first to perceive, in his intuitive way, that one of the most besetting dilemmas of the modern civilizing process lay in the constant increase of the individual sense of guilt, which, emerging as a noxious by-product of cultural progress, actually threatened to nullify its many gains for humanity. His prescription for the cure of this oppressive guilt complex must surely be considered inadequate as a *spécifique*, for, influenced by the psychological optimism of his age, he did not reckon properly the depth and urgency—indeed the tragic fatefulness—of the psychic forces involved. But the man-machine theme allowed him at least to move toward a correct diagnosis of the malady.

It was on this general issue, moreover, that La Mettrie finally fell out with the philosophes, who, so long as the concept of natural law had been upheld, were quite unperturbed by the man-machine doctrine, even if it did contain the seeds of the *Discours sur le bonheur*. Their theory of natural law had been built on the premise that human behavior was essentially rational and hence could be judged by universally valid norms. But it was no idle quip when La Mettrie said about the consequences of his scientific inquiry: "A force de Raison, on parvient à faire peu de cas de la

Raison." The single-minded exploration of the biological labyrinth that is man resulted, predictably enough, in the subordination of reason to instinct as the controlling factor in psychology. Seen from this new perspective, the moral restraints imposed by social education seemed far less to regulate the instincts than to introduce stresses into the "machine" that impeded its automatic pursuit of happiness. La Mettrie, prompted as always by his medical loyalties, therefore became more eager to restore the optimum operation of the man-machine than to preserve the social value of its malfunctioning. In dispensing thus with the utility of a universal moral code (except perhaps as a vague and distant ideal of the human race), he definitely took his stand against the optimistic rationalism of eighteenth-century ethics. The answer that Voltaire made to all this in his *Poème sur la loi naturelle* was a brilliant summary of the natural-law conception, but it can hardly be said to have cleared away the difficulties raised by La Mettrie. As for Diderot, his attack against La Mettrie's "counterethics" betrayed an acerbity that sprang really from desperation; for, having long since grasped the full seriousness of the challenge it posed, he had himself, in *Le Neveu de Rameau* and *Le Voyage de Bougainville*, already struggled more or less in vain to surmount the dilemma growing out of the clash of reason and instinct which, in the higher civilizations, defeats man's hope of happiness.

Another work by La Mettrie, *Les Animaux plus que machines*, was in the main a polemical piece aimed at a certain Dr. Balthasar Tralles, who had published a lengthy refutation of *l'Homme machine*. On this occasion La Mettrie's tactic was to elaborate an ironic defense of the animistic position, in the course of which he managed to expose indirectly its various weaknesses and absurdities. Such being the case, *Les Animaux plus que machines* adds little of moment to the thesis of *l'Homme machine*, although it does help to clarify several points of detail. La Mettrie takes pains, for instance, to rectify the false impression left by *l'Homme machine* that he wished to place human beings and animals on exactly the same level. What he had meant to say, of course, was that human and animal intelligence depended alike on the same sort of organic causation, but that such a common derivation did not prevent the capacity of man's mind from being vastly superior to that of the beasts.[23]

In the *Système d'Epicure*, which contained a theoretical sketch of organic evolution, La Mettrie's materialism took on a wholly new dimension. The problem of the origin of living forms, which he had first tried to solve metaphysically in the *Histoire de l'âme*, only to discard it completely in *l'Homme machine*, was now taken up once more, but this time within the framework of naturalistic science. La Mettrie's efforts mirrored in this respect the influence exerted by the current of transformistic thought which, only a year or two before, had been initiated by such works as de Maillet's *Telliamed* and Diderot's *Lettre sur les aveugles*. The *Système d'Epicure* sought to explain the formation of living things in terms of an agglomeration of certain "graines ou semences, tant animales que végétales" presumed to be present in the atmosphere, and which were obvious counterparts of the "molécules organiques" newly publicized by Buffon's *Histoire naturelle*. In La Mettrie's opinion, the successive combinations of these "semences" have brought about, in the course of time and by a process of natural selection, the evolution of organic beings from the simplest to the most complex forms, and from seriously defective to more or less perfect structures. He observes: "Les premières générations ont dû être fort imparfaites. Ici l'oesophage aura manqué; là l'estomac, la vulve, les intestins, &c. Il est évident que les seuls animaux qui auront pu vivre, se conserver, & perpétuer leur espece, auront été ceux qui se seront trouvés munis de toutes les pieces nécessaires à la génération, & auxquels en un mot aucune partie essentielle n'aura manqué. Réciproquement ceux qui auront été privés de quelque partie d'une nécessité absolue, seront morts ou peu de tems après leur naissance, ou du moins sans se reproduire. La perfection n'a pas plus été l'ouvrage d'un jour pour la nature, que pour l'art."[24] But the *Système d'Epicure*, which is little more than a collection of random réflexions, does not attempt to work these very promising ideas into a consistent hypothesis, as perhaps La Mettrie would have done if he had lived long enough. Never-

[23] *ibid.*, pp. 78-80, 82-84. This question had already been discussed briefly in *l'Homme plante, ibid.*, pp. 23-24.
[24] *ibid.*, III, 220-21.

theless his materialism did arrive at a coherent, if somewhat cursory, vision of the *homme machine* set within the appropriate context of an evolutionary, naturalistic biology: "Comme, posées certaines loix physiques, il n'étoit pas possible que la mer n'eût son flux & son reflux, de même certaines loix du mouvement ayant existé, elles ont formé des yeux qui ont vu, des oreilles qui ont entendu, des nerfs qui ont senti, une langue tantôt capable & tantôt incapable de parler, suivant son organisation; enfin elles ont fabriqué le viscere de la pensée. La nature a fait dans la machine de l'homme, une autre machine qui s'est trouvée propre à retenir les idées & à en faire de nouvelles. . . . Ayant fait, sans voir, des yeux qui voient, elle a fait sans penser, une machine qui pense."[25] This brief synthesis, with which La Mettrie's speculation came to an immature end, still traces the path along which the sciences of life are able to approach, and slowly to push back, the mystery of the psyche.

[25] *ibid.*, pp. 226-27.

CHAPTER IV

THE HISTORICAL BACKGROUND OF *L'HOMME MACHINE*

THE sources of the man-machine idea are so diversified that the present account of them must concern itself with only those that proved to be of some special importance. For the sake of convenience, the influences that acted on La Mettrie will be discussed under the separate headings of philosophy, free thought, and medical science, although it should be stressed from the start that in their concrete reality the ideas present in La Mettrie's mind, far from falling into such neat categories, often cut across all three.

The philosophical germ from which *l'Homme machine* grew, as the author's insistence on the point makes perfectly clear, was the Cartesian doctrine of the *bête machine*. From Descartes's time until that of La Mettrie, the paradox of a nonconscious animal-automaton had given rise to endless metaphysical controversy about whether or not beasts possessed a soul, and, if they did, of what sort it was.[1] But of greater significance for the problem now facing us was the relationship of the *bête machine* concept, not so much to the dualist metaphysics from which it had been deduced, as to the Cartesian "science of man," which was exemplified by the mechanistic biology of the *Traité de l'homme* and by the system of physiological psychology given in the *Passions de l'âme*. When seen from this standpoint, it would appear that the beast-machine was simply absorbed into the broad current of iatromechanist thought, and all the more naturally because the latter, despite its independent origins in seventeenth-century medicine, had found its strongest stimulus and most comprehensive statement in Descartes's writings.[2] The *bête machine* underwent

[1] On this subject, cf. Leonora C. Rosenfield, *From Beast-Machine to Man-Machine: Animal Soul in French Letters from Descartes to La Mettrie*, New York, 1941.
[2] For Descartes's contribution to iatromechanism, see Auguste-Georges Berthier, "Le mécanisme cartésien et la physiologie au xviie siècle," *Isis*, II (1914), 37-89; III, (1920), 21-58.

a gradual transformation in this special context until it came to mean, not that animals were pure automata devoid of sensation and self-awareness, but rather that the various manifestations of consciousness, instinct, sensibility, and even intelligence, all of which seemed empirically to typify animal behavior, ought to be explained exclusively in terms of the organic machine. But such a method was equally applicable to human psychology, if one only took the trouble, as Descartes had done, to conciliate the theologians by allowing beforehand that, in the unique case of man, the organism functioned in concert with a rational soul which alone defined his essence. This essence, however, could only grow less and less essential as the method of psychophysical inquiry progressively sought, in particular with the growing aid of comparative anatomy, to clarify the mechanics of mental activity without calling it into use.

In *l'Homme machine* La Mettrie extended to the human species, by force of analogy, the meaning that animal automatism, following its separation from Cartesian metaphysics, had eventually come to have in the iatromechanist school. He remarked about this step: "enfin [Descartes] a connu la Nature Animale; il a le premier parfaitement démontré que les Animaux étoient de pures Machines. Or après une découverte de cette importance ... le moien sans ingratitude, de ne pas faire grace à toutes ses erreurs! Elles sont à mes yeux toutes réparées par ce grand aveu. Car enfin, quoi qu'il chante sur la distinction des deux substances, il est visible que ce n'est qu'un tour d'adresse, une ruse de stile, pour faire avaler aux Théologiens un poison caché à l'ombre d'une Analogie qui frappe tout le Monde, & qu'eux seuls ne voient pas. Car c'est elle, c'est cette forte Analogie, qui force tous les Savans & les vrais juges d'avouer que ces êtres fiers & vains, plus distingués par leur orgueil, que par le nom d'Hommes ... ne sont au fond que des Animaux, & des Machines perpendiculairement rampantes." In his praise for Descartes's presumed duplicity, La Mettrie tends, of course, to interpret Cartesianism somewhat anachronistically in the light of eighteenth-century literary tactics. Accordingly, he chides himself elsewhere about his own imprudence in *l'Homme machine*, and appears to envy Descartes's slyness: "Il falloit être aussi rusé que votre compatriote, c'est-à-dire, laisser tirer aux autres de si dangereuses conséquences. . . . Ce grand philosophe a dit, l'animal est ainsi fait; l'homme est ainsi fait: il a montré les deux tableaux, mais il n'a pas dit, voyez combien ils se ressemblent! Au contraire, il s'est fort bien passé d'ame dans les animaux pour expliquer leurs mouvemens, leurs sentimens, & toute l'étendue de leur discernement, mais il ne s'en est point passé dans l'homme; il a voulu paraître orthodoxe aux yeux du peuple, & philosophe aux yeux des philosophes."[3]

The contemporaries of Descartes had already objected that if the *bête machine* concept were accepted, it would be very difficult in the end to prove that man himself was not a machine. The sheer absurdity of such a consequence—for the term "machine" was understood by these critics to exclude the possibility of consciousness—continued to be cited by later thinkers, in particular by Leibniz, as a self-evident refutation of animal automatism. However, the conversion of the *bête machine* into the *homme machine* lost much of its implausibility when Descartes's doctrine was taken in its alternate sense; and this was in fact how La Mettrie saw the matter when he announced exultantly: "Avant Descartes, aucun Philosophe n'avoit regardé les animaux comme des machines. Depuis cet homme célebre, un seul moderne des plus hardis s'est avisé de réveiller une opinion, qui sembloit condamnée à un oubli, & même à un mépris perpétuel, non pour venger son compatriote, mais portant la témérité au plus haut point, pour appliquer à l'homme, sans nul détour, ce qui avoit été dit des animaux."[4] La Mettrie exaggerates here the boldness and novelty of what he did, for there was actually, as I have described elsewhere,[5] an extensive movement of ideas which, prior to the appearance of *l'Homme machine*, had already derived from Cartesian biology a more or

[3] In "Epître à mon esprit, ou l'anonyme persiflé," *Oeuvres*, II, 215-16.
[4] In *Les animaux plus que machines, ibid.*, p. 29. This interpretation of Cartesian influence was echoed by contemporary observers, one of whom, D-R. Bouillier, wrote: "Les esprits forts . . . ne veulent rien admettre que de matériel. . . . Ils veulent qu'absolument l'homme soit une machine; machine pensante à la vérité, mais pur automate après tout. C'est une extension du roman de Descartes sur les animaux, avec cette différence, qu'au lieu que ce roman-ci tendoit à relever l'excellence de l'homme, l'autre n'a pour but que de le dégrader" (*Pièces philosophiques et littéraires*, 1759, p. 22).
[5] *Diderot and Descartes: A Study of Scientific Naturalism in the Enlightenment*, Princeton, 1953, especially Chap. IV.

less consistently mechanistic view of man. In order to explore the subject further with the aid of new information, I propose to deal in this chapter with those influences which La Mettrie specifically acknowledged, or which were so immediate to his milieu as to be unavoidable. It will appear from such a study that, while the man-machine idea had been expressed in a variety of ways before 1747, La Mettrie's rehandling of the theme was in a class by itself with respect to depth and originality.

Among the philosophical intermediaries between Descartes and La Mettrie, one may begin by mentioning Malebranche. Though he regarded the latter's system of occasionalist metaphysics as made up of "l'erreur, l'illusion, les rêves, le délire,"[6] La Mettrie realized that no one else had shown more relentless ingenuity in working out the details of a mechanistic psychophysiology. As a result, he was tempted to divorce Malebranche's dualism from the whole system of scientific explanation and conjecture that accompanied it in the *Recherche de la vérité*: "Quoiqu'il admette dans l'homme deux substances distinctes, il explique les facultés de l'ame par celles de la matière."[7] Such a materialist interpretation was, La Mettrie believed, encouraged to some extent by Malebranche himself, who had stated that, while the concepts of mind and will were essentially independent of the notion of matter, they were nonetheless abstractions that could be rendered distinct and palpable only by reference to the material world: "Parce que ces idées sont fort abstraites et qu'elles ne tombent point sous l'imagination, il semble à propos de les exprimer par rapport aux propriétés qui conviennent à la matière, lesquelles, se pouvant facilement imaginer, rendront les notions qu'il est bon d'attacher à ces deux mots *entendement* et *volonté,* plus distinctes et même plus familières."[8] In carrying out this proposal Malebranche became, in La Mettrie's words, "le premier des Philosophes qui ait mis fort en vogue les esprits animaux"[9]—those imperceptible "spirits" which, by their ubiquitous and instantaneous activity, seemed to link body and soul together in a single entity. But whereas for Malebranche this linkage was merely *occasional* in character, we

---
[6] *Oeuvres*, I, 171.   [7] *ibid.*, p. 242.
[8] Nicolas Malebranche, *De la recherche de la vérité*, éd. G. Lewis, Paris, 1946, I, i; I, 2.
[9] *Oeuvres*, I, 242-43.

have seen that for La Mettrie it came to have a causal value. Such a transition was hardly unusual, for the entire tendency of science since the second half of the seventeenth century, as shown particularly by Newtonian physics and the experimental method it fostered, had been to view causation in the light of an empirical correspondence of events rather than of substance and its modes of being. Thus if mental phenomena were, as Malebranche had said, concretely knowable and describable qua matter, there could be in the end no scientific reason for assuming the separate existence of an immaterial soul.

Among those who elaborated the *bête machine* idea in a manner favorable to materialism, La Mettrie himself singles out for comment—although there were others—Claude Perrault and Thomas Willis. The contribution of each was, however, somewhat different. Perrault's general position may properly be described as animistic, for he believed that the sensations experienced by animals could not be fully explained in terms of mechanism alone. But the soul which he felt it necessary to call into service was one that no longer retained its substantial distinctness, inasmuch as it combined the role of thinking with that of regulating the organic functions and was defined, moreover, as coextensive with the body. Perrault's animism consequently appeared to La Mettrie to have reached the threshold of materialism. This appraisal does seem largely justified when one examines the *Mechanique des animaux*, in which Perrault's animistic reservations do not in the least interfere with his "dessein . . . d'expliquer par la mechanique les principales fonctions des animaux,"[10] and where the notion of soul has in fact no concrete place whatever in his scrupulously mechanistic explanations. Willis' standpoint, on the other hand, represented in the main an Epicureanism that had been modernized in accordance with the iatrochemical doctrines current in the seventeenth century. In *De anima brutorum* he undertook to clarify the vital, sensitive, instinctual, and emotive behavior of animals—and of man as well, who was, however, further endowed with a noncorporeal rational principle—by means of a soul that consisted of "very fiery and active particles" emanating from the "sulphureous

[10] Claude Perrault, *Essais de physique, ou recueil de plusieurs traitez touchant les choses naturelles*, Paris, 1680-88, III, 15.

element" of the blood and the "nitreous element" of the air (see "Notes," no. 103).

Together with his age, La Mettrie also owed a great deal to the general influence of Locke. The *Histoire de l'âme*, permeated by Lockean teachings, had established its author as the chief forerunner of Condillac in the introduction of sensationalist psychology into France. Despite this, the materialism of *l'Homme machine* did not derive in a fundamental sense from Locke. As La Mettrie himself saw it, his main affinity with the British philosopher resulted from the latter's insinuation that the soul was material in nature, "quoique sa modestie ne lui ait pas permis de le décider. 'Nous ne serons peut-être jamais, dit-il, capables de décider, si un être purement matériel pense ou non . . . parce que nous ne concevons ni la matière, ni l'esprit.' "[11] But this skeptical proposition, which had been merely incidental to Lockean thought, owed its materialist career in France (which will be discussed soon) chiefly to Voltaire's distortion of its intended meaning. In the meanwhile, it would be correct to say that La Mettrie was indebted to Locke above all for having destroyed the Cartesian doctrine of innate ideas, which had served as the epistemological basis of the definition of mind as a separate substance. Furthermore, both the enthusiasm for experimental science and the antimetaphysical zeal that compose the very atmosphere of *l'Homme machine* and fashion La Mettrie's sense of reality, are in large part traceable to Locke, who, for his having replaced the practice of a priori reasoning by the investigation of secondary causes, was recognized as the first to have "débrouillé le chaos de la métaphysique."[12] And while it is true that the mechanistic thesis which is at the core of *l'Homme machine* had no counterpart whatever in the *Essay Concerning Human Understanding*, La Mettrie nevertheless did combine his own special standpoint with Locke's theory of knowledge in such a manner that each found its natural extension and completion in the other.

Although La Mettrie himself confessed his debt to Spinoza, the latter's responsibility for the man-machine idea remains somewhat problematical in character, mainly because of the variety of inter-

[11] *Oeuvres*, I, 261-62.
[12] *ibid.*, p. 263.

pretations, most of them misleading, that the Enlightenment gave to Spinozist philosophy. On the one hand, Spinoza's metaphysics (or at least what La Mettrie understood of it) seemed, with its Scholastic concerns about God and substance, to have "tout confondu & tout embrouillé en attachant de nouvelles idées aux mots reçus."[13] On the other hand, *l'Homme machine* was described by its author as a confirmation of the doctrine of human bondage advocated by the sage of Amsterdam. In this equivocal situation, it is not impossible to accept a recent critic's characterization of La Mettrie's thought as "le développement le plus cohérent du néo-spinozisme,"[14] provided, however, that neo-Spinozism is equated, as it was by the philosophes generally, with an atheistic materialism that pictured man and the world as mechanistically determined, and did away with the existence of moral freedom. But La Mettrie was certainly not a Spinozist in the full sense of the term, for he nowhere stated, or even suggested, that behind matter and mind there lay hidden the one true substance of which the other two were merely modal aspects. While nothing in *l'Homme machine* explicitly barred the way to such a development, the fact remains that the author himself chose not to take it; and this for what must have seemed to him the excellent reason that such an underlying and unifying substance, being far less accessible to positive knowledge than the notions either of matter or of mind, could be of no value whatever to a materialism that was scientifically motivated. Inasmuch as La Mettrie reached his conclusions by way, and in the interests, of medical science, while wholly rejecting the metaphysical method and goal of the *Ethica*, his agreement with Spinoza must be regarded as largely superficial and to some extent coincidental.

The dynamist conception of matter that underlies *l'Homme machine* would indicate that La Mettrie was indebted, even if indirectly, to Leibniz, with whose philosophy he must have been well acquainted as a result of independent reading and of his personal contacts with its leading French exponent at the time, Mme du Châtelet. A radical feature of his materialism—the inclusion

---

[13] *ibid.*, p. 268.
[14] Paul Vernière, *Spinoza et la pensée française avant la révolution*, Paris, 1954, II, 537.

of "force motrice" among the essential properties of matter, in opposition to the passive-mechanical definition of *res extensa* given by Descartes—had already appeared in the *Histoire de l'âme*. But this "puissance motrice de la matière" had been presented with an eclectic indiscrimination, for La Mettrie, while discussing it within an Aristotelian-Scholastic frame of reference, had given it a materialist meaning, claiming at the same time that, as such, it was a doctrine that had flourished unchallenged from early antiquity down to the seventeenth century.[15] There is, moreover, some reason to believe that he had adopted this manner of interpretation at the suggestion of Leibniz himself.[16] But more important, the latter's own theory of inherent motion, completely divorced from its monadological context and, of course, suitably materialized, was adduced in support of the dynamist viewpoint present in the *Histoire de l'âme*: "Leibniz a reconnu dans la matière... non seulement une force *d'inertie*, mais une force *motrice*, un *principe d'action*, autrement appellé *nature*."[17] That the teaching of Leibniz contributed to the naturalism of *l'Homme machine* is revealed particularly well by La Mettrie's appreciation of Christian Wolff, the popularizer of Leibnizianism: "Je viens encore un moment à la force motrice. 'C'est,' comme dit Wolf, 'le résultat des différentes forces actives des élémens, confondues entr'elles; c'est un effort des êtres simples, qui tend à changer sans cesse le mobile de lieu. Ces efforts sont semblables à ceux que nous faisons pour agir.' Wolf en fait lui-même de bien plus grands sans doute, pour que Dieu, témoin de cette action de la nature (qui fait tout dans le système de ce subtil philosophe) ne reste pas oisif, & pour ainsi dire, les bras croisés devant elle: ce qui tend *à l'athéisme*. Mais dans ce partage il n'est pas plus heureux que son maître. C'est toujours la nature qui agit seule, qui produit, & conserve tous les phénomènes."[18] Despite these remarks, *l'Homme machine* differed from the *Histoire de l'âme* in that it did not propose the Leibnizian concept of force either as a uniformly physical, or as a metaphysical, principle of nature. We have seen that, as a result of the strictly biological orientation of 1747, La Mettrie identified the self-moving power of the organism with the concrete phe-

[15] *Oeuvres*, I, 77-82.   [16] *ibid.*, pp. 250-51.   [17] *ibid.*, p. 250.
[18] *ibid.*, p. 257.

nomenon of muscular irritability. Nevertheless, it may be assumed that his previous understanding of Leibniz's ideas had predisposed him to evaluate the data concerning irritability in terms of a general dynamism of organic bodies.

It will perhaps seem odd that no mention has yet been made of Hobbes among La Mettrie's philosophical sources. Between the mechanistic psychology of the former's *De homine* and that of *l'Homme machine*, there surely exists a marked resemblance. It is therefore all the more frustrating that we cannot ascertain if La Mettrie was familiar with Hobbes's natural philosophy, which enjoyed, incidentally, far less currency in the French Enlightenment than did his political doctrines. In the *Abrégé des systèmes*, which consisted of brief analyses of the major philosophical systems of the seventeenth century, La Mettrie did not bother even to name Hobbes; while elsewhere in his writings, despite a great fondness for citing works and authors known to him, there is scant evidence that he realized his proximity to the English atheist's position. It appears unlikely, under the circumstances, that such a glaring omission could have been owing to anything but ignorance. Although there is still the possibility that La Mettrie deliberately kept silent about his affinities with Hobbes, the absence of positive proofs makes it necessary here to leave the entire question moot.

What has been said in the foregoing pages leads us to conclude that, although various foreshadowings and ingredients of La Mettrie's thought were present in the general background of philosophy in his time, the theory of the man-machine itself did not come directly from that quarter. To encounter the idea prior to 1748, we must turn to the literature of free thought, which, while it too derived in many ways from the philosophical sources that have just been reviewed, differed in spirit from them by its primary interest in sapping the theological pillars of the *Ancien Régime*. In this current of intellectual libertinism, the notion of the man-machine—or rather, different approximations of it—soon took form as an effective weapon against religious belief. It will suffice here to illustrate that development with a few representative examples, selected from among many others for the anticipatory light they cast on *l'Homme machine*.

Voltaire, on several occasions that were not typical of his deistic outlook, had viewed human destiny through the disabused optic of naturalism. For instance, at a climactic moment in his polemic with Pascal he had observed: "Je conçois fort bien sans mystère ce que c'est que l'homme; je vois qu'il vient au monde comme les autres animaux ... qu'il y a quelquefois des enfants mal organisés qui vivent privés d'un ou deux sens et de la faculté du raisonnement ... que nos idées sont justes ou inconséquentes, obscures ou lumineuses, selon que nos organes sont plus ou moins solides, plus ou moins déliés, et selon que nous sommes plus ou moins passionnés; que nous dépendons en tout de l'air qui nous environne, des aliments que nous prenons, et que, dans tout cela, il n'y a rien de contradictoire."[19] Along with this, the *Lettres philosophiques* of 1734 interpreted Locke in such a manner as to give French readers the impression that he had asserted that matter could think—which was to be, in fact, the immediate reason for La Mettrie's early estimate of him as a materialist.[20] The *Essay Concerning Human Understanding* had observed that we will never be able to know if God, in his omnipotence, had not superadded to matter the faculty of thinking (see "Notes," no. 18). In the famous "Lettre sur Locke," Voltaire made this more or less neutral remark the basis of his own supposition that the soul was material, admittedly not without some abuse of logic: "Je suis corps et je pense: je n'en sais pas davantage. Irai-je attribuer à une cause inconnue ce que je puis si aisément attribuer à la seule cause seconde que je connais... ? Dieu a donné aux organes des bêtes, qui sont matière, la faculté de sentir et d'apercevoir.... Eh! qui peut empêcher Dieu de communiquer à nos organes plus déliés cette faculté de sentir, d'apercevoir et de penser, que nous appelons raison humaine... ? Ne vous révoltez donc plus contre la sage et modeste Philosophie de Locke...."[21]

The opinion that matter might well have properties seemingly incompatible with its essence was promoted not only by Voltaire's presentation of Lockean philosophy, but also—and with no less authority—by Newton's theory of gravitation. Attractionist phys-

---

[19] Voltaire, *Lettres philosophiques*, éd. Naves, Garnier, Paris, p. 144.
[20] *Oeuvres*, I, 199.
[21] Voltaire, *op.cit.*, pp. 66-68.

ics, by modifying the narrow conception of *res extensa* that Descartes had sought to establish within the strict limits of intelligibility, had the effect during the eighteenth century of restoring to matter much of its perennial mystery—that is, its harboring of radical properties that remained unknown and were not deducible from a logical definition. Just as the inexplicable force of attraction was proved empirically to inhere in matter, La Mettrie was encouraged to suppose by analogy that matter might also be capable of consciousness, however incomprehensible such a notion might seem. A similar line of reasoning had, in fact, already prompted in 1738 an affirmation by Voltaire of the doctrine of "thinking matter" which, this time, had come significantly close in form to the man-machine idea: "Quant à la matière, vous enseignez gravement qu'il n'y a en elle que l'étendue et la solidité; et moi je vous dis modestement qu'elle est capable de mille propriétés que ni vous ni moi ne connaissons pas. ... Vous êtes à peu près comme un régent de collège qui, n'ayant vu d'horloge de sa vie, aurait tout d'un coup entre ses mains une montre d'Angleterre à répétition. Cet homme, bon péripatéticien, est frappé de la justesse avec laquelle les aiguilles divisent et marquent les temps, et encore plus étonné qu'un bouton, poussé par le doigt, donne précisément l'heure que l'aiguille marque. Mon philosophe ne manque pas de trouver qu'il y a dans cette machine une âme qui la gouverne et qui en mène les ressorts."[22] It must surely have been because of reflections like these that La Mettrie came to regard Voltaire as a fellow exponent of materialism, and did him the dubious honor of affixing several appropriately chosen verses of his to the title page of *l'Homme machine*.

It has already been noted that the image of the clock, which Voltaire employs in the lines just quoted, was the technical criterion that inspired La Mettrie's mechanical model of man. In the repeater-watch the eighteenth century was apt to see not only a most admirable piece of machinery but a mechanism whose entire structure tended organically toward a single supreme function—and one which, in the telling of time, seemed to imitate the rational intelligence of man. Of equal importance in this respect were the many ingenious automata so popular at the time, such as Vaucan-

[22] Voltaire, *Oeuvres*, XVII, 150.

son's famous flutist and duck, which embodied the engineering equivalent of the man-machine theory and undoubtedly prepared the imagination of La Mettrie and his contemporaries for the idea of psychophysical automatism. The extent of their influence is made quite plain, for example, by the text of an anonymous book review that appeared in the *Bibliothèque raisonnée* during 1744. It dealt with Saint-Hyacinthe's *Recherches philosophiques*, a work now wholly forgotten, which had claimed that the soul, although extended in nature, was not identical with matter because if matter, in the form of the human body, were supposed capable of thought, it would have to possess this property in each one of its particles —which was obviously not the case. In pointing out the speciousness of this argument, the reviewer of the *Bibliothèque raisonnée* was led to give an outline of the man-machine hypothesis which emphasized the superiority of organicist reasoning over Saint-Hyacinthe's atomistic logic. The passage in question offers a striking illustration of the background of *l'Homme machine*: "Si vous n'aviez jamais vu que des masses de Plomb, des pièces de Marbre, des Cailloux, des Pierres, & qu'on vous présentât une belle Montre à répétition, & de petits Automates qui parlassent, qui chantassent, qui jouassent de la flûte, qui mangeassent, qui bussent, tels que d'habiles Artistes en savent faire, qu'en penseriez-vous, qu'en jugeriez-vous, avant que d'avoir examiné les ressorts qui les font agir? Ne seriez-vous pas porté à croire qu'ils ont une Ame de la nature de la vôtre, ou du moins comme celle des Bêtes, & ne seriez-vous pas porté à parier que cette même Ame est la cause de leur *activité*? Cependant il n'y a dans tous ces Automates que matière, & toutes les merveilles qu'elles opèrent ne sont que le résultat de leur composition, de leur structure, de leur organisation.... Vous aviez beau auparavant considérer, examiner les masses de Plomb, les pièces de Marbre, les Pierres, les Cailloux; vous aviez beau réfléchir sur la nature des Parties ... qui forment ces *Composés*, vous ne pouviez jamais vous figurer qu'elles fussent capables d'exécuter tout ce que font ces Automates.... Appliquez cela à l'admirable Machine, à cet Organe, que je suppose être dans l'Homme & dans les Animaux, le principe de nos actions. Posons que cet Organe soit le Cerveau.... On vous somme de dire si vous connoissez la structure & le mécanisme du Cerveau.... Cet Organe vous étant donc inconnu, n'êtes-vous pas dans le cas de celui qui n'ayant jamais vu que des masses de Plomb, des Pierres, des Cailloux, ne sauroit s'imaginer qu'on en pût former des Machines hydrauliques, sans y introduire & y placer une Ame, ou un Etre pensant pour les gouverner, les faire agir, les faire parler, chanter toutes sortes d'airs? ... D'ailleurs, en soutenant que la Matière ne puisse être le sujet de la pensée, pouvez-vous dire ce que c'est qu'une pensée...? Vous sentez qu'il y a en vous-même un Principe actif, qui produit tels & tels Actes, mais vous ne sauriez expliquer la nature de ces Actes, parce que le mécanisme de ce Principe, sa nature même, ou du moins une bonne partie de son essence vous est inconnue. ... L'effet, l'action, l'opération d'une Machine, ne sauroient être l'effet, l'action, l'opération de chacun des ressorts ... de cette Machine."[28]

There are several reasons why this excerpt from the *Bibliothèque raisonnée* is important with respect to La Mettrie. Its date—1744—precedes that of *l'Homme machine* by only three years; its argument is patently set forth in a hypothetical spirit; and the materialist accent peculiar to it results from the author's attempt to conceive of a mechanical organicism. Because of the wide circulation of the journal in which it appeared, there is a good chance that La Mettrie actually saw it. Although the text presents the man-machine notion rather casually in the course of criticizing someone else's ideas, its readers were for the most part alert enough to perceive in it a surreptitious propagation of materialism. We are led in fact to wonder how such a piece, notwithstanding its anonymity and the open-mindedness of the *Bibliothèque raisonnée*, was printed at all. Its appearance may be taken as evidence that the man-machine philosophy, favored by the intellectual freedom of Holland, was in the 1740's approaching the point of open avowal. This, in turn, probably encouraged La Mettrie and his publisher to believe that the moment had come to entrust the unguarded assertions of *l'Homme machine* to the judgment of an enlightened public.

No less typical of the climate of opinion which brought La Mettrie's thinking to maturity was a work such as abbé Jacques Per-

---

[28] *Bibliothèque raisonnée des ouvrages des savans de l'Europe*, Amsterdam, XXXII (1744), 48-53.

netti's *Lettres philosophiques sur les physionomies*, published in 1746. If in its pages the man-machine concept was expressed somewhat less incisively than in the passage cited above, the book had at least made a sufficiently strong impression on La Mettrie to be remembered by him in *l'Homme machine* (see below, p. 157). His interest was aroused, no doubt, by the materialist presuppositions on which the abbé's method of physiognomical reading was based. For in assuming that the correlation of facial and character traits was traceable to the underlying influence of purely physiological factors, Pernetti proved to be (without wishing, if we believe him, to champion materialism) one of the immediate precursors of *l'Homme machine*.

Pernetti started, promisingly enough, with an admission of metaphysical ignorance concerning the nature of the soul, of matter, and of motion. In such a dilemma, he saw no better approach to psychology than to frame an empirical hypothesis capable of coordinating psychophysical data: "comment connoitrois-je l'ame, que je n'ai jamais aperçue; qui est d'une nature si particuliere que nos sens, qui sont les seuls moïens de perception que nous aïons, ne peuvent en aprocher; dont je ne puis me tracer la plus légere ressemblance, par aucun des objets qui m'environnent; dont je ne sçais, ni l'essence, ni la maniere d'agir? . . . Je crois qu'il n'y a qu'une façon de parler de l'ame, qui est de parler de ses opérations entant qu'elles dépendent du corps. . . . Il arrivera, par ce sage moïen, que ceux qui ont eu la présomption de vouloir connoitre l'ame par elle-même, n'en sçauront rien, pour s'être guindez trop haut; & que ceux qui, plus timides, se sont bornez à voir ses effets, examiner ses opérations, je dirois presque matérielles, en auront porté un jugement beaucoup plus assuré. . . . Qu'on ne s'épouvante [donc] pas de ceux qui, la regardant à travers un voile sur lequel elle se peint, à la vérité imparfaitement, nous rendent, par l'étude qu'ils ont faite de cette peinture, l'image la plus ressemblante de l'ame qu'on puisse donner."[24]

Although these remarks, in phraseology no less than in content, are suggestive of *l'Homme machine*, it is obvious that La Mettrie did not owe his materialism as such to the *Lettres sur les physiono-*

---

[24] Jacques Pernetti, *Lettres philosophiques sur les physionomies*, La Haye, 1746, pp. 83-86.

mies, since the *Histoire de l'âme* had appeared earlier. But Pernetti's orientation sharply emphasizes the experimental and provisional status of the psychophysical conception—an emphasis which will, in fact, also typify *l'Homme machine,* in contrast to the more or less systematic materialism expounded by La Mettrie in 1745. The heuristic validity claimed by him for the man-machine theory would seem to echo the words of Pernetti, who had written: "Il est plus facile, à la vérité, d'établir ces Principes, que de les expliquer. C'est avoir diminué d'autant l'obscurité du sujet, que d'avoir découvert des Raisons d'établir un Principe plutôt que l'autre, quoiqu'on ne puisse pas rendre compte du Principe même. C'est une lueur au moins: & avons-nous autre chose que des Lueurs dans les choses naturelles?"[25] This pragmatic acceptance of the inexplicable attached likewise to Pernetti's affirmation of man's physiological destiny: "je suis comme forcé à dire, sans m'entendre bien moi-même, que la diversité des caractères ne peut avoir pour Principe que la diversité de l'organisation, & que tout ce qu'il y a de bon ou de mauvais dans l'homme . . . dépend de la matiere différemment pétrie & combinée."[26] Such being the case, Pernetti was bound to criticize, in a tone reminiscent of La Mettrie's, the false pride that largely motivates the popular hostility to materialism, and to urge that it be replaced by a readiness to employ biological methods in the education of the higher faculties: "nous nous nuisons beaucoup, en nous spiritualisant comme nous faisons, & en dédaignant les secours mécaniques & matériels, que nous croïons, et qui sont en effet, inférieurs à la dignité de notre esprit. La Nature a voulu vainement nous le persuader: nous nous roidissons contre ses Leçons, que nous croïons faussement humiliantes. . . . Je desirerois que, pour former un Homme . . . on étudiât d'abord . . . son tempérament; que pendant quelque tems, on laissât là son ame, pour ainsi dire, & qu'on n'agît que sur la Matiere. . . . Et qu'on ne croïe pas, que ce soit là un mauvais chemin: il me semble impossible de faire une bonne Education, sans égard à la Constitution matérielle du Corps."[27]

In the domain of clandestine literature, there is even stronger evidence that the decade of the 1740's witnessed a quickening of interest in the mechanistic view of man. Perhaps the best instance

[25] *ibid.*, p. 90.   [26] *ibid.*, pp. 94-95.   [27] *ibid.*, pp. 159-61.

of this trend was the anonymous *Nouvelles libertés de penser* of 1743, which anticipated with clarity and vigor many of the leading themes of *l'Homme machine*. Considering its subject matter and date of publication, we can assume that the work soon came to La Mettrie's attention. The man-machine idea, which runs like a leitmotiv through the *Nouvelles libertés de penser* and binds together the several essays that make it up, is for the most part supported by information drawn from the sphere of medical science. For example, the piece entitled "Sentimens des philosophes sur la nature de l'âme" describes the contribution of the iatromechanist thinkers who brought about the final transformation of the animal-automaton into the human-automaton: "ils soutiennent que ce qui produit ces opérations [i.e. de l'intelligence] dans les animaux est ce qui fait dans l'homme celles par lesquelles on prétend établir la différence de son âme avec celle des bêtes. . . . Le propre du cerveau est, disent-ils, dans tous les animaux, de penser, de juger des rapports qui lui sont faits par les autres sens & de les combiner . . . , le plus ou moins de perfection dans toutes ces opérations n'étant que l'effet de la différente composition ou arrangement des parties dans les organes qui en sont les instruments."[28] In order to show that "le raisonnement dans l'homme est uniquement l'effet de la disposition des organes de son cerveau," various illustrations are given of the concrete relationship between the physical condition of the brain and the exercise of the mental faculties.[29] The author of another essay, bearing the title: "Réflexions sur l'existence de l'âme et sur l'existence de Dieu," seeks and finds a justification of materialism in the marvelous complexity that the advance of science has revealed concerning the nature of matter: "Tous les jours [la matière] nous découvre des propriétés jusqu'alors inconnues; elle acquiert, pour ainsi dire, de nouvelles qualités & paroît à nos yeux sous des formes dont nous ne la croyons pas susceptible . . . & si nos vues sont bornées pouvons-nous en faire un titre pour borner ses propriétés? Il est un axiome convenu, c'est qu'il ne faut point multiplier les êtres sans nécessité. Si l'on conçoit que les opérations attribuées à l'esprit peuvent

[28] Anon., *Nouvelles libertés de penser*, in *Examen de la religion*, Trévoux, 1745, p. 80.
[29] *ibid.*, pp. 81-82.

être l'ouvrage de la matière agissant par des ressorts inconnus, pourquoi imaginer un être inutile, & qui dès-lors ne résoud aucune difficulté?"[30] Besides, what would be the point of defining mind as an independent substance, when the dualists themselves must resort for purposes of psychological individuation to the "organes matériels," and must assume that "ces organes étant différens dans tous les hommes, l'intelligence qui est la même en effet, paroît par-là aussi différente chez chacun d'eux, que réellement leurs organes respectifs sont différens?"[31] Last but not least, the article called "Sur la liberté" sets out to prove that all acts of volition spring from organic necessity, and comes to the same general conclusions that La Mettrie will express on the subject of moral determinism.

All of these materialist themes are also present in the manuscript literature that circulated "sous le manteau" in the period leading up to *l'Homme machine*. As one might expect, such writings usually took the form of blunt attacks against the dogma of spiritual immortality, on which the Christian view of human destiny was based. Typical of them is the anonymous *l'Ame matérielle*, which probably dates from the second or third decade of the century.[32] Although there is no special reason for believing that La Mettrie had seen this manuscript, it is of interest to us because, like the works already mentioned, it reflects well the quality of thought and conversation to be found in the social circles that someone of La Mettrie's intellectual sympathies was bound to frequent. Its author, incidentally, regarded Malebranche's *Recherche de la vérité* as the best general treatise on physiological psychology, and felt free to say about his own efforts: "on ne trouvera pas mauvais que je joigne ici mes idées à celles de ce grand philosophe, et que je me serve de ses lumières pour traiter une matière si abstraite."[33] The conclusions reached in *l'Ame matérielle* are summarized as follows: "que l'ame est une espece de feu très tenu, ou une espece de petite flamme qui circule avec le sang; que l'Esprit n'est

[30] *ibid.*, p. 131.
[31] *ibid.*, p. 134.
[32] Concerning this work, see: I. O. Wade, *The Clandestine Organization and Diffusion of Philosophic Ideas in France from 1700 to 1750*, Princeton, 1938, pp. 222-25.
[33] Anon., *l'Ame matérielle*, MS Arsenal 2239, p. 115.

autre chose que la configuration des parties du cerveau, et le mouvement des Esprits animaux . . ; que la pensée n'est qu'une trace, ou qu'une image que les objets ou les Esprits animaux ont formée dans le cerveau; que le raisonnement ne consiste que dans la differente situation de quelques petits corps qui s'arrangent diversement dans la tête . . ; que le sentiment est l'ébranlement des Fibres, causé par les Esprits animaux qui sont renvoyés au cerveau; enfin que c'est la matiere dont le cerveau est composé, qui pense, qui raisonne, qui veut, qui sent, &c."[84] While all this seems close enough to the standpoint of *l'Homme machine*, a special feature of the materialism of *l'Ame matérielle*, namely, its uncritical throwing together of Epicurean and mechanistic ideas, explains why La Mettrie was to take care to distinguish his own theory of the man-machine from the outmoded conception of soul as "subtle matter" ("une espèce de feu très tenu," etc.), echoed by such moderns as Willis and Perrault.

It would be tedious to consider the various other texts which anticipated, in one sense or another, the *homme machine* philosophy, since these are rather numerous and their contents, beyond a given point, become repetitious. For further documentation, it would be profitable to consult a work such as *De l'âme, et de son immortalité*, attributed to Jean-Baptiste de Mirabaud, which had long circulated in manuscript form before its publication in 1751. Of special interest, too, is the anonymous *Essai sur les facultés de l'âme*, which has survived only in MS (Mazarine 1192).

The examples discussed so far recreate sufficiently the setting of free thought in which *l'Homme machine* was nurtured to establish the fact that many of its major ideas were already in the air. The problem arises, consequently, of deciding in what ways *l'Homme machine* went beyond the historical situation that produced it. In answer to this, La Mettrie's thought may be said to stand out from its immediate background in several important respects. First, it represents a far more coherent and consistent statement of the man-machine doctrine than anything that can be found in the works anticipating it. Secondly, its most original and interesting trait is the use that La Mettrie makes of the irritability principle in order to arrive at an organicist definition of

---

[84] *ibid.*, pp. 169-70.

the human machine as a self-sufficient dynamic system of interdependent parts. It is precisely this manner of viewing the phenomena of life and consciousness that differs so markedly from the "dead mechanism" approach which, harking back to Cartesian biology, still characterizes the efforts of his predecessors. In *l'Homme machine*, moreover, the scientific motivation of materialism, which is largely absent from the texts preceding it, has become predominant over the aim of antireligious subversion, even though the latter purpose was by no means neglected and was perhaps, for the eighteenth century, the more apparent one. Because of the paramount desire to win acceptance for his method of physiological psychology, La Mettrie's arguments for the man-machine idea are drawn more extensively and more decisively than those of his forerunners from the domains of anatomy, physiology, and pathology. And the scientific goal which it envisages causes La Mettrie's philosophy to unfold within a hypothetical context that cannot be said to typify the other works generally, although it is present in some of them. All these differences point, in effect, to an intellectual formation that was peculiar to La Mettrie. It is therefore time to consider the crucial role of his medical training and interests.

The strongest influence exerted on *l'Homme machine* in the field of medicine—an influence which it would be hard to overrate—was that of Boerhaave, under whom La Mettrie had studied during 1733 and 1734. The famous professor's reputation as an inspiring teacher was fully confirmed by the behavior of his pupil, who left Leyden with a sort of apostolic zeal to spread the Boerhaavian gospel in France. We have seen that from 1735 to 1743 he set himself the formidable task of translating—and often of annotating—the bulk of Boerhaave's writings. There is, then, slight cause for wonder that La Mettrie should have been deeply imbued with the iatromechanist method which they championed. But if in the application of mechanics to medicine Boerhaave had inherited the mantle of Descartes, fortunately he had not been unduly awed by his inheritance. An essay like *De comparando certo in physicis* makes it clear how little his iatromechanist commitments prevented him, when he had occasion to stress the value of empirical criteria, from becoming almost an adversary of the

Cartesian school. An admirer of the English experimentalists—of Sydenham in particular—Boerhaave did his best to expand the already impressive role of clinical instruction at the Medical Faculty of Leyden. The advantages of such an education were not lost on La Mettrie, who was to corroborate the man-machine doctrine with a large number of pathological observations, some of the most curious of which pertain to neuropsychiatry.

However, it is not enough to say merely that Boerhaave taught La Mettrie the usefulness of experience, important as this aspect of his influence was. Actually, the content of his teaching—which may be described as a highly eclectic iatromechanism—was sufficiently many-sided to provide nourishment for a variety of aptitudes and leanings among his students, and this was in fact one of the secrets of his extraordinary success as a teacher. In the case of La Mettrie, it was not only, nor even primarily, the clinical competence of Boerhaave that left its lasting imprint on him; in reality, he was well aware that the celebrated professor of medicine, for all his fervent empiricism, lacked the true gift of experimental discovery, and that Nature was something known to him mainly "par autrui... & presque de la seconde main." But what impressed the young French doctor above everything else was Boerhaave's stature as a theoretician; and it proved to be this phase of his achievement that the disciple mirrored most faithfully in *l'Homme machine*. Scrupulous as Boerhaave had been about the amassing of reliable data, his scientific ambitions had not stopped there. His principal aim, as La Mettrie saw it, had been to construct with the materials offered by experience a comprehensive theory of medicine which would conform to the general laws of mechanics—a theory capable of raising that discipline from the more or less tentative art it had always been to the full dignity of a science. This syncretism of rationalist and empiricist tendencies in Boerhaave's thought was perhaps best revealed by his *De usu ratiocinii mechanici in medicina*. Carefully observed and well-established facts, he tells us, are basic, "mais si, partant de ces données premières clairement aperçues, on en déduit ensuite, selon la méthode géométrique, toutes les conséquences qu'en peut tirer une déduction évidente et ininterrompue, on pénétrera beaucoup plus avant dans la recherche, que ne l'eût permis le seul auxiliaire des sens."³⁵ In particular, the advances made since the time of Descartes in the fields of hydrostatics and microscopic anatomy strengthened Boerhaave's hopes of setting up a thoroughly mechanistic body of medicine. As a result, he declared that it was "seuls les Mécaniciens ... qu'il faut entendre, et eux seuls; c'est leurs oracles qu'il faut consulter; leurs principes à qui il faut avoir recours; leur méthode qu'il faut adopter, exclusivement, dès qu'il s'agit de recherches sur les effets d'un organe donné."³⁶ The "given organ" to which La Mettrie applied this vehement advice was, of course, the brain, and its primary "effect" was consciousness. In taking such a step, he had simply gone beyond "la médecine du corps, pour se donner à la médecine de l'âme."³⁷ With that, La Mettrie transposed to the new domain he intended to explore the same consistently mechanistic method by means of which Boerhaave, as seen from one of his typically optimistic remarks, had hoped to elevate medical theory in all its branches to the status of eighteenth-century physics: "Qu'on étende à toutes les matières, comme on le fera d'ailleurs avec le temps, l'application de cette méthode; et l'on finira par obtenir une science médicale certaine, non plus réduite aux hypothèses, non plus soumise à des changements perpétuels, mais une médecine éternelle."³⁸

His evaluation of Boerhaave's place in the history of medicine makes it clear that what La Mettrie prized most in his teacher was "le grand théoricien." The "Dédicace" of the *Traité du vertige* acknowledged in the following terms the nature of its author's debt to the Dutch professor: "si j'ai fait quelques progrès dans ce grand Art dont vous êtes le réformateur, c'est principalement à vous que je les dois; puisque c'est dans vos sçavantes Leçons & dans vos divins Ouvrages que j'ai puisé cette Théorie qui a répandu sur la Médecine une clarté que deux mille ans d'études & d'expériences n'avoient pû lui procurer; Théorie lumineuse, qui seule suffiroit au moins expérimenté & le feroit marcher à pas sûrs dans la pratique, tandis que sans elle le Praticien le plus consommé est

---

³⁵ Hermann Boerhaave, *De usu ratiocinii mechanici in medicina* (1703), in *Opuscula selecta neerlandicorum de arte medica*, Amsterdam, 1907, p. 147.
³⁶ *ibid.*, p. 159.   ³⁷ Voltaire, *Oeuvres*, xxvi, 510.
³⁸ Boerhaave, *op.cit.*, p. 179.

presque toujours réduit au tatonnement & à la divination."[39] La Mettrie had doubtless been all the more impressed by Boerhaave's theorizing talents because in eighteenth-century France, where the iatromechanist movement had made definitely less headway than in Holland, Italy, and Germany, the general level of medicine was comparatively backward and unscientific—a state of affairs which was to furnish, incidentally, much of the impetus for La Mettrie's scathing satires on the French doctors. Having come to the "truth" relatively late, he was inclined (as often happens in such cases) to make up for it by adopting the mechanistic doctrine more enthusiastically and applying it more broadly than those to whom it had been familiar from the start. But in extending mechanical norms of interpretation from organic to psychic phenomena, La Mettrie remained loyal to the special synthesis of rationalist and empiricist procedures that he admired so much in Boerhaave. He gave in—perhaps more easily than he should have —to the urge to simplify which the latter had already shown when, at one point, he had claimed confidently: "La complication des causes de la vie humaine est moins grande que nous ne le pensons nous-mêmes. Si la structure des organes était exactement connue ... la mécanique nous ferait apparaître comme les conséquences de principes très simples, des phénomènes dont le mystère excite aujourd'hui au plus haut degré notre étonnement."[40] In brief, the crux of Boerhaave's methodological influence on La Mettrie may be said to consist in the fact that the pupil, even while he based his arguments first and foremost on concrete data, nevertheless sought in *l'Homme machine* a means of encompassing the fund of available data in its totality, and of erecting on the bedrock of mechanism the foundations of an exact science of the mind.

But how far had Boerhaave himself already applied his principles to the solution of the body-mind problem? While his writings surely contained many hints of a radically mechanistic approach to psychology, this was actually a subject on which La Mettrie tended to understand the Dutch professor's words some-

---

[39] La Mettrie, *Abrégé de la théorie Chymique. . . . Auquel on a joint le Traité du Vertige*, pp. 164-65.
[40] Boerhaave, *op.cit.*, p. 173.

what in his own fashion. He well knew that Boerhaave's teleological appreciation of the animal anatomy was typical of "a perfect Deist": "au fond, autant qu'on en peut juger par ses ouvrages, personne ne fut moins spinosiste: partout il reconnoît l'invisible main de Dieu, qui a tissu, selon lui, jusqu'aux plus petits poils de notre corps."[41] Yet such a taste for natural theology did not necessarily exclude an inclination to treat the mind-body correspondence in more or less materialist terms. La Mettrie could also say of him: "Il explique par le seul mécanisme toutes les facultés de l'âme raisonnable; & jusqu'à la pensée la plus métaphysique, la plus intellectuelle, la plus vraie de toute éternité, ce grand théoricien soumet tout aux loix du mouvement,"[42] even though it was not forgotten that, on appropriate occasions, Boerhaave's thinking had shown a far greater respect for orthodox metaphysics than such a statement would suggest. The materialism imputed to the latter was really an inference which La Mettrie had drawn on his own initiative: "Il divise l'homme en corps, & en âme, & dit que la pensée ne peut être que l'opération de l'esprit pur; cependant non seulement il ne donne jamais à l'âme les épithètes de spirituelle & d'immortelle, mais lorsqu'il vient à traiter des *sens internes*, on voit que cette substance n'est point si particulière, mais n'est que je ne sais quel sens interne, comme tous les autres, dont elle semble être la réunion."[43]

To see more clearly how La Mettrie found in Boerhaave precisely what he was predisposed to find, it will suffice to consider for a moment the *Institutiones rei medicae*, which, in paragraphs 566 through 586, dealt with neurophysiological subject matter under the general heading of "De sensibus internis." Although this entire section, which describes the neural mechanisms associated with the various forms of sensory activity, offers a rich background for La Mettrie's own treatment (mostly in the *Histoire de l'âme*) of the same problems, it is necessary, because of the extent of the topic, to limit ourselves to a single telling example. In his terse manner, Boerhaave had said about the process by which memory supplies the mind with the ideas it needs for thinking: "Tout

[41] *Oeuvres*, I, 265. Cf., also, La Mettrie's "Vie de Boerhaave," *Institutions de médecine*, Paris, 1740, II, 43-44.
[42] *Oeuvres*, I, 265.   [43] *ibid.*, pp. 264-65.

cela ne dépend uniquement que de cette simple disposition du *sensorium commune,* laquelle n'est qu'une pure disposition méchanique du cerveau."[44] If this proposition was philosophically rather ambiguous, the commentary that Haller gave in his edition of the *Institutiones* developed the professor's meaning along the conventional lines of a psychophysical parallelism, but was careful not to imply a materialist dénouement: "Les enfans qui ont le cerveau mol; la plupart des oiseaux & des insectes, qui l'ont petit, se souviennent à peine d'aucune idée, ou du moins d'un très-petit nombre. La même âme retient parfaitement & facilement les idées dans un cerveau plus âgé & plus solide; l'âme se développe avec le corps de l'enfant; à quatre ou cinq ans il raisonne déjà, il montre quelque esprit; jusqu'à l'adolescence, c'est un prodige de facilité à apprendre, tant les idées se gravent aisément; la dureté des solides vient-elle à prévaloir, de nouvelles idées entrent à peine. . . . Le vieillard ne démord pas de ses anciennes idées, qui sont, pour ainsi dire, racornies avec les fibres de son cerveau. Dans l'âge décrépit, on perd enfin toutes ces idées, on ne connaît plus le monde, ni ses amis, ni soi-même, on végète."[45] All of this, which was to find its use in *l'Homme machine,* is reproduced accurately enough in La Mettrie's translation of the *Institutiones.* But soon afterward, apropos of a reference to the causes of imbecility and mental aberration, La Mettrie inserts into the commentary the following remarks of his own coinage, which, allowed to stand undistinguished from Haller's text, give the reader the impression that Boerhaave's precept must in the end lead logically to materialism: "Ce défaut de jugement dépend si fort d'une disposition physique dans le cerveau, à la première origine des nerfs, qu'il n'y a qu'à la rétablir, pour avoir l'esprit sain; & tous les jours la perte de la mémoire n'est-elle pas dépendante du sommeil, du vin, de la chaleur même excessive, de l'apoplexie, qui endommage presque toujours cette faculté, laquelle se rétablit avec le temps par les remèdes méchaniques . . . ? Mais puisqu'elle revient aussi méchaniquement qu'elle se dissipe, *elle appartient donc au corps; elle est donc corporelle.*"[46] As regards Boerhaave's relation to the man-

---

[44] Boerhaave, *Institutions de médecine,* trad. par M. de La Mettrie, 2e édn., Paris, 1743-50; §581; v, 118-19.

[45] *ibid.,* pp. 120-21.   [46] *ibid.,* p. 122. (Italics are mine.)

machine concept, it may be said in general that, although he had furnished most of the scientific materials and much of the methodological incentive needed for its formulation, we have in the case of La Mettrie an imaginative disciple who went beyond the explicit sense and intent of his master's doctrines.

La Mettrie's presumption that Boerhaave had, for all practical purposes, identified the soul with the *sensorium commune*, evokes a physiological theme which played an important part in the rise of the *homme machine* philosophy. Descartes had set a fateful precedent when, as a physiologist, he had undermined his own distinction between *res cogitans* and *res extensa* by placing the seat of the soul specifically in the pineal gland. While this particular hypothesis was soon rejected by informed opinion as altogether fanciful, the history of physiology during the next hundred years and more was to witness many similar attempts to find a locality of the brain that could be regarded, more or less plausibly, as the immediate instrument of mental life—that is, as the common center where all sense perceptions and ideas converged into the unified and simple state of consciousness. Such speculation indirectly owed a great deal to the progress of microanalysis. In laying bare for the first time the extremely complex structures of even the crudest organisms, the microscope had profoundly altered the scientific imagination of the period. As a result matter seemed to lose much of its classic grossness and, in proportion to the anatomical perfections it displayed, became capable of functions which, owing to their apparent excellence, had traditionally been placed beyond the range of merely material factors. Concrete references in *l'Homme machine* to the *sedes animae* theme have to do with the theory of Willis, who fixed the *sensorium commune* in the *corpora striata*, and with that of Lancisi and La Peyronie, who were both pleased to confer the same honor (with as little accuracy) on the *corpus callosum* (see "Notes," nos. 39, 40). The over-all effect of such theorizing was not lost on the *esprits forts*, who were naturally receptive to technical corroboration of their views about the soul's materiality. To give but two instances of this among many in the literature of free thought, the author of *l'Ame matérielle* observed: "Je ne peux trouver que très extraordinaire que l'on ait agité cette question, *De la place que doit occuper l'âme*, lors même qu'on la supposait spirituelle: car il me semble que rien n'implique tant contradiction que de dire que l'âme est spirituelle, et de vouloir en même tems qu'elle réside quelque part, surtout dans un lieu particulier."[47] Exactly the same point was made by one of the contributors to the *Nouvelles libertés de penser*: "J'ai peine à concevoir comment un être, tel qu'on suppose l'âme, pourroit être susceptible d'ubication & pourroit exister respectivement à telles & telles portions de matière."[48] Thus La Mettrie was simply taking for granted the historical linkage between this problem of physiology and the origin of the man-machine idea, when he wrote: "Un être inétendu ne peut occuper aucun espace; & Descartes qui convient de cette vérité, recherche sérieusement le siège de l'âme, & l'établit dans la glande pinéale. . . . Il est évident par-là que Descartes n'a parlé de l'âme, que parce qu'il étoit forcé d'en parler & d'en parler de la manière qu'il en a parlé, dans un tems où son mérite . . . étoit . . . capable de nuire à sa fortune."[49] While the author of *l'Homme machine* hesitated to accept any one of the then current theories about the seat of the soul, he had undoubtedly been encouraged by such investigations to conceive of the brain in general as the self-sufficient organ of psychic life.

In the scientific background of the man-machine, the sources of the irritability principle have, of course, a place of unique importance. Concerning this subject, the main problem for us will be to evaluate La Mettrie's contribution in relation to Haller's. Most historians of science, who have recognized Haller as the chief discoverer of irritability, have simply ignored La Mettrie altogether. On the other hand, a few admirers of La Mettrie, misled by certain chronological facts, have tended to exaggerate his originality at the expense of Haller's. Actually, the truth of the matter, which neither side has understood, is rather involved and lies somewhere in between. An examination of the available evidence will show that La Mettrie's conception and use of irritability was a brilliant step forward in the history of general physiology. Although he benefited greatly from the pioneering work of Haller, La Mettrie soon arrived at a position of his own which, without exactly rivaling or eclipsing the other's achievement, went beyond it in some ways with respect to depth and correctness. Since it would be

---

[47] *op.cit.*, p. 159.   [48] *op.cit.*, p. 134.   [49] *Oeuvres*, I, 240-41.

awkward to discuss here the origins of the irritability idea in the light of all the pertinent experimental data, these latter will be found to a large extent in the notes on the text of *l'Homme machine*.

From about the mid-seventeenth century on, the growing application of mechanical and chemical notions to the sphere of medical science had aroused firm hopes that, by these promising means, the cause of muscle action would finally be disclosed. At the iatromechanist pole were those who, from Descartes down to Boerhaave, had sought to explain contraction pneumatically in terms of an influx of animal spirits from the nerves into the muscle mass; while at the chemiatric pole were those who, like Willis, had ascribed it to some sort of explosive reaction between various components of the nerve fluid and the blood. And, to be sure, there were many others who had arrived at compromise solutions which combined features belonging to the two different schools of thought.[50] Each mode of explanation had the merit of empirical support, for it was known experimentally that motion could be arrested in a given muscle by ligaturing either its efferent nerve or blood vessel, and that the motion could be restored with removal of the ligature. But despite these proofs, both types of theory (apart from many technical difficulties that need not concern us here) showed a serious inadequacy: it was known also that muscle fibers, even when cut off completely from the nervous and vascular systems alike, could, by artificial stimulation, be made to contract in regular fashion for an indefinite length of time. Because such experiments with the phenomena of irritability pointed up the underlying defect of every one of the prevalent theories of contraction, they became a subject of much fascination and, over the years, were performed on many types of animal (and with different methods of stimulation) by a long line of investigators. But while the facts of irritability thus became well known before the end of the seventeenth century, and attempts were usually made to fit them in somehow with one or another of the existing theories

---

[50] For a general discussion, consult E. Bastholm, *The History of Muscle Physiology, from the Natural Philosophers to Albrecht von Haller* (*Acta historica scientiarum naturalium et medicinalium*, Vol. VII), Copenhagen, 1950.

of contraction, their real significance for physiology was not to be understood until much later.

La Mettrie was thoroughly versed in these matters, and, although in *l'Homme machine* he refers by name only to Bacon, Harvey, Steno, Boyle, and Cowper, he knew that observations of autonomous muscle action had been made also by a number of others, including Lower, Glisson, Peyer, Wepfer, Baglivi, Stuart, and Gorter (see "Notes," no. 89). But the background of La Mettrie's *principe d'oscillation* was not restricted to factual information. Tentative efforts had been made on more than one occasion to derive from the data of irritability a fundamental law of biology. Such attempts had been greatly aided, in turn, by two decisive developments in physiological science. First, when Steno had finally shown in 1663 that the heart functioned simply as a muscle, and had thereby destroyed the ancient view of it as a "source of vital heat," the long-range effect of his demonstration proved to be the raising of the contraction problem to a level of unequalled importance in the study of the living organism. Secondly, after Leeuwenhoek had seen through the microscope the fibrous composition of muscle tissue, it became possible to explain the behavior of the organism as a whole in terms of the properties shown by its structurally basic fibrils. The combined result to which both of these events led found its first full expression in *l'Homme machine*, when La Mettrie traced back to the individually self-activated muscle fibers what he took to be the vital principle of the organic machine. But in so doing, he was not far from the position already taken in the 1670's by Francis Glisson, who not only had claimed that movement, in contrast to the clock-like idea of mechanism held by the Cartesians, was innate to all the parts (even the fluids, bones, and fat) composing the animal body, but had been the first to describe this capability by the term *irritabilitas*. Although he thus deserves credit for having initiated the modern conception of irritability,[51] Glisson received almost no recognition in his own period, nor for more than half a century afterward. The reason for this was not so much that his doctrine was too advanced, as that it came buried in Scholastic jargon and meta-

[51] Cf. Max Verworn, *Irritability, a Physiological Analysis of the General Effect of Stimuli in Living Substance*, New Haven, 1913, pp. 2-5.

physical confusion which all but obliterated its meaning and importance; moreover, it was offered as a vague speculative opinion which, at the time, could not be supported properly by experimental data. Notwithstanding this, La Mettrie probably owed something to Glisson's example when he conceived of irritability as a general property of all living tissue, nonmuscular no less than muscular.

The more immediate source of La Mettrie's principle of irritability was Haller. Because the latter's classic treatment of the subject in *De partibus corporis humani sensibilibus et irritabilibus* was not known until 1752, some scholars have come to the erroneous conclusion that *l'Homme machine* anticipated Haller's discovery of the physiological law commonly linked with his name. Actually, Haller's interest in muscular irritability and his exhaustive observation of its nature long antedated the famous memoir of 1752. He himself gives 1746 as the year when he began his frequent vivisections in connection with the study of the sensitive and irritable reactions of different organs; but the entries in his journal make it clear that, as far back as the 1730's, he had been making significant experiments on the artificial stimulation of muscle fibers under a variety of conditions.[52] It is therefore understandable why Haller, in the commentary he added to his edition of Boerhaave's *Institutiones* (published from 1739 to 1743), called attention again and again to the facts and problems of irritability, and went so far as to suggest the theory that he was later to work out in fuller detail. A scrutiny of these comments leaves little doubt that La Mettrie, who brought out his abridged translation on the heels of Haller's edition, was able to find in them many of the leads necessary for arriving at his own doctrine of irritability. In the *Institutiones*, Boerhaave himself had tried to explain the contraction mechanism quite conservatively in terms of a flow of animal spirits into the muscle mass, even though he had had before him the facts of autonomous motion and had been sufficiently puzzled by them to imagine, for a moment, the presence of occult powers in the heart. The footnotes supplied by Haller, who in this regard possessed far keener insight than his teacher, repeatedly stressed

[52] Albrecht von Haller, *Mémoires sur la nature sensible et irritable des parties du corps animal*, Lausanne, 1756, I, 3-4, 296-393, *passim*.

the shortcomings, particularly in the case of cardiac function, of Boerhaave's explanations. Not only did Haller dwell on the various inadequacies of the *esprits animaux* hypothesis, but he took the unexplained and tantalizing data of irritability as prima-facie evidence that the underlying cause of muscular action had as yet been completely overlooked.[53] Judging by the portions of Haller's commentary which La Mettrie chose to preserve or emphasize, it may be said that the translator well realized the scientific value of the materials he had before him. One proof of this, among others, was the prominence he gave to a remark, buried in Haller's sub-footnotes, which bluntly ascribed Boerhaave's failure to offer a satisfactory theory of cardiac motion to his neglect of the irritability factor: "M. Boerhaave est le premier . . . qui ait bien développé ce mystère [i.e. the heartbeat]; & les trois causes qu'il nous expose,[54] sont très-véritables. Que manque-t-il à l'opinion de ce grand Théoricien? Cette cause du mouvement dans le coeur, qui dans les expériences dont nous avons parlé tant de fois, reste encore après la mort dans les nerfs, les artères, & le sang des oreillettes, séparés du corps. Mais cette cause, qui est peut-être analogue au ressort naturel des fibres, tel qu'il se trouve dans les insectes, ne peut s'expliquer dans l'homme; de plus, elle est trop faible, pour que toutes nos expériences puissent nous la montrer bien clairement."[55]

Still more auspicious was Haller's discussion of peristaltic movement. Boerhaave had reviewed the facts generally known about the subject, only, however, to become so perplexed by them that, despairing altogether of an interpretation in terms of mechanical laws, he had at length attributed peristalsis to that supreme refuge of human ignorance—"the omnipotent power of the Creator." Haller's comment at this point, which sought to fathom the mystery of vital functioning, amounted to a recapitulation of the experimental history of muscular irritability. In the course of it, he formulated in essence what was soon to be elaborated into his

---

[53] Boerhaave, *Praelectiones academicae in proprias institutiones rei medicae*, edidit, et notas addidit Albertus Haller, Naples, 1754-55; see especially II, 25-26 (§159), 55 (§187), 58 (§189); III, 173-74 (§406).
[54] See "Notes," no. 102.
[55] Boerhaave, *Institutions de médecine* (§409), IV, 57.

famous theory: "Caeterum tota theoria ista simplicissimo illo phaenomeno, a nemine negabili, nititur, omnem fibram musculosam animalis vivi, irritatam a quacunque causa, continuo in contractionem ire, ita ut haec ipsa ultima nota sit, qua animalia imperfecta a vegetabilibus dignoscantur."[56] Although La Mettrie did not translate verbatim the long passage containing this sentence, he did summarize Haller's opinions in a manner that seemed to take their truth for granted.[57] We can be certain that he was all the more eager to adopt them as his own, because he noticed that they permitted Haller to cut the ground from under the chief enemies of materialism—the exponents of animistic biology: "Je rejette donc l'empire de l'*âme* de Stahl, de l'*archée* de Van Helmont, & le *principe présidant* de Wepfer ... sur toutes les actions du corps humain."[58]

Furthermore, there is reason to suspect that, at the time of writing *l'Homme machine*, La Mettrie had first-hand information about the researches then in progress on the subject of muscular irritability, which by 1747 had become a topic of lively interest in more than one quarter. Haller, who finally came to resent the reputation for originality which La Mettrie had gained among some readers, charged that everything *l'Homme machine* had said about irritability had been derived either from his own publications, or from certain experiments performed by Bernhard Siegfried Albinus.[59] The latter, another of Boerhaave's students, was a Professor of Medicine at Leyden and a respected authority in the field of descriptive anatomy—a science which La Mettrie had, in fact, studied under him in the past. The curiosity of Albinus having shifted in 1745 from anatomy to physiological theory, his lectures after that date dealt often with muscular irritability, which, rather academically, he termed *principium movens* or *facultas movendi*. Under the circumstances it is fair to assume that through his acquaintance with Albinus, La Mettrie, who was in Leyden

---

[56] Boerhaave, *Institutiones rei medicae*, IV, 239; see also IV, 248-50 (§600).
[57] *op.cit.*, V, 209.   [58] *ibid.*, p. 210.
[59] Haller, *op.cit.*, I, 90. The passage in question (see below, p. 202) is rather confusing in that it speaks of "un jeune Suisse" who supposedly informed La Mettrie about Haller's writings. Such an intermediary was, of course, quite unnecessary, for La Mettrie already had a thorough acquaintance with Haller's opinions, as the latter should well have realized.

during most of 1747, learned about the latest investigations of irritability, and received some hint of the radical findings which Haller was soon to offer to the world as an experimentally proved law of physiology.

As regards La Mettrie's debt to Haller, it may be concluded that the latter had made available much of the technical data and an outline of the general theory which served as the basis of the irritability doctrine given in *l'Homme machine*. But Haller's own *Irritabilitätslehre*, though presented in an experimentally impeccable form, remained inferior to La Mettrie's in that it was confined to only one type of living substance, the muscle. While this defect has led one critic to say that "Haller's theory represents a great regression in comparison to the correct fundamental thoughts of Glisson,"[60] it is necessary here to take a more balanced view of the matter. For if it is true enough that modern physiology does not limit the irritable process to muscle cells, Haller's "error," on the other hand, was a positive advance when it is seen in proper historical perspective. Inasmuch as irritability, around 1750, could be experimentally verified only in the case of muscular contraction, the real contribution of Haller was that, having discovered such a property where it actually existed, he described its nature as it actually was—which proved to be much more than Glisson's speculations had done. Haller can hardly be blamed because he did *not* claim to perceive irritability in tissues where neither he nor anyone else at the time had the means of proving its presence. But once the factor of irritability had been clearly isolated and defined by him, others were free to extend its operation to the nonmuscular parts of the organism. And it is in fact to La Mettrie's credit that, without delay, he did precisely that, showing a higher degree of scientific imagination and insight than Haller had shown. Consequently, his conception of irritability may be said to have combined the best features of Glisson's and Haller's theories. Judged in the light of present-day knowledge, it impresses us as superior to both because it achieved a synthesis between the experimental proof of muscular irritability on the one hand, and, on the other, the generalization of that property with respect to all living systems.

[60] Verworn, *op.cit.*, p. 6.

In this way La Mettrie avoided making Haller's misleading distinction between irritability and sensitivity, which, though valid in a purely psychological sense, was erroneous insofar as nerve cells are known to be, in their fashion, no less irritable than muscle cells. Yet even this error had been of great indirect profit to La Mettrie, for without it the nature of irritability could not then have been understood. Only by stimulating muscles separated from their efferent nerves was it possible to show that their response represented an elementary force—a specific energy—in the organic substance itself. If the irritable reaction had been studied only (or even primarily) in relation to nerve stimuli, this would simply have confirmed, in the intellectual setting of the period, the conventional view that organic activity was produced by a soul (or by some equally vague "vital principle") which, from its seat in the brain, presumably moved the body via the nervous apparatus. It was by the demonstration of contractility entirely apart from the nerve impulse that La Mettrie and his contemporaries were able to grasp the true meaning of that physiological phenomenon; or, put differently, that irritability at long last replaced the soul or the vital principle as a concept essential to biology, and, still more significantly, became with La Mettrie the basis for investigating the psychic aspects of the life process. This crucial development first took place in *l'Homme machine*, despite the fact that both Haller and La Mettrie, knowing nothing as yet about reflex mechanisms nor about the fine ramifications of the nervous system into the muscle walls, had assumed the absence of a nerve impulse in many instances of contraction where such was actually not the case. However, their ignorance proved to be benevolent enough, for under the circumstances it really served to better characterize the irritable reaction, which, as it has since come to be known, is of course essentially free of nervous stimulation.

Before bringing this chapter to an end, something should be said about the relationship of *l'Homme machine* to a certain trend of thought which emerged during the 1740's in what we would now call the psychiatric field. Once physiology, by adhering closely to the mechanistic ideal, had begun to assume the form of a tolerably exact science, the hope arose that medicine, if it used its new resources properly, might be able to treat not merely the major mental disorders (which it had always done), but also the great variety of lesser aberrations of the "soul"—roughly comparable to the modern neuroses—which until then had fallen almost exclusively to the lot of the priest and the moralist to cope with as best they could. Such a comprehensive practice of psychiatry had already been made a medical goal in Descartes's *Discours de la méthode*, which was a fact known to La Mettrie when he presented the man-machine idea under the Cartesian aegis: "Autant de tempéramens, autant d'esprits, de caractères & de moeurs différentes. Galien même a connu cette vérité, que Descartes a poussé loin, jusqu'à dire que la Medecine seule pouvoit changer les Esprits & les moeurs avec le Corps."

But in this tendency La Mettrie was not alone. An important example (particularly with respect to *l'Homme machine*) of a similar line of reasoning was the academic oration pronounced by Hieronymus Gaubius in 1747, entitled *De regimine mentis quod medicorum est*. The author, trained under Boerhaave, held a chair of medicine at Leyden. The purpose of his remarks was to help in opening up a relatively new area of inquiry, one that seemed to him as useful and challenging as it had remained uncultivated in the past—the very same area, in fact, that Descartes had already staked out.[61] Gaubius argued that it was within the legitimate scope of medicine to concern itself with all psychic troubles of a type not ordinarily equated with disease. The scientific basis offered for such an inclusive mental hygiene and therapy was the known or knowable effects of bodily states on the mind and the emotions. The physician could be expected to maintain the "soul" in a condition of maximum health and efficiency by regulating the organic temperament on which its functions depended. Although Gaubius was careful not to be lured by this objective into the camp of the materialists, his professed dualism appeared somewhat compromised by the intransigence with which he foresaw the control of all mental phenomena by physical means.

We know that when Gaubius delivered his oration on February 8, 1747—only a few months before the composition of

[61] Hieronymus Davidus Gaubius, *Sermo academicus de regimine mentis quod medicorum est*, Leyden, 1747, p. 54.

THE HISTORICAL BACKGROUND OF L'HOMME MACHINE

l'Homme machine—La Mettrie was seated nearby in the audience. That the proposed extension of psychiatry into the moral domain immediately struck a responsive chord in him is made quite apparent not only by the broad analogies between the contents of *l'Homme machine* and those of *De regimine mentis*, but also by the fact that La Mettrie illustrated his thesis with several curious case histories taken directly from Gaubius (see "Notes," nos. 64, 65, 66, 67). The latter who, like many scientists at the time, held orthodox opinions in religion, was understandably embarrassed and annoyed when, on reading *l'Homme machine*, he realized suddenly the close affinity which existed between his own medical projects and the materialism of a decried author whom it was obvious he had strongly influenced. Years later, in a letter to Charles Bonnet, whose *Essai analytique sur les facultés de l'âme* pursued the same line of inquiry initiated by himself, Gaubius, still embittered by *l'Homme machine*, took the occasion to voice his fears about the final outcome of such psychophysical investigations. "Quant aux principes que vous y adoptez," he wrote, "je suis trop partial pour en oser juger: témoins mon discours académique De Regimine Mentis quod Medicorum est, publié l'an 1747, et ma *Pathologie* [*Institutiones pathologiae medicinalis*, 1758]. Et comme je regarde votre analyse pour un développement mathématique de ce que j'ai avancé, ainsi je pourrais en fournir des preuves innombrables et des plus frappantes, soit de ma propre expérience, soit des observations d'autres médecins.... C'est principalement la médecine, dont la physique de l'âme peut puiser ses lumières. Des esprits malins en tirent des conséquences irréligieuses. M. de La Mettrie était assis sur les degrés de la chaire fort attentif, quand je prononçais ce discours à la fin de mon rectorat, et peu après il publia son *Homme Machine*. C'est ce qui me rendit cauteleux par rapport à cette matière dans ma *Pathologie*. Et peut-être que votre *Essai* ne manquera de faire une pareille impression, en confirmant quelques-uns dans leur matérialisme de l'âme et en induisant d'autres à vous croire adonné au même système."[62] While he assured Bonnet that the drawing of such conclusions would be quite unjustified, it seems that Gaubius had

[62] Raymond Savioz, *Mémoires autobiographiques de Charles Bonnet de Genève*, Paris, 1948, p. 194.

thoroughly learned his lesson, for when the opportunity arose in 1763 to give a "Sermo alter de regimine mentis," he reversed his point of view and discoursed this time about the effects of the mind on the body.

That Gaubius and La Mettrie were not isolated spokesmen for the new conception of psychiatry may be seen by another work: Antoine Le Camus's *Médecine de l'esprit*. Although published in 1753, it was written actually around 1744.[63] Because there is no evidence that La Mettrie knew anything about Le Camus or his ideas, our interest in the book, which displays many impressive parallels with *l'Homme machine*, will be limited to the fact that it reflects the same advanced trend in medical thought of which Gaubius and La Mettrie, each in his way, were also examples. Le Camus's general plan was essentially in agreement with that of Gaubius: "Après avoir réfléchi attentivement sur les causes physiques qui, modifiant différemment les corps, varioient aussi les dispositions des esprits, j'ai été convaincu qu'en employant ces différentes causes, ou en imitant avec art leur pouvoir, on parviendroit à corriger par des moyens purement mécaniques les vices de l'entendement & de la volonté."[64] The author of the *Médecine de l'esprit* was aware of adding a whole new dimension to the practice of psychiatry: "nous nous sommes appliqués à considérer l'état parfait & les vices soit de l'entendement, soit de la volonté lorsque les hommes paroissent jouir de la meilleure santé. Jusqu' [ici on n'a] trouvé d'autre remède pour obvier à ces vices que les avis, les préceptes, l'éducation, les leçons. Pour nous, envisageant de plus près les loix de l'union de l'âme & du corps, nous prétendons les déraciner par des causes Physiques."[65] The serious pursuit of such an aim often prompted language that might well have come from *l'Homme machine*, as when Le Camus declared: "Ouvrons la barrière . . . & pénétrant dans les labirinthes les plus secrets de notre

---

[63] Antoine Le Camus, *Médecine de l'esprit; où l'on cherche 1° le méchanisme du corps qui influe sur les fonctions de l'âme. 2° Les causes physiques qui rendent ce méchanisme ou défectueux, ou plus parfait. 3° Les moyens qui peuvent l'entretenir dans son état libre, & le rectifier lorsqu'il est gêné.* 2e édn., Paris, 1769, Préface, p. v. While the second edition represents a complete reworking of the original in regard to technical details, the statements of theoretical purpose (which alone concern us here) are the same in both versions.

[64] *ibid.*   [65] *ibid.*, p. 335.

constitution, saisissons, s'il se peut, le mécanisme de nos corps, déchirons le voile qui couvre nos âmes. . . . Ici la Physique & la Métaphysique semblent s'unir si intimement, qu'en voulant les séparer on ne peut atteindre le but qu'on s'étoit proposé. Il n'appartient qu'à la science qui doit connoître également & les esprits & les corps, de traiter de ces combinaisons abstraites. Or cette science n'est autre chose que la Médecine."[66] The striking resemblance between the man-machine philosophy and the scientific objectives of the *Médecine de l'esprit* did not escape the notice of the reading public, for, in a second edition of the book, Le Camus was obliged to proclaim his loyalty to dualist metaphysics in order to satisfy those who had accused him of teaching that "l'âme n'est qu'une simple machine qui ne va que par ressorts, ou du moins une simple modification de la matière si elle n'est matière elle-même."[67] It is clear from the cases of Gaubius and Le Camus that we must count among the sources of *l'Homme machine* a tendency of thought which, during the 1740's, sought to give to psychiatry a far wider scope than it had ever known before, and a scope that was asserted largely at the expense of the moral authority of religion.

In the foregoing pages, I have tried to analyze the main components of the soil from which *l'Homme machine* drew its substance. Although these tell us a good deal about its origins, they do not completely explain its originality, which, by definition, is something that transcends the historical method. But it is possible now to describe briefly the nature of the synthesis which La Mettrie made of the materials that were available to him. Philosophically, the *homme machine* had become a potential outgrowth of Descartes's *bête machine*, once the latter had become detached from its metaphysical antecedents and, owing partly to Locke's discrediting of a priori psychology, had begun to serve as the basis of a physiological theory of mind. The man-machine idea which subsequently came into being appeared first in the clandestine literature of free thought; as such, it was aimed chiefly at the Christian dogmas of the spirituality and immortality of the soul, and beyond them at the political and social order of which the Catholic Church was the ideological prop during the *Ancien*

[66] *ibid.*, p. 2.   [67] *ibid.*, p. viii.

Régime. Having inherited the idea from this background, La Mettrie retained its antireligious and subversive connotations, but at the same time he appraised it anew in relation to the medical sciences from which it had received its initial impetus. Benefiting from certain decisive developments in the fields of comparative anatomy, physiology, and psychiatric medicine, he succeeded in conferring on the idea a new scientific vitality which it has not lost since 1748. Although for La Mettrie the medicophilosophical meaning of the man-machine was of primary value in comparison to its anti-religious uses, in a practical sense these two aspects of his doctrine were inseparable, for, given the general conflict of science and religion in the eighteenth century, the one necessarily involved the other. As a result, the author of *l'Homme machine* became the first to launch the medical sciences fatefully and creatively, as others had already done with mathematics, physics, and astronomy, onto the vast and brightly lit stage of Enlightenment thought.

CHAPTER V

THE CRITICAL REACTION OF LA METTRIE'S CONTEMPORARIES

So LIVELY was the hostility aroused by the appearance of *l'Homme machine* that it ranks as perhaps the most heartily condemned work in an age that saw the keenest competition for such honors. As was to be expected, these attacks served merely to compound and prolong the book's *succès de scandale*. It would be tedious to examine singly the many reviews and rebuttals of *l'Homme machine* that bore witness to its popularity, if only because their repetitiveness is in keeping with their bulk. The majority of them will be mentioned here briefly in connection with some special topic of criticism, while only the few significant refutations will be discussed at any length. The reader who desires to explore the subject more fully may consult the Bibliography.

The promptest and strongest reaction to *l'Homme machine* came in Germany, where, besides being reviewed extensively in the periodical press, it was the cause of voluminous polemics. One reason for this lay in the provocative "Dedication" to Haller, which did not fail to excite mixed feelings of shock and indignation among his numerous German following. Another reason—once the author's identity had become known—must surely have been Frederick II's protection of La Mettrie, and the latter's newly won official position in Berlin. But of no less importance was the fact that for a decade or two the materialistic question had already, as Lange puts it, been "powerfully raised in Germany, when suddenly the 'Homme machine' fell upon the literary scene like a bomb hurled from an unknown hand."[1] The particulars of the critical response occasioned by this dramatic event have been reconstructed

---

[1] Frederick Albert Lange, *The History of Materialism*, New York, 1950, Bk. 1, Sect. 4, p. 137.

in their main lines by the researches of Lange,[2] Poritzky,[3] and Bergmann.[4]

La Mettrie's book had a very different career in France, where its sale was forbidden from the start. In view of the author's dubious standing with the French censorship, this repressive measure probably resulted from a simple police order; in any event, no record of a court decree has been found. The prohibition, as was customary, encouraged the clandestine circulation of both printed and manuscript copies of *l'Homme machine*. But the aura of illicitness surrounding it apparently prevented the work from being reviewed in any of the French periodicals, and also spared La Mettrie the annoyance of finding himself the object of a series of refutations like those published in Germany. It is because of this situation that scholars have remained quite unaware of the French critical reaction to *l'Homme machine*. Such a reaction did, however, occur in an indirect way, but in terms which, if one looks into the question, leave little doubt that La Mettrie was its real cause. At first, the French must have decided that the best policy was to ignore the book altogether and hope it would sink into oblivion. Once this tactic had failed and the man-machine doctrine had come to have a widespread appeal, the apologists of Church and State became busy. During the 1750's there appeared a number of lengthy tracts in which the *homme machine* philosophy figured either as the specific, or at least as a prominent, target of attack. Among these were such now-forgotten titles as Lelarge de Lignac's *Elémens de métaphysique tirés de l'expérience*, Hubert Hayer's *La spiritualité et l'immortalité de l'âme*, and Laurent François's *Défense de la religion contre les difficultés des incrédules*. A curious feature common to all these works is that, while they assailed the man-machine idea quite openly, they remained reluctant to refer by name either to La Mettrie or to his book. It is as if their authors were taking extreme care to shield from that notorious source of contagion anyone who might until then have had the good fortune to remain uncontaminated.

[2] *ibid.*, pp. 137-39.
[3] J. E. Poritzky, *Julien Offray de Lamettrie, sein Leben und seine Werke*, Berlin, 1900, pp. 180-207.
[4] Ernst Bergmann, *Die Satiren des Herrn Maschine*, passim.

THE CRITICAL REACTION OF LA METTRIE'S CONTEMPORARIES

Relatively little in the mass of criticism leveled at *l'Homme machine* actually came to grips with its meaning. There were even some critics who, taking the smug view that the book's absurdities did not merit a serious reply, simply heaped abuse on the author and his ideas. They renewed with fervor the tiresomely illogical argument—hardly weakened, it would seem, by Bayle's paradox of the "virtuous atheist"—that every materialist must necessarily be a debased and vicious person, bent on destroying the authority of religion and, by the same stroke, the whole fabric of the social and political order. Among several such denunciations of La Mettrie, the following sample from a British magazine is offered for the self-righteous resonances of its magisterial prose: "Writers of this kind, who advance principles of such malignant influence, and so evidently subversive of the interests of society, and of every individual, must be lost not only to all the generous feelings and sentiments of men, but even to a becoming sense of their own happiness; and can be looked upon in no other light than as public enemies. And surely every one, who has the spirit of a man, and any regard for the interests of truth and virtue in the world, will feel a generous indignation rise in his breast, against every puny infidel, that would endeavor to weaken or undermine those fundamental principles which are their only support, and treat him, be his rank or character ever so great, with utter neglect and scorn."[5]

By banning *l'Homme machine* in Leyden and burning it in the public square of The Hague,[6] some Protestants had shown that they had hardly more respect for freedom of thought than did the frankly intolerant Catholics. Mainly as a commentary on these events, La Mettrie was to include in the 1751 edition of his *Oeuvres philosophiques* a pithy "Discours préliminaire," which argued that speculative opinions, however unorthodox, ought not to be suppressed, if only because they had almost no practical effect either on existing moral notions or on social behavior. But even before that date, the controversy over *l'Homme machine* had involved a general discussion of the freedom of the press, which for a moment had seemed to be endangered within its European citadel of Holland. Elie Luzac, wishing to justify his publication

[5] *The Monthly Review*, 1 (1749), 124.
[6] Cf., Pierre Clément, *Les Cinq Années littéraires*, Berlin, 1756, 1, 121.

of the book, had in 1749 brought out anonymously the *Essai sur la liberté de produire ses sentimens*. It was a crisp and well-reasoned work, which contended, rightly enough, that the honest search for truth requires us to give a hearing to every possible point of view, and that such a procedure must in the long run be advantageous to both the public weal and the political authority of an enlightened nation. Luzac was simply reiterating the theme of the "Avertissement" which he had prefixed to La Mettrie's book, when he stated: "Si la défense de produire ses Sentimens ne peut que jetter les hommes dans un doute sur les propositions qui en font l'objet, quel moïen que le public soit jamais persuadé sur sa religion, tant qu'on défend la plume aux Athées, aux Esprits forts &c? C'est une vérité qui saute aux yeux, & que l'Imprimeur de l'Homme Machine, qu'on ne peut assurément taxer de partialité, a bien remarqué."[7]

Such logic doubtless failed to convince those whose authoritarian temper was well illustrated by a review of *l'Homme machine* from the pen of the Swiss pastor, Pierre Roques. But for all his eagerness to castigate from a fitting sense of outrage, Roques hardly got around to discussing La Mettrie's thesis itself. Quarreling chiefly with the self-exonerating remarks of the "Avertissement de l'Imprimeur," he revealed himself as one of those Protestants whose sympathy for free expression extends to so-called heretical literature, but not to works "où l'audace se soulève contre la Religion en général," or which threaten what he complacently termed "les règles incontestables de la plus pure Morale."[8] This review was answered by Etienne Luzac, speaking for his brother. He declared the freedom of the press to be indivisible, for if reasons of religious or political expediency could in principle justify suppression, then why "plutôt réprimer l'audace contre la Religion en général, que contre la Religion en particulier?"[9] He added that, in order to condemn books for going against "la plus pure Morale," we would first need universal agreement as to just what

[7] E. Luzac, *Essai sur la liberté de produire ses sentimens*, Au Pays libre, Pour le Bien Public, 1749, p. 59.
[8] *Nouvelle bibliothèque germanique*, Tome v, 2e partie (1748-49), Amsterdam, 1750, p. 330.
[9] *ibid.*, Tome vi, 2e partie (1750), p. 433.

that is. Finally, in answer to the charge that his brother had let himself be influenced by merely mercenary motives, Etienne Luzac replied that it was the commercial policy of the Dutch to consider themselves "autorisés à toute entreprise, dès que les probabilités nous font entrevoir qu'à notre défaut l'Etranger y suppléera."[10] The episode of *l'Homme machine* thus proved to be, in one of its many facets, a good example of the cooperation that took place in the eighteenth century between the ideal of economic *laissez-faire* and that of intellectual liberty.

Among the weakest rejoinders to *l'Homme machine* were those that substituted religious dogma for philosophical argument. An instance of this was given by one Adam Wilhelm Franzen, who opposed to the man-machine doctrine a series of scriptural revelations "proving" the immateriality of the soul.[11] Similarly, a pamphlet by Francisco Neumayr, S. J., entitled *Ob der Mensch weiter nichts seye als eine Maschine* and originally given as an Easter sermon, sought to refute La Mettrie by finding an impudent blasphemy in the suggestion that a mere machine could have been the object of Christ's act of redemption, and that the Son of God himself should have condescended to become one.[12] But the high point of irrelevancy was reached with a tract by a certain Daniel Pury, supposedly written against two of La Mettrie's works: *l'Homme machine* and the *Discours sur le bonheur*. Disregarding completely the contents of either of these, Pury went off on a tangent and argued rather self-consciously that the atheist is unable to prove the nonexistence of God.[13]

As a rule, the replies to *l'Homme machine* did not go so absurdly wide of the mark. But even the more intelligent rebuttals failed regularly to meet La Mettrie's argument on its own ground. Insofar as their authors resorted to metaphysical reasoning to disclaim what was wrongly imagined to be a system of materialist

[10] *ibid.*, p. 439.
[11] A. W. Franzen, *Widerlegung der französischen Schrift*: L'Homme Machine, nebst dem Beweis der Gegensätze, Leipzig, 1749, pp. 39-94.
[12] F. Neumayr, *Frag: Ob der Mensch weiter nichts seye als eine Maschine? Beantwortet wider die Freydenker und Materialisten* [Augsburg], 1761, pp. 11-13.
[13] D. Pury, *Pensées pour et contre les écrivains mécréants, à l'occasion de deux écrits nouveaux, intitulés; l'un, l'Homme machine; l'autre, Discours sur le bonheur*, Neuchatel, 1752, passim.

metaphysics, their remarks may be said to have amounted to a collective *ignoratio elenchi*. In fact, the refutations of *l'Homme machine* make it quite clear that in the general view of the eighteenth century a scientific hypothesis was still expected to conform to a set of presumably unchanging metaphysical axioms as well as to observable data. The thought never seriously occurred to La Mettrie's critics that the fate of metaphysical truth might itself depend on the activities and triumphs of the scientific imagination. They believed without question in the possibility of defining a priori the natures of matter, motion, consciousness, etc., and it followed all too easily from the definitions they offered that the concept of mechanism was logically incompatible with that of mind. What the foes of *l'Homme machine* failed from the first to realize was that La Mettrie, precisely because he had already assumed the unknowableness—either a priori or a posteriori—of the essences of matter, mind, or motion, was proposing the man-machine as the hypothesis which seemed to him to accord best with the limits of explanation imposed by such a state of ignorance. Blind to this, his critics confidently set about spinning metaphysical webs in the hope of destroying a no less metaphysical fly, when all the time what La Mettrie had really put in doubt was the competence of their own method to deal meaningfully with the concepts of mind and matter. The raising of such a problem was, apparently, still too foreign to the mentality of that pre-Kantian age, for us to expect that La Mettrie's challenge would have been taken up in earnest.

Typical of the tendencies just described was Gottfried Plouquet's *Dissertatio de materialismo*. Inspired by the Wolffianism then popular in the German universities, it rejected the man-machine philosophy out of hand on the basis of such prepossessions as the harmony of two substances in man, the incompatibility of matter and perception, and so forth. Plouquet failed altogether to see that the antimetaphysical postulates of *l'Homme machine* were themselves the ground of La Mettrie's hypothetical materialism: "The author frankly admits in his book that he does not know what matter is, what motion is, how matter can become active, how the organism is generated, what perception is and how it arises, &c., and nonetheless he hopefully and trustingly arrives at [his] conclusions."[14] Like Plouquet's, the refutation by Franzen also kept revolving within the circle of its own assumptions. Having decided that between "äusserliche, und innerliche Erfahrung" only the latter type of cognition can yield any genuine knowledge of the soul, Franzen dismissed anatomy and physiology outright as irrelevant to the problem of mind. Although he admitted all the concrete correlations between mental and physical states cited by La Mettrie, he denied that these implied a causal relationship in the proper sense.[15] On the other hand, the real distinction between mind and body was said to be knowable only rationally and a priori.[16] And since such a distinction would show that matter is essentially incapable of thought, Franzen concluded that the former could not possibly acquire that capability merely by a special arrangement of its parts.[17]

Samuel Christian Hollman, a professor at Göttingen, took a somewhat more pedantic and patronizing stand. Classing the man-machine doctrine as an offshoot of Spinoza's monism, he remarked about the idea of Nature in *l'Homme machine*: "As soon as I had read this, I formed in regard to our philosopher's proficiency, of which I already had no very advantageous opinion, a far lower one still.... A Spinozist is in my view a wretched and confused person, whom we ought to pity; and if he can still be aided, we ought to help him with a few not too profound observations taken from Logic, and with a clarification of what *One* and *Many* mean, and what manner of thing a SUBSTANCE is."[18] It was Hollman, incidentally, who injected some humor into the polemics by charging that the author of *l'Homme machine* must be, according to his own principles, nothing but a machine, and that therefore one should not be surprised if, under the circumstances, he had no control over the nonsense that escaped him.[19] The fantasy of a

[14] Gottfried Plouquet, *Dissertatio de materialismo, cum supplementis et confutatione libelli: l'Homme machine: inscripti*, Tübingen, 1751, p. 48.
[15] Franzen, *op.cit.*, pp. 103-04ff., 159-60.
[16] *ibid.*, p. 170.
[17] *ibid.*, pp. 20-22.
[18] *Göttingische Zeitungen von gelehrten Sachen*, 1748, p. 427. The rebuttal in question was soon translated from German into French and published separately under the title: *Lettre d'un anonyme pour servir de critique ou de réfutation au livre intitulé: l'Homme machine*.
[19] *ibid.*, p. 411.

"Monsieur Machine" having appealed to La Mettrie, he accepted the name and composed three anonymous pamphlets which, by way of mystifying his enemies, satirized the life of so remarkable a personage.[20]

As proof that the French were not less adept than the Germans in the *ars confutandi*, there is Père Hayer's *La spiritualité et l'immortalité de l'âme*, published in 1757 in three volumes. The author took a rather sweeping view of the man-machine philosophy, projecting it backward in time so as to include among its representatives Epicurus, Lucretius, Hobbes, Locke, Bayle, and a few others. Although in this assorted company La Mettrie was mentioned by name only occasionally, it is clear enough that he was the immediate cause of Hayer's concern.[21] Yet the discussion of mechanistic psychology in terms, not of a specific work or author, but of a set of general propositions, makes it evident that by 1757 the *homme machine* idea had become prevalent enough in France to characterize an entire school of thought. Hayer's refutation began with a priori definitions in the Cartesian manner: the essence of matter was divisibility, configuration, passivity; that of the soul was nonextension, indivisibility, activity. Thereupon, the type of argument against the man-machine doctrine for which Hayer showed a decided weakness went as follows: A machine consists of matter; matter is divisible; but how can one divide an idea? Since one cannot, the mind is not a machine. Or else: If the mind is a machine, then a given idea would have to correspond to a given material shape, say, a square; similarly, the opposite of the idea must correspond to the opposite geometrical form. But the opposite of a square does not exist. *Ergo*, the mind is not a machine. Convinced that only such syllogistic subtlety can reveal the true nature

---

[20] These pamphlets, which all appeared in 1749, were: *Epître à mon Esprit ou l'Anonyme persiflé; Epître à Mlle A. C. P. ou la "Machine terrassée"*; and *Réponse à l'auteur de la Machine terrassée*. For a discussion of them, consult Bergmann, *op.cit.*, pp. 21-38; and Lemée, *J. O. de La Mettrie*, pp. 205-19.

[21] Abbé Trublet, who knew both La Mettrie and Hayer personally, confirmed this fact in his review of the latter's book. Regarding it as a refutation of *l'Homme machine*, he remarked: "Le P. Hayer a ... la complaisance de suivre M. de la Mettrie dans ses pretendues explications; & il lui est aisé d'en faire voir l'absurdité, & même le ridicule. M. de la Mettrie n'étoit pas un Adversaire digne de lui, & nous croyons que sans manquer à sa cause, il pouvoit être beaucoup plus court sur un pareil Ecrivain" (*Le Journal Chrétien*, June 1758, pp. 10-11).

of things, Hayer is not surprised that to most people, whose grasp of logic is far less sophisticated, the man-machine idea should appear altogether plausible. His recognition of its success indicates that the *homme machine*, a decade after its promulgation, no longer seemed as absurd as it had in 1748: "Ce qui concilie au Matérialisme le plus de suffrages, c'est l'idée fausse que s'en font des gens inattentifs; ils se le figurent comme un système tout simple auquel l'esprit livré à lui-même se porte naturellement, & comme nécessairement; ils se représentent au contraire l'Anti-matérialisme comme le fruit d'une Métaphysique qui s'évapore en subtilités. Je sçais que ce mot, *l'homme n'est qu'une machine*, est bientôt prononcé; je sçais encore que les sens, que l'imagination & conséquemment tous les préjugés de l'enfance déposent en faveur d'Epicure."[22]

Among the refutations of *l'Homme machine* that are of greater interest to us, there was the work by the Breslau physician, Balthasar Tralles, *De machina et anima humana prorsus a se invicem distinctis commentatio*, published in 1749. It was dedicated to Haller, whom the author wished to avenge in some measure for La Mettrie's perfidious "Dédicace." Pursuing this aim, Tralles endeavored above all to show that the medical profession was far from being, as La Mettrie had insinuated, a breeding ground for atheistic materialism. The issue thus raised was indeed an important one, for it serves to clarify the motives for much of the outcry—too violent not to have betrayed a secret fear—which *l'Homme machine* had met with even from those who were best qualified to judge it impartially. The truth of the matter is that, by 1748, the prevailing desire to harmonize scientific knowledge with religious dogma had finally reached the stage of futility. The desperateness of the situation had already called forth a marked tendency among both theologians and scientists to link (rather myopically, as it soon turned out) the fate of religion itself with that of certain scientific opinions, particularly in the fields of geology, biology, and psychology. *L'Homme machine* had, in its blunt way, proclaimed the end of this fragile entente, maintained during the preceding decades by an impressive array of natural theologies.

[22] Hubert Hayer, *La spiritualité et l'immortalité de l'âme, avec le sentiment de l'Antiquité tant sacrée que profane, par rapport à l'une & à l'autre*, Paris, 1757, I, xv.

The challenge to that entire mode of thought had, in fact, found expression indirectly in the guileful "Dedication" to Haller. In pretending to be the disciple and friend of the celebrated physiologist, La Mettrie had known perfectly well that his action would undermine the vulnerable position of a man who, in the eyes of all Europe, was one of the most respected personifications of the fusion of scientific eminence and orthodox piety. Such was the blow that Tralles sought to parry, and to do so effectively, he had at least to view La Mettrie's materialism in a proper light. But if Tralles proceeded to evaluate the man-machine as a psychophysical theory, he did so in as negative a spirit as possible, stressing not what it might conceivably explain in the end, but what it was incapable of explaining from the very start. Admitting, for instance, La Mettrie's correlation of brain mass and intelligence, he demanded a concrete elucidation of mental ability in terms of the size and conformation of the brain. Similarly, to La Mettrie's remark that the competent doctor counts on physical causes in preference to the "soul," Tralles replied that there are some forms of insanity without a trace of organic damage, and asked in what apothecary shop drugs were to be found for such inner enemies. In a consistent vein of scientific defeatism, he cited as arguments against *l'Homme machine* many of the unsolved problems which it was La Mettrie's hope that his theory would be able to solve in the long run.

A Wolffian on the metaphysical plane, Tralles advised La Mettrie to consult the *Psychologia empirica et rationalis* concerning the distinction between the mechanics of sensation and the subjectivity of thought. Moreover, *l'Homme machine* had attributed natural law to animals on the evidence of their behavior: but did beasts have any notion of the divine source or moral end of the law they supposedly followed? Animals might well have, as La Mettrie had said, a language of their own: but speaking animals clearly did not belong to the best of possible worlds, or we should have had them long ago. La Mettrie had claimed that apes, if taught to speak, could some day reach the status of human beings: in that event, surely no one would deny him the right to rule over his new Ape-Republic. But it was less by such poor jokes than by disparaging the heuristic value of the man-machine hypothesis that Tralles brought retaliation on himself. In *Les animaux plus que machines*, as we have seen, La Mettrie elaborated mockingly on Tralles's dualist conception, in order to convince the reader that it explained infinitely less about psychic phenomena than did the *homme machine*. His ire still not cooled by this, La Mettrie gave a prominent place to the Breslau doctor in his crowning satire against Haller—the delightfully outrageous *Petit homme à longue queue*.

Another refutation, *l'Homme plus que machine*, has been described by some scholars as an attempt by La Mettrie to bemuse his enemies. However, its real author was Elie Luzac, who wrote it to counter the accusation that he approved personally of the opinions expressed in *l'Homme machine*.[23] What remains peculiar to it is Luzac's concern about the naturalistic framework in which La Mettrie had set forth the man-machine theory. The objection is raised that, even if man were actually a self-determining mechanism, it would by no means follow that the universe is similarly constituted, for such an inference would require a knowledge about the totality of things which no one in effect possesses. In answer to La Mettrie's assertion that "la raison de l'existence de l'univers se trouve dans l'univers," Luzac contends that if such were the case the existence of the universe, being a part of its essence, would be necessary; and furthermore, that if the universe did exist by necessity, it would have to do so in a definite form—in other words, its formal existence would be not only necessary but immutable, which is a proposition obviously contrary to fact.[24] With respect to the problem of human existence, the idea of necessity is likewise transposed from La Mettrie's physical, to a Scholastically metaphysical, realm of discourse. If man, says Luzac, contained within himself the reason for his being, he would exist changeless from all eternity—that is, he would be God.[25] Consequently, the concept of a Nature which, lying between the two extremes of God and Chance, creates itself by virtue of the "causes

[23] Luzac's work was included in the Amsterdam 1764 and 1774 editions of La Mettrie's *Oeuvres philosophiques*. Concerning the problem of its authorship, see my "Elie Luzac's Refutation of La Mettrie," *Modern Language Notes*, LXIV (1949), 159-61.
[24] La Mettrie, *Oeuvres*, III, 175-77.
[25] *ibid.*, pp. 177-79.

cachées dans son sein," is rejected as intrinsically meaningless.[26] The differences on this question between Luzac and La Mettrie reflect an underlying crisis in the nature of meaning itself. For Luzac, the meaningful remained ultimately suprasensible and demonstrable; for La Mettrie, it consisted primarily in the hypothetical ordering by reason and imagination of empirical data.

Perhaps the most original and suggestive response to the man-machine philosophy was Lelarge de Lignac's *Elémens de métaphysique tirés de l'expérience*, published in 1753. Though made up of letters which seek to convert a materialist who believes that "man is a machine," the work mentions neither La Mettrie nor any of his writings, for it was the author's avowed policy to "ménager la délicatesse du public" in the case of "les Auteurs universellement décriés."[27] But a number of quoted passages which are said to come from the "oracle" of modern materialism turn out, on examination, to be by none other than La Mettrie. Unlike other critics, Lelarge de Lignac is sufficiently aroused by the challenge of the man-machine doctrine to arrive at a new philosophical position of his own, founded on the evidence of what he terms the *sens intime*. Agreeing from the start with La Mettrie's demand that philosophy rely fundamentally on experience rather than on a priori logic, he conceives of the *sens intime* as a sort of sixth sense which, notwithstanding its inwardness, is no less empirical than the other senses. Functioning in a mood of *recueillement* and self-contemplation, it is said to disclose the existence of a simple and continuous state of consciousness, which remains essentially distinct both from the sense impressions brought to it from the external world, and from the modifications produced in it by bodily changes. This introspective separateness of the *moi*, perceived in the inaccessible depths of one's own being, forms the basis of Lelarge de Lignac's objection to La Mettrie's identifying the psyche with the organic machine: "Ceux qui aiment à méditer ne conviendront point . . . qu'ils y soient dans un état purement machinal, puisqu'ils sçavent au contraire, qu'ils ne se mettent dans

[26] *ibid.*, pp. 184-85.
[27] Abbé Joseph-Adrien Lelarge de Lignac, *Elémens de métaphysique tirés de l'expérience: ou Lettres à un matérialiste sur la nature de l'Ame*, Paris, 1753, p. 159. Of special pertinence to our discussion are pp. 159-223.

une situation propre à méditer, que par un effort qui ferme, pour ainsi dire, aux esprits les avenues du cerveau, & les empêche d'y porter des nouvelles de ce qui se passe dans la machine. Mais dans ces rêves de *la veille*, où l'âme est véritablement réduite à l'inertie, il est évident que tous les effets de la machine sont suspendus par rapport à elle, que les impressions du dehors ne lui parviennent point, qu'aucune image n'est peinte devant elle, parce que les esprits ne jouent plus dans le cerveau. Alors la machine marche seule sans l'aveu de l'âme: alors l'âme est réduite à sentir purement son existence, c'est la seule idée qui lui soit présente, & sa façon d'exister est alors de ne sentir que soi; jamais elle n'est plus dégagée de la machine."[28] The *sens intime* conception, thus offered as a metaphysical solution of the spiritualist-materialist impasse, was an attempt to go beyond both the man-machine thesis and the innatist psychologies of Descartes and Malebranche. In postulating the essential autonomy of the self without, however, implying anything about the validity of particular notions, it translated the distinction of mind and matter from a supposedly demonstrable proposition into an elemental fact of experience. This promising orientation in philosophy, which owed its foreshadowing of Miran de Biran and personalism to Lelarge de Lignac's encounter with the *homme machine* theory, was later developed more fully in the latter's *Témoignage du sens intime* (1760).

Lelarge de Lignac's critique did not, however, diminish the value of the *homme machine* considered as a scientific hypothesis. To do that, it was necessary to prove that the *sens intime* could not result, in its turn, from a special neural mechanism that isolated consciousness, under certain circumstances, from the influences of the nervous system as a whole. Lelarge de Lignac sought, in fact, to rule out such a possibility by attributing (this time without any support in experience) certain cognitive capabilities to the *sens intime* which were, in the final analysis, quite unrelated to its basic role. He contended against La Mettrie that if a mental image really coincided with the mechanical apparatus producing it, then by reason of the *sens intime* we would have simultaneously as clear a perception of the one as of the other; and since this was obviously not the case, the soul and the body had to be distinct

---

[28] *ibid.*, pp. 24-25.

entities. But this specious line of reasoning was actually motivated, as the author himself reveals, by a stubborn indifference to scientific progress which made it difficult for him to judge sympathetically any "revolutionary" hypothesis: "C'est notre fureur [que] de reprendre les sciences par les fondemens; on a raison pour quelques parties: mais de prétendre qu'on est encore au point d'inventer. . . . En vérité, c'est une extravagance qui tend évidemment à la ruine des sciences."[29]

Reflecting in some ways the argumentation of Lelarge de Lignac, abbé Antoine-Martin Roche's *Traité de la nature de l'âme* devoted many of its pages to a criticism of the man-machine doctrine.[30] Roche's main disagreement with La Mettrie lay in the claim that the multiple ramifications and operations of the nervous system could in no manner be reconciled with the absolute simplicity of consciousness. In his view, the "partisan de l'homme machine" had tried to surmount this obstacle by imagining an "Ame matérielle" which, being free to move about at will within the body, could at once maintain contact with each of its constituent parts and unify all conscious activity at the "origine des nerfs." But such a misconstruing of La Mettrie's meaning clearly resulted from Roche's failure to differentiate between the material soul of the *Histoire de l'âme*, and the man-machine idea proper. Having embroiled the two, he complained that the *âme matérielle* created more difficulties than it solved, for according to such a notion a voluntary motor act would require (contrary to what ordinary experience teaches) not only that the soul be present in several places at the same time, but also that it know the complex organic means of carrying its wishes into execution.[31] In short, Roche did not realize that La Mettrie, faced with just such problems as these, had sought in *l'Homme machine* to harmonize physiological multiplicity and psychological oneness in terms of the structural and functional unity of the organic mechanism rather than in terms of the material unity of a "soul substance."

Another example of the French reaction to *l'Homme machine* was Laurent François's *Défense de la religion contre les difficultés*

[29] *ibid.*, pp. 255-56.
[30] *Traité de la nature de l'âme, et de l'origine de ses connoissances*, Paris, 1759, I, 1-106.
[31] *ibid.*, 56-62.

des incrédules. The first of its four volumes began with a lengthy description of the background and status of materialist thought in France at the mid-eighteenth century. La Mettrie, who figured prominently in the discussion, was quoted often enough, although he was not actually referred to by name. The remainder of Volume I (pp. 133-349) contained a general refutation of materialism, in which La Mettrie was again present as a major target, in the company of several other freethinkers who also received their due. Owing to this eclecticism, François's rebuttal may be said to have suffered from the tendency to efface the individual character of the man-machine theory by submerging it in a welter of materialist and pseudomaterialist doctrines, the various authors of which seemed to his indiscriminate gaze "si uniformes dans leurs pensées, que je serois tenté de les regarder comme des écrivains qui se copient les uns les autres."[32] Nevertheless, his remarks are of some interest to the historian of ideas because of the link they establish between La Mettrie's concept of Nature and the rise of transformistic naturalism in the Enlightenment. In this respect, François classed materialists according to three main types, which he termed "Epicuriens," "Spinozistes," and "Naturalistes." It was the last category that he reserved for those who posited, along with La Mettrie, the existence of "les *causes physiques cachées dans le sein de la nature,* desquelles ils ont reçu la faculté de sentir & de penser par l'organisation de quelque portion de matière."[33] But François, like Luzac before him, could make nothing of the postulate of a creative Nature, which to his mind was an ambiguous and unstable notion that had finally to crystallize into that of God, or dissolve into that of Chance: "Que peut-on entendre par ce terme de *nature?* Il ne reste plus que d'entendre les corps eux-mêmes; ce sont donc les corps qui sans art se façonnent avec le plus grand art..., qui sans aucune connoissance d'eux-mêmes & des autres, s'arrangent avec le plus bel ordre, qui sans loix, suivent les loix les plus sages?"[34] These enigmas led François, by an easy transition, to examine critically the evolutionist materialism which Diderot

---

[32] Laurent François, *Défense de la religion contre les difficultés des incrédules,* Paris, 1755, I, 6.
[33] *ibid.,* p. 29.   [34] *ibid.,* p. 66.

had expressed through "Saunderson's speech" in the *Lettre sur les aveugles*. He was aware that the latter's speculations followed the "Naturaliste" impulse already shown by La Mettrie, and that the "fermentation de la matière" from which Diderot's organic world took shape remained essentially akin to the "causes cachées dans le sein de la nature."[85] But if François's critique of La Mettrie and Diderot rightly stressed the general paradox that underlay their naturalism, it failed to understand the deeper sense in which such a paradox, implicit in the encounter of human reason and physical contingency, represented in their thinking, not so much the illogical outcome of a false premise, as the point of departure for a hypothetical explanation.

It would appear from what has been said that both the French and German critics of *l'Homme machine* overlooked its most original and important features; or that when one of these—such as the idea of a creative Nature—was singled out for comment, it was summarily dismissed as nonsensical. The common tendency was to assimilate what La Mettrie had said to some earlier, more familiar version of materialist philosophy—either Epicureanism, Hobbesianism, or (as happened most often) "Spinozism"—in order that a ready-made refutation might be applied to it. Haller, for instance, was content to describe *l'Homme machine* as an "epitome of the poem of Lucretius... merely augmented by a few observations and discoveries of the modern period."[86] Those with less classical tastes were apt, on the other hand, to believe that La Mettrie's "Athéisme est celui de Spinosa, quoique partout il semble vouloir passer pour original."[87] The journalist Clément, willing to give La Mettrie some credit for originality, brought himself to admit at least that "à travers la fumée de ses raisonnemens on voit

[85] *ibid.*, p. 98; see also, pp. 23-27, 67-84.
[86] *Göttingische Zeitungen von gelehrten Sachen*, 1747, p. 907. The comte de Tressan hardly did better to read into the book some gratuitous notions of Epicurean origin: "L'homme est une machine/ Que le concours des atomes forma,/ Et que l'éther plus rapide anima" ("Réponse à un de mes Amis, qui avait fait l'Apologie de l'Homme-Machine de la Métrie," *Oeuvres*, Paris, 1823, x, 238).
[87] P. Roques, in *Nouvelle bibliothèque germanique*, v, 2e partie, p. 335. Another reviewer wrote: "He speaks throughout the language of a Spinozist, asserting that there is in the whole world only one substance modified in different ways" (*Acta historico-ecclesiastica*, Weimar, XIII [1749], p. 468).

percer des étincelles d'imagination, des idées même qui *auroient envie* d'être neuves & justes."[38]

The crucial significance of irritability for the *homme machine* thesis, when it was noticed at all, met as a rule with two sorts of objection. The first of these questioned whether the facts cited by La Mettrie sufficed to establish a faculty of self-motion in matter, and claimed instead that autonomous muscle action was produced by the temporary momentum of the animal spirits trapped in the resected organs or fibers. The second and more frequent reply conceded that matter might well possess, under certain conditions, the power to move itself purposively; but it rejected the inference that such automatic properties were in any way responsible for consciousness and the mental functions. This was, for example, the gist of abbé Pluquet's disagreement with La Mettrie: "Mais supposons pour un moment que l'irritabilité des fibres des animaux soit l'effet d'une force motrice attachée à leurs parties; peut-on en conclure qu'elles pensent? n'a-t-on pas prouvé que l'activité qui fait l'essence de l'être pensant, est essentiellement différente de la force motrice qui transporte les corps? il ne suffit donc pas de disséquer, & d'observer, pour éclairer le labyrinthe de l'homme; il faut y porter le flambeau de la métaphysique."[39] Haller embellished this point of view when, ignoring the real issue raised by La Mettrie and taking the existence of an immaterial principle for granted, he argued that the contractions observed in excised muscle fibers were in themselves an indication that irritability remained basically unrelated to the soul: "En effet puisque l'Irritabilité subsiste après la mort, qu'elle a lieu dans les parties séparées du corps, & soustraites à l'empire de l'âme, puisqu'on la trouve dans toutes les fibres musculaires, qu'elle est indépendante des nerfs, qui sont les satellites de l'âme, il paroît qu'elle n'a rien de commun avec cette âme, qu'elle en est absolument différente, en un mot que l'Irritabilité ne dépend point de l'âme, & que par conséquent l'âme n'est point l'Irritabilité."[40]

As late as the 1760's, rejoinders to the man-machine philosophy

[38] Clément, *Cinq Années littéraires*, Berlin, I, 122.
[39] Abbé François-André-Adrien Pluquet, *Examen du fatalisme*, Paris, 1757, II, 498.
[40] Haller, *Mémoires sur la nature sensible et irritable des parties du corps animal*, I, 90-91.

kept appearing sporadically in France. Though adding little of value to the controversy, they indicated at least that La Mettrie's thought continued to make headway in the latter half of the century. One of these was the rather inane pamphlet by the theologian Pichon, entitled truculently: *Cartel aux philosophes à quatre pattes*, which deserves no further description here.[41] Another example was the long and strident rebuttal of the man-machine and allied doctrines which abbé Gauchat, that tireless and tiresome antiphilosophe, included in his multitomed *Lettres critiques*.[42] Typically enough, he chose to pass La Mettrie over in complete silence, and based his discussion instead on the contents of the *Nouvelles libertés de penser*, which, as we have seen, had anticipated several of the major themes that were taken up and developed more fully in *l'Homme machine*. Gauchat's procedure would suggest that, in the 1760's, the man-machine had already become a broad generic concept, which was no longer clearly associated in the mind of the public with the thinker who had first given it a truly European status. This curious situation was attested by still another defense of traditional metaphysics: Denesle's *Examen du matérialisme*.[43]

Among the belated refutations of La Mettrie's book, the most interesting was perhaps that by Jacques François de Luc, which formed a chapter in his *Observations sur les savans incrédules* (1762). Motivated by an awareness that science had become deeply alienated from religion, the author felt the need to "se fortifier par la réflexion contre les Ecrits des Savans incrédules de tout genre, dont le nombre augmente chaque jour."[44] An outstanding member of that dangerous group was of course La Mettrie, whose writings were held to demonstrate perfectly "le pernicieux effet que produit l'orgueil des Sciences humaines sur les Savans nés Chrétiens."[45] For an apologist of the established order

[41] Its author proposed to debate the question: "L'homme est-il une simple machine? l'homme est-il un pur esprit?"

[42] Gabriel Gauchat, *Lettres critiques, ou analyse et réfutation de divers écrits modernes contre la religion*, Paris, Tome xviii (1763), passim.

[43] Denesle, *Les préjugés des anciens et nouveaux philosophes sur la nature de l'âme humaine, ou Examen du matérialisme*, Paris, 1765, see especially 1, 210-412.

[44] *op.cit.*, p. 8.

[45] *ibid.*, p. 384. *L'Homme machine* is dealt with on pp. 373-92.

of things thus to have admitted from the start that scientific pursuits might well conflict with a pious outlook on life was in effect to recognize the end of an entire era of Western culture that went back to the Middle Ages. Events now threatened to come full circle since the still recent date when Tralles, stressing the religious orthodoxy of the leaders of European science, could haughtily dismiss La Mettrie and the materialists as mere second-raters and vulgarizers in the scientific sphere. The reversal of that state of affairs served now to discredit the age-old axiom that Truth must be one and indivisible under the supreme control of theology. This profound change in the orientation of the modern mind, which the efforts of many others had gradually prepared before him, was perhaps proclaimed first by La Mettrie in a decisive and revolutionary manner.

CHAPTER VI

L'HOMME MACHINE SINCE 1748

THOUGH CRITICAL STUDIES of La Mettrie have not been lacking, the problem of his place in the history of ideas has never been adequately treated, nor even, for that matter, seriously posed. But important as the subject is, it will not be possible, if the present work is to remain within its prescribed limits, to discuss in detail the influence of the man-machine philosophy. Such a task must be left to others. In this final chapter, I shall merely attempt to set in proper perspective La Mettrie's relationship to those who followed in his intellectual wake, and to suggest that the minimizing of his contribution by cultural historians has perpetuated, up to now, a distortion of Enlightenment thought on some fairly consequential points. It will be necessary to recognize also some practical limits in time to the development of the man-machine doctrine. The current of ideas—represented particularly by Diderot and D'Holbach—for which *l'Homme machine* may be said to have provided the main impetus, shows a plausible degree of distinctness until, roughly speaking, its culmination around 1800 in the school of Cabanis. But thereafter, the general premises of physiological psychology become so widely prevalent that the career of the man-machine theory overlaps with much of the history of philosophy, medicine, psychology, and the biological sciences. As a result, it will seem more profitable to shift our interest, during the nineteenth century, to the fortunes of *l'Homme machine* itself and to the growth of La Mettrie's reputation.

The difficulty in the past of arriving at an objective appraisal of La Mettrie's rank among the philosophes has had as its principal cause the strongly negative attitude taken toward him by his contemporaries for reasons which, in the last analysis, are not relevant to the permanent value of his writings. From the preceding chapter, the conclusion has arisen that the enemies of the man-machine succeeded in maintaining a conspiracy of silence around La Mettrie (at least in France), which was broken now and then by the berating of his talents and character, in order that his opinions might be dismissed more readily as worthless. Such tactics would, of course, have proved fruitless enough, had not the philosophes themselves on that occasion joined forces with the reaction. Their reasons for doing so, if not quite honorable, were at least understandable. Because La Mettrie's "bad name" was exploited more than once to bring into disrepute those who had been associated with him, the philosophes soon decided to disown their *enfant terrible*. Moreover, such a step was made relatively easy by the fact that La Mettrie, who had always cut the figure of an *isolé*, lacked the sort of footing in French society which was needed to consolidate his fame in the world of letters; and also, no doubt, because he had died at an opportune time. A few examples will give an adequate notion of the kind of disparagement to which La Mettrie was regularly subjected by the philosophes no less than by their foes. The marquis d'Argens said of him: "Cet homme étoit de la plus grande ignorance, n'avoit aucune lecture; toute son érudition consistait en quelques vers de comédie. Il écrivoit en françois comme un énergumène et savait à peine assez de latin pour entendre les livres de médecine."[1] So transparent a calumny, which a mere glance at La Mettrie's works would have sufficed to refute, was eagerly passed on by others.[2] Elsewhere D'Argens made it clear that the antagonism of the philosophes toward La Mettrie was not an outgrowth of the man-machine standpoint, which several of them (including D'Argens himself) accepted in a greater or lesser degree. It was because the *Discours sur le bonheur* had appeared to sap the basis of all morality by its arguments against remorse, that the author was posthumously ejected from the philosophic fold: "Les philosophes ont vu avec horreur dans toute l'Europe, de quelque secte qu'ils ayent été, un homme aussi pernicieux à la société oser prendre le nom de philosophe, & jeter une honte éternelle sur la philosophie."[3]

[1] Jean Baptiste de Boyer, marquis d'Argens, *Ocellus Lucanus*, Berlin, 1762, p. 245.
[2] See, for instance, Chaudon, *Anti-Dictionnaire philosophique*, Paris, 1775, II, 54.
[3] D'Argens, *Histoire de l'esprit humain, ou Mémoires secrets de la république des lettres*, Berlin, 1765-68, XII, 301.

From precisely the same motives, and with the *Discours sur le bonheur* specifically in mind, Diderot later recited almost a litany of the slanders that had become inseparable from the name of La Mettrie, whom he qualified, among other things, as "dissolu, impudent, bouffon, flatteur; fait pour la vie des cours et la faveur des grands. Il est mort comme il devoit mourir, victime de son intempérance et de sa folie; il s'est tué par ignorance de l'art qu'il professait."[4]

The purpose of emphasizing here this special antipathy aroused by La Mettrie is not to imply that he was blameless, even though the philosophes' censure of him must be regarded as grotesquely overdone. The importance of these facts for us is that, unless a very ample allowance is made for them, it is not possible to take a correct view of the role played by *l'Homme machine* in the eighteenth-century milieu. The very nature of the situation makes it apparent that we cannot hope to discover La Mettrie's true position in the history of ideas by any direct means: that is, by acknowledgments of affinity on the part of those who were to be in any way indebted to him. On the contrary, there is every reason to expect that those who will be his immediate successors will keep the strictest silence about their relationship to the author of *l'Homme machine*—an expectation which events will fully justify. Thus it is reasonable to assume that La Mettrie's actual influence could only have been greater—perhaps much greater—than his contemporaries were willing to admit publicly. There would be no need to insist on this obvious point, if not for the fact that students of the French Enlightenment, in evaluating La Mettrie's contribution, have generally tended to see things through the eyes of the eighteenth century itself. In contrast to such a method, the historical status of La Mettrie can be ascertained only by indirect (but not necessarily unreliable) means. To this end, two types of evidence are pertinent: the chronology and diffusion of La Mettrie's writings and ideas; and the resemblance of his doctrines to those of his presumed continuators, chief among whom, as already noted, were Diderot, D'Holbach, and Cabanis.

There can be little doubt that La Mettrie was the first to have

[4] In the *Essai sur les règnes de Claude et de Néron; Oeuvres complètes de Diderot*, éd. Assézat & Tourneux, Paris, 1875-77, III, 218.

worked out a coherent and authoritative theory of the man-machine from the highly varied materials furnished by the background of philosophy, science, and free thought. Moreover, with the literary success of *l'Homme machine*, his theory was propagated openly and on a European scale. That subsequently it continued to have an appeal in France among an ever growing public is attested, not only by the criticisms which it elicited in the course of the 1750's and 1760's, but even more unequivocally by the number of editions of La Mettrie's *Oeuvres philosophiques* that were issued from 1751 to 1796—eleven of them in all, of which ten had appeared by 1775. In comparison with this, Diderot, who came next after La Mettrie in expounding a system of materialist psychology, did not give full expression to his ideas until the *Rêve de D'Alembert*, which, however, was withheld from publication during his lifetime. Actually, it was not before 1770 that D'Holbach's *Système de la nature* initiated a new and broader phase of publicity for the man-machine doctrine. Consequently, it was La Mettrie who, for more than two decades after 1748, had dominated the intellectual scene as the most original, forceful, and widely read exponent of the *homme machine* philosophy; so that it is fair to suppose that the extent of his impact on those who followed him must have been in keeping with so clearcut an advantage. A passing confirmation of this (one of the few that exist) was offered by Jean Paul Marat, the future Jacobin, when he recognized that La Mettrie's book—"ce livre qui a tant fait de bruit chez les Athées"—represented, despite the faults he found with it, the principal link between Descartes's psychophysiology and his own lucubrations in *De l'Homme, ou des principes et des loix de l'influence de l'âme sur le corps, et du corps sur l'âme* (1775).[5]

If we now consider, even briefly, the works of those who gave fresh developments to the man-machine thesis, our presumptions about their debt to La Mettrie will find strong support. In the case of Diderot, the underlying similarities between his thought and that of La Mettrie are not far to seek, although the relationship between the two eighteenth-century materialists, to be under-

[5] *op.cit.*, I, xiii-xiv.

stood as it should, demands a detailed and discriminating study.[6] As early as the *Interprétation de la nature*, but more particularly in his *Rêve de D'Alembert, Eléments de physiologie*, and *Réfutation d'Helvétius*, the *homme machine* served as a general presupposition of Diderot's biological and psychological speculations. In fact, precisely because, thanks to La Mettrie, it could be taken for granted rather than as an object of proof, Diderot was freer than his colleague had been to explore the complexities of the vital process, and to push the mechanistic explanation of life to its farthest limits. To this end, he applied the man-machine idea within a richly promising context of evolutionary biology, which, as we have seen, was a synthesis that La Mettrie too had arrived at, though less successfully, just before his death. Likewise, Diderot became deeply concerned with the problem of the transition of matter from the inorganic to the organic state—a question that La Mettrie, after the unsatisfactory efforts of the *Histoire de l'âme*, had put aside as too obscure to be attacked profitably with the scientific means then available. But perhaps the most original and far-reaching change that Diderot wrought in the man-machine idea was his radical translation of it to the microcosmic level. In that regard, the chief merit of the *Rêve de D'Alembert* lay in its conception of cellular structure, which was made the basis of the various special theories that Diderot elaborated to explain the formation and behavior of the organism as a whole. Thus he was led to seek the ultimate mystery of the living machine in the interdependent harmony of its elemental units: the "pointes sensibles et vivantes."

Sensibilité itself, the distinctive property of living substance, was regarded by Diderot as generally inherent, either passively or actively, in all matter as such; but this assumption, it must be granted, did not bring him any closer to a positive solution of the problem that perhaps fascinated him most: the origin of life. La Mettrie's restriction of the properties of functional motion and sensibility only to matter that already exhibited the necessary organization, may be said, in comparison with Diderot's somewhat speculative approach, to have been of more immediate theo-

---

[6] The recent effort of Jean Perkins ("Diderot and La Mettrie," *Studies on Voltaire*, Geneva, x [1959], 49-100) is unfortunately impaired by a consistent neglect of La Mettrie's originality.

retical value. In a broader sense, however, the concept of *sensibilité*, which had a fundamental role in Diderot's biological thought, suggests some analogy with the use made by La Mettrie of the notion of irritability. On superficial reading, a work like the *Rêve de D'Alembert* may well give the impression of being properly vitalistic, or even hylozoistic, in its emphasis. A closer look at the text will reveal, on the other hand, that the *sensibilité* which it posits as a general property of matter is not to be confused with the sort of mysterious *principe vital* that true vitalists oppose categorically to the mechanistic method in biology. By *sensibilité* Diderot actually means the automatic mode of reactivity that is peculiar to living systems, and he consistently proposes to explain its emergence quite mechanistically in terms of physicochemical factors: "avec une matière inerte, disposée d'une certaine manière, imprégnée d'une autre matière inerte, de la chaleur et du mouvement on obtient de la sensibilité, de la vie, de la mémoire, de la conscience, des passions, de la pensée."[7] There is thus a generic resemblance between the elemental structures to which both Diderot and La Mettrie trace the specific capabilities of the organism. Whereas the one speaks of *sensibilité* as characterizing the "pointe vivante," and the other conceives of the irritable process as the essential property of "chaque fibre du corps animal," their suppositions serve much the same purpose. For both Diderot and La Mettrie attempt, at least theoretically, to derive from the arrangements of these primary histological units all the higher organic functions, including consciousness, volition, and intelligence. As a result, it is possible to say that the dynamic organicism which is held to typify the standpoint of the *Rêve de D'Alembert* already had a significant anticipation in the parallel tendency of *l'Homme machine*.[8] The psychophysiological doctrines of La Mettrie and Diderot alike would seem, in fact, to have sprung from a common desire to bridge the conventional gap between mechanism and vitalism by assuming that deeper investigation of the phenomena peculiar to each of those concep-

[7] Diderot, *Oeuvres*, II, 115.
[8] Cf., Paul Delaunay, "L'Evolution philosophique et médicale du biomécanisme: de Descartes à Boerhaave, de Leibnitz à Cabanis," *Le Progrès médical*, 1927, p. 1377.

tions would, in the end, wipe out the dichotomy erected arbitrarily between them.

With respect to D'Holbach, his *Système de la nature* (on which, incidentally, Diderot had collaborated) grounded its materialism quite squarely on the man-machine thesis, which it reasserted with methodic diffuseness.[9] Despite this, the work actually said little about the *homme machine* that had not already been said by La Mettrie, even though the latter was not mentioned once in its pages. But D'Holbach did make his predecessor's conception the starting point of a more systematic, not to say dogmatic, exposition of the materialist philosophy. In particular, he worked out the logical and moral implications of the idea of a self-sufficient Nature which, encompassing the totality of things, produces in endless sequence the necessary effects of determinable causes. Along with this, unfortunately, his interest in the man-machine took on the doctrinaire quality of a foregone conclusion, since it lacked from the start the purpose, so prominent in La Mettrie, of serving as a general hypothesis for the scientific study of man. Instead, D'Holbach used mechanistic psychology chiefly to promote the militant atheism which, comprising the very spirit of his book, attacked the authority of the established religion and that of the obsolete and corrupt *régime* it buttressed.

Although Condillac does not belong among the representatives of the *homme machine* theory, a review of his relationship to La Mettrie will help to render more distinct the historical identity of the latter's ideas. It is apparent, in the first place, that La Mettrie could hardly have been influenced by Condillac, because the *Histoire de l'âme*, which was its author's main contribution to sensationism, appeared earlier than Condillac's first philosophical work, the *Origine des connaissances humaines* of 1746. As for *l'Homme machine*, whatever it had in common with Condillac's writings had already been present, almost without exception, in the *Histoire de l'âme*; whereas its points of difference with the *Histoire de l'âme* had no counterpart at all in the *Origine des connaissances humaines*. One could reverse the problem, perhaps, and wonder about La Mettrie's effect on Condillac; but that would lead mostly to fruitless speculation, in view of the

[9] See especially Vol. 1, Chaps. vi-xi.

latter's extremely close ties to Locke. Consequently, the most valid procedure is to compare the philosophies of La Mettrie and Condillac apart from any question of historical influence.

The psychological method of Condillac, like that of Locke, was primarily concerned with the rational analysis of ideas in terms of the sensory perceptions from which they had arisen. As such it assigned no differential role to either the physical apparatus of sensation or to the organism in general, but regarded the experiencing mind as an abstract receptacle in contradistinction to a living organ. The Lockean-Condillacean psychology was carried to its extreme form by Helvétius, who, though he affirmed *en passant* that "l'Homme est une machine qui, mise en mouvement par la sensibilité physique, doit faire tout ce qu'elle exécute,"[10] actually made no use whatever of that principle in his study of human behavior. Instead, assuming that the influence of the organism was constant in all normal persons, he sought to explain the specific differences among individuals solely by reference to sense impressions in a given physical and social environment. In the *Réfutation de l'Homme d'Helvétius*, Diderot felt obliged to correct this grossly one-sided and patently false interpretation of the mental process; and to that end he insisted on the primacy of those differentiae based on the machine which Helvétius had stubbornly excluded from consideration. Thus it may be said that in the eighteenth century the man-machine theory involved the subordination of sensationism to a psychological method that was rooted not so much in sensory experience as in the facts of physiology. Such a standpoint had enormous consequences of a practical and even humanistic sort, for the man of La Mettrie and the man of Condillac were to be quite different. In its presentation of psychic reality, the *homme machine* approach will show less interest in ideas as abstract entities than in the instincts, emotions, differences of temperament and intelligence that impart to ideas a concrete meaning and force. While, in its own domain, the analysis of sensation will succeed better in explaining the formation of knowledge from the common store of human experience, this epistemological advantage will have the effect of minimizing the individual variant, with

[10] Claude-Adrien Helvétius, *De l'Homme*, Londres, 1774, I, 130.

the result that Condillac's man is, basically, a statue possessed of a *tabula rasa* for a brain—in brief, a depersonalized general man. Compared with this, in a psychology built on the man-machine conception it is the instinctual and emotive reactions, the inborn temperament of the individual which, from the start of life, give to the sum of his experience the special inner quality by virtue of which sensation becomes more than the means of forming abstract ideas: it yields the *personal* ideas which, through the shaping of personality as a whole, determine his psychological fate.

From the vantage point of the present time, it is evident that the sensationist method of Condillac and the physiological method of La Mettrie—*l'expérience* and *la machine*—are complementary rather than antithetical, for no system of psychology could hope to do justice to the complexity of mental phenomena unless it employed both methods simultaneously, each in its proper sphere. But even in such a synthesis, it is inevitable that either the *sens externes* or the *sens internes* (to use an eighteenth-century distinction) will play the dominant role. Thus the primacy given by La Mettrie to the organic aspect need not, and does not, exclude the importance of the experiential aspect. Actually, if the *Histoire de l'âme* is taken together with *l'Homme machine*, one realizes that La Mettrie's orientation in psychology has a fullness of perspective and a scientific completeness which serve to correct the one-sided approach of the school of Locke, Condillac, and Helvétius. The value of La Mettrie's contribution to the history of psychology—a contribution which has not been recognized as it deserves to be—consists precisely in the fact that he was the first, in the age of Enlightenment, to investigate the problem of mind from the double standpoint of physiology and sense perception.[11]

[11] In the seventeenth century, of course, Hobbes's *De Corpore* and *De Homine* had shown a similar tendency. But apart from the fact that Hobbes's explanations were much cruder and less comprehensive than La Mettrie's, the emphasis of his materialism was on the equating of sensation and feeling with motions rather than with definite organic structures. The physiological psychology of David Hartley, which may be regarded as an independent product of the same scientific interests that produced *l'Homme machine*, appeared in his *Observations on Man* of 1749. Though Hartley maintained a formal distinction between mind and matter, the associationism linked with his name was based on a vibration theory which he applied with singular persistence to every sort of mental and

L'HOMME MACHINE SINCE 1748

In this respect, the most significant development of the *homme machine* may be said to have come at the end of the century with Cabanis's *Rapports du physique et du moral de l'homme*. Because it was mostly through Cabanis that La Mettrie's general theory entered into the mainstream of modern scientific and philosophical thought, the work merits a somewhat fuller discussion here.

Like that of *l'Homme machine*, the thesis of the *Rapports du physique et du moral* is that thinking and behavior are constantly determined by physiological causes: "Les opérations de l'intelligence et de la volonté se trouveroient confondues, à leur origine, avec les autres mouvemens vitaux: le principe des sciences morales, et par conséquent ces sciences elles-mêmes, rentreroient dans le domaine de la physique; elles ne seroient plus qu'une branche de l'histoire naturelle de l'homme."[12] Erecting his psychology on this basis, Cabanis examined separately, and in a far more methodical and technically controlled manner than La Mettrie had done, the influence of such physiological factors as the organs of sensation and the central nervous system; pathological states; age; sex; temperament; diet, exercise, mode of work, hygienic habits; drugs and stimulants; climate; and so forth. In a famous parallel between the functions of the brain and those of the stomach, which would doubtless have delighted a gastronome like La Mettrie, the *Rapports* pictured the mind as a sort of machine that manufactures thought: "Pour se faire une idée juste des opérations dont résulte la pensée, il faut considérer le cerveau comme un organe

---

biological process, and which led him in the end to a determinist view of behavior. But like Hobbes's before him, Hartley's physiology fell short of an organicist conception, and he differed with La Mettrie, among other ways, in treating the organism mainly as a kind of elastic instrument played on by external stimuli, rather than as a system possessing innate and purposive motion. Finally, it should be stated that Charles Bonnet, in the *Essai analytique sur les facultés de l'âme* (1760), sought also to work out a psychology in terms of both sensory data and physiological conditions. But while his ideas ran parallel at many points with those of *l'Homme machine*, Bonnet's method was radically different from La Mettrie's in that he adopted a firm dualist position, and interpreted psychic events as resulting from an interaction between the soul and the body.

[12] *Oeuvres philosophiques de Cabanis*, éd. C. Lehec & J. Cazeneuve, Paris, 1956, I, 115.

particulier, destiné spécialement à la produire, de même que l'estomac et les intestins à opérer la digestion. . . . Nous voyons les alimens tomber dans ce viscère, avec les qualités qui leur sont propres; nous les en voyons sortir avec des qualités nouvelles. Nous voyons également les impressions arriver au cerveau, par l'entremise des nerfs: elles sont alors isolées et sans cohérence. Le viscère entre en action; il agit sur elles: et bientôt il les renvoie métamorphosées en idées. . . . Nous concluons que le cerveau digère en quelque sorte les impressions; qu'il fait organiquement la sécrétion de la pensée."[13] Needless to say, Cabanis ruled out all reference to a soul. If it is true that in the *Lettre sur les causes premières* he sought to go beyond a reductive materialism, his psychology was not for that reason any less materialistic in its premises and conclusions.

The underlying concept of the psychophysiology worked out in the *Rapports* is "sensibilité physique," an irreducible property of all animal substance, which represents a special facet of the mechanistic order of things: "la sensibilité se rattache, peut-être, par quelques points essentiels, aux causes et aux lois du mouvement, source générale et féconde de tous les phénomènes de l'univers."[14] Viewed as an elementary organic force inhering in the nervous system, Cabanis contrasts it with irritability, which, in accord with Hallerian doctrine, he regards as both independent of nerve stimuli and restricted to muscular contraction. He thereupon tries to unify the two principles by conceiving of the nervous network as present everywhere in the body, even in the individual muscle fibers, which he in fact describes as outgrowths of nerve tissue.[15] This allows Cabanis to define the irritable process as a form of *sensibilité*, while the latter remains in his eyes the generic and basic phenomenon in biology.[16] Such a viewpoint suggests an interesting parallel with La Mettrie's notion of irritability. Inasmuch as *sensibilité physique* does not correspond to Haller's distinction between *sensibilis* and *irritabilis*—for Cabanis states that "il y a bien certainement *sensibilité sans sensation*"—it apparently refers, like the concept of irritability in *l'Homme machine*, to the automatic reactions of "chaque partie du corps

[13] *ibid.*, pp. 195-96. [14] *ibid.*, p. 173.
[15] *ibid.*, p. 171; see also p. 240. [16] *ibid.*, p. 171.

organisé," from which, in turn, all the vital and conscious operations of the organism are held to be derivable. The only difference here between Cabanis and La Mettrie was that the former thought of the property in question as fundamentally of a reflex type, while the latter saw it as a reactive energy which was present in living matter on a level more general and primitive than that of nerve structures proper. Except for this, Cabanis was right enough to remark: "Quand on examine attentivement la question de l'*irritabilité* et de la *sensibilité*, l'on s'aperçoit bientôt que ce n'est guère qu'une question de mots."[17]

It is hardly surprising that the *Rapports* should have been addressed as much to the *moraliste* as to the *médecin*, for its author followed *l'Homme machine* in affirming that "le point de vue sous lequel je considère la médecine, la fait rentrer à chaque instant dans le domaine des sciences morales."[18] Indeed, Cabanis was much more insistent than La Mettrie on the theme of physiological salvation, and his book strove throughout to substantiate the claim that "c'est dans l'organisation même de la race humaine, qu'est placé le principe de son perfectionnement."[19] But not only did Cabanis link the *médecin* indissolubly to the *moraliste*: he extended the scope of the latter term to include the *législateur*, so that in his thinking the man-machine theory may be said to have acquired a positive political meaning. With many of the *idéologues*, the aim of ameliorating human nature fitted in appropriately enough with the post-revolutionary fervor of achieving the social and moral regeneration of mankind. Going beyond that, however, Cabanis foresaw a specifically Republican use for his investigations, when he suggested that applied physiology would make it possible for the citizens of France to attain a measure of personal equality sufficiently great to provide a natural basis and safeguard for their political equality.[20]

Cabanis's elimination of finalistic logic from the sphere of science was no less complete than La Mettrie's.[21] His psycho-

---

[17] *ibid.*, p. 167; see also pp. 535-39.   [18] *ibid.*, p. 127.
[19] *ibid.*, p. 578. Similarly happiness was seen as a product of "le bien-être physique": "c'est encore en cela que réside le bonheur moral, qui en est un résultat particulier" (*ibid.*, p. 260).
[20] *ibid.*, p. 357.   [21] *ibid.*, pp. 296, 550.

physical theorizing, as a consequence, unfolded within the framework of a general biological naturalism, which had, moreover, an evolutionary dimension.[22] Seeming to echo La Mettrie, he pointed out that scientific explanation had no choice but to begin with the recognition that, in the external world, blind forces are capable of engendering forms and beings which manifest purpose and intelligence, so that the history of living things appears to be, from our vantage point, the paradox of a continual self-transcendence on the part of matter: "Quoique la sensibilité développe dans les corps des propriétés qui ne ressemblent en aucune manière à celles qui caractérisoient leurs élémens, il faut cependant se garder de croire que la tendance à l'organisation, la sensibilité que l'organisation détermine, la vie qui n'est que l'exercice, ou l'emploi régulier de l'une et de l'autre, ne dérivent pas elles-mêmes des lois générales qui gouvernent la matière. On se jetteroit dans un abîme de chimères et d'erreurs, si l'on s'imaginoit avoir besoin de chercher la cause de ces phénomènes, ailleurs que dans le caractère de certaines circonstances, au milieu desquelles les principes élémentaires, en vertu de leurs affinités respectives, se pénètrent, s'organisent, et, par cette nouvelle combinaison, acquièrent des qualités qu'ils n'avoient point antérieurement."[23] Such an estimate of natural process was associated, logically enough, with a positivistic ideal that placed first causes beyond the limits of human knowledge: "Quand même nous parviendrons à lever quelques coins du voile, c'est-à-dire, à faire dépendre une partie des phénomènes propres aux corps organisés, d'autres phénomènes plus généraux déjà connus, nous nous retrouverions toujours dans le même embarras relativement au fait principal, qui ne peut reconnoître pour cause, que les forces actives et premières de la nature, desquelles nous n'avons ni ne pouvons avoir aucune idée exacte."[24] In renouncing metaphysical truth, Cabanis was no less satisfied than La Mettrie had been to restrict the goal of science to the correlation of secondary phenomena, with the result that he took essentially the same view of psychophysical causation as that expressed in *l'Homme machine*: "Nous n'expliquons les phénomènes que par leurs rapports de ressemblance, ou de succession, avec

---

[22] *ibid.*, pp. 514-33, *passim*. [23] *ibid.*, p. 527.
[24] *ibid.*, p. 514.

d'autres phénomènes connus.... Quand l'un succède constamment à l'autre, nous supposons qu'il est engendré par lui; et nous établissons entre eux, les relations exprimées par les deux termes d'*effet* et de *cause*. C'est là ce que nous appelons expliquer."[25]

In the divergence already noted between the sensationist school of Locke-Condillac-Helvétius, and the physiological psychology of La Mettrie and his followers, the position taken by Cabanis may be inferred from his own comments. There runs through the *Rapports* a marked opposition to the Condillacean method, and indeed a rather incisive criticism of its unilateral grasp of mental reality: "Les philosophes analystes n'ont guère considéré jusqu'ici, que les impressions qui viennent des objets extérieurs, et que l'organe de la pensée distingue, se représente et combine: ce sont elles seulement qu'ils ont désignées sous le nom de *sensations*; les autres restent pour eux dans le vague."[26] Among the types of psychic data which Condillac is blamed for having neglected are the instincts in general, imagination, dreams, all emotions and affective states, automatic actions, hereditary dispositions, temperamental traits, the language of gesture and facial expression, sympathetic reactions, the differences between childhood, adolescence, manhood, old age, and so forth. It is precisely to these that Cabanis was to attribute the primary place in his own investigations; meanwhile, he recognizes that the psychologist is obliged to choose between the physiological and the sensationist approach: "C'est ici, je le répète, que l'on peut suivre deux routes différentes. Comme elles mènent à des résultats, en quelque sorte opposés, on ne saurait choisir au hasard."[27] Like La Mettrie, Cabanis takes the position that the influences which remain independent of sense perception—all of which he classes loosely under the heading of instinct—are the deeper, more constant, and, in the end, more significant factors in deciding an individual's behavior and psychic destiny. The sensationist method, by comparison, is incomplete and superficial, because it rests on a false conception of the mind. In correcting Cartesian innatism, Locke and his followers went to the opposite extreme, and with

[25] *ibid.*, p. 198.
[26] *ibid.*, p. 174. For the conflict of views between Cabanis and Condillac, see pp. 174-88, 551-58.
[27] *ibid.*, p. 174.

the *tabula rasa* hypothesis replaced one distortion with another, for the pre-experiential nature of the mind is plainly not "cette table rase, que se sont figurée plusieurs idéologistes. Le cerveau de l'enfant a déjà perçu et voulu: il a donc quelques faibles idées; et leur retour, ou leur habitude a produit en lui des penchants. Tel est le point d'où il faut partir, si l'on veut, en faisant l'analyse des opérations intellectuelles, les prendre véritablement à leur première origine."[28] Condillac's "statue" receives no better treatment: "Rien, sans doute, ne ressemble moins à l'homme, tel qu'il est en effet, que ces statues qu'on suppose douées, tout-à-coup, de la faculté d'éprouver distinctement les impressions attribuées à chaque sens en particulier; qui portent sur elles des jugemens, et forme en conséquence, des déterminations."[29] The statue simply corresponds to Condillac's erroneous aim of deriving a psychology from the external senses alone; it is the antithesis and denial of the living, active machine. Moreover, Cabanis argues that such a hypothesis offers an entirely unrealistic analogy, or model, of how the mind functions, because none of the senses acts altogether separately from the others, nor does the apparatus of sensation ever operate independently of the internal environment of the whole organism. As a result of these basic disagreements with the sensationist tradition that dominated the eighteenth century, Cabanis regards the *Rapports* as initiating a new era in the scientific study of man. In this claim, however, he tended to exaggerate his originality, for it is apparent that La Mettrie, not to mention Diderot and D'Holbach, had already adopted a very similar stand in psychology.

It is perhaps unnecessary to say that, despite the many parallels noted above, Cabanis maintained the most complete silence about any kinship between his doctrines and those of *l'Homme machine*. Apart from the desire to appear original, his reasons are not difficult to imagine. At the time, the *idéologues* were working in a political and cultural atmosphere that tended to condemn the more radical aspect of the Enlightenment, and this tendency was to grow stronger with the rise to power of Napoleon. In such a situation, they were eager to remain neutral by dissociating themselves as much as possible from the atheistic group of

---

[28] *ibid.*, p. 547. [29] *ibid.*, p. 552.

philosophes. Thus Cabanis was no more willing to be placed in the lineage of Diderot and D'Holbach (with whose thought he also had much in common) than in that of La Mettrie. The motives for this attitude are further disclosed by the fact that, despite the profound conflict between its psychophysiological naturalism and Christian theology, the *Rapports* refrained from drawing any antireligious or atheistic conclusions. But, while Cabanis's reluctance to recognize La Mettrie as a forbear is understandable, it is far less easy to understand why most historians have placed the background of *idéologie* almost exclusively in the school of Locke, Condillac, and Helvétius. Such a view of things may apply well enough to Destutt de Tracy and many other *idéologues*, but it is a patent misreading of history in the case of Cabanis. Yet Picavet makes only the most casual sort of reference to La Mettrie as a precursor of Cabanis's physiological psychology;[30] and Cailliet, who undertakes to trace the origins of *idéologie* all the way back to Protagoras, somehow manages not to mention La Mettrie at all in the line of descent.[31] It is to be hoped that henceforth the subject will be viewed in a more balanced fashion by students of the French Enlightenment and its aftermath.

During the first half of the nineteenth century, *l'Homme machine* came nearest to being forgotten. This was owing partly to the fact that the doctrines of Cabanis and the *idéologues* replaced the earlier, less developed ideas of La Mettrie, and partly to the rapid transformation of the cultural milieu after 1800. The idealistic and neoreligious attitudes that accompanied the spread of Romanticism proved to be, of course, quite antagonistic to the man-machine psychology, and in particular to the atheistic materialism with which it was bound up. Likewise, the restoration of the monarchy and the political and social conservatism that came to typify the French scene—at least officially—until the Revolution of 1848, powerless though these were to harm the reputations of Voltaire, Rousseau, Montesquieu, and even Diderot, proved sufficient to suppress for a time the memory of a lesser figure like La Mettrie. Nevertheless, the same period saw the steady increase of the intellectual trends that were soon to bring

[30] François Picavet, *Les idéologues*, Paris, 1891.
[31] Emile Cailliet, *La tradition littéraire des idéologues*, Philadelphia, 1943.

about the vindication of *l'Homme machine* and its author. In France these were, above all, the positive advances being made in the sciences, especially in biology, neurophysiology, and psychiatry, as evidenced by the pioneering efforts of such investigators as Bichat, Pinel, Esquirol, Broussais, Magendie, Flourens, and others. Concurrently, the physiological psychology represented by the school of Cabanis began to exert an influence on literature—most notably in the novels of Balzac. In the philosophical sphere, the appearance between 1830 and 1842 of Comte's *Cours de philosophie positive* came as a sweeping confirmation of the non-metaphysical, heuristic criteria with which La Mettrie's man-machine hypothesis had long ago envisaged psychologic truth. In Germany, too, the stage was being set for La Mettrie's rehabilitation. The years leading up to and following 1850 witnessed there, for the first time, the development of an indigenous school of materialism, nurtured by the aforesaid currents in French science no less than by their German counterparts, and having among its proponents such names as Feuerbach, Vogt, Moleschott, Czolbe, and especially Büchner, the author of *Kraft und Materie* (1855).[32] The appearance of this book, which had a dramatic and far-reaching impact, was in its day a literary event comparable to the publication of *l'Homme machine* more than a century earlier.

Before long, the rediscovery of La Mettrie took place almost simultaneously in France and in Germany. Assézat published his edition of *l'Homme machine* in 1865, and in the following year Lange's monumental *History of Materialism* gave a long overdue reassessment of La Mettrie's thought. In the second half of the nineteenth century, the complex of determinist theories developed by such figures as Claude Bernard and Taine brought about an ascendancy of the naturalistic outlook in philosophy and literature no less than in science. The climate of opinion created thereby strongly favored the further growth of La Mettrie's reputation. To this period belong, incidentally, a number of translations of *l'Homme machine* into German and Italian. In 1873 there appeared the first book-length study of La Mettrie, by René Paquet,[33] who largely set himself the task—apparently still for-

---

[32] Cf. Lange, *History of Materialism*, Bk. 2, Sect. 1, pp. 235-94.
[33] *Essai sur La Mettrie, sa vie et ses oeuvres*.

midable—of stripping way the many prejudices and calumnies encrusted around the philosophe's name, and of acquainting the general public with some of the more salient merits of *l'Homme machine*. Shortly thereafter, Du Bois-Reymond, the well-known German physiologist, delivered before the Prussian Academy of Sciences an incisive oration on La Mettrie, in which the erstwhile member of that learned society was hailed as an early founder of the monistic conception of things which, in the speaker's view, typified the spirit and methodology of modern science.[34] The spread of Darwinian ideas also brought new respect for La Mettrie when it was realized that his speculations, once so odious, concerning the common origin and mental resemblance of *Homo sapiens* and the anthropoid ape were unusually farsighted. This was especially true in Germany, where the influence of a popular evolutionist like Haeckel found no immediate equivalent in France. In fact, as German scholars began to take the lead in the critical study of La Mettrie, some of their French colleagues grew a bit wary. Picavet, at any rate, wrote a pamphlet in 1889 challenging the high estimate of La Mettrie being given across the Rhine.[35] Suspecting that this estimate must spring from motives of cultural chauvinism because of the philosophe's ties with Frederick the Great and the Berlin Academy, Picavet sought to relegate La Mettrie among the mediocre writers of the Enlightenment. Such negative reactions were rare, however, and it may be said that with the appearance in 1900 of Poritzky's well-grounded and comprehensive study, *Lamettrie, sein Leben und seine Werke*, *l'Homme machine* advanced finally from the status of a curiosity, to that of a classic—albeit not in absolutely the first rank—of philosophical literature.

Research on La Mettrie has continued its course in our own century, with new editions or reprintings of *l'Homme machine*, in the original and in translation, being issued from time to time. Bergmann, who unraveled the story of the satirical skirmishes between La Mettrie and a number of German critics, succeeded thereby in restoring some light and shadow to his personality and

[34] *Monatsberichte des königlich Preussischen Akademie der Wissenschaften zu Berlin*, 1875, pp. 85-112.
[35] *La Mettrie et la critique allemande*, Paris, 1889.

in modifying the caricature of him that had been handed down from the past.[36] R. Boissier, in *La Mettrie, médecin, pamphlétaire et philosophe*, emphasized particularly the eighteenth-century medical background of his subject; but his discussion, while generally informative, unfortunately remained, like the essays of Vézeaux de Lavergne, Maître, and Tuloup (see Bibliography), too often on the level of standard histories of medicine to be of much value on specific problems. Finally, Pierre Lemée has managed to clear away some of the vagueness and confusion that have long attached to the biography and bibliography of La Mettrie.[37] But despite this broadening of interest in the man and his work, no attempt was made to give a fully critical edition of *l'Homme machine*.

Since the basic ideas of *l'Homme machine* have become so broadly diffused and so completely absorbed into the main currents of modern thought, the book itself may be said today to concern chiefly the historian. However, certain events of recent years have given special meaning to the status of La Mettrie in the historical consciousness of our time.

During the 1920's, there took place a curious re-enactment of the man-machine debate, prompted by the challenge that the neovitalism set in vogue by Bergson, Hans Driesch, and others, opposed to the mechanistic school of biology. Typical of this development was Eugenio Rignano's *Man not a Machine, A Study of the Finalistic Aspects of Life* (1926). The book soon brought a rebuttal from Joseph Needham, entitled *Man a Machine, in Answer to a Romantical and Unscientific Treatise*, etc. The controversy spun itself out primarily on the biological, rather than the psychological, plane. Rignano advanced the familiar argument that, since living things showed essential properties having no equivalents in the behavior of inanimate bodies, it was a fundamental mistake to regard the organism as a machine. These properties, teleological in nature and deriving variously from the homeostatic tendency of any system that is alive, were seen to consist in such uniquely vital functions as the self-conserving results of the metabolic process; the ontogenetic growth of the organism; its pre-estab-

---

[36] *Die Satiren des Herrn Maschine*, Leipzig, 1913.
[37] *J. O. de La Mettrie, médecin, philosophe, polémiste*, 1954.

lished morphological and physiological adaptation at birth, no less than its later adaptations in pursuit of an environmental optimum; the purposive character of reflex actions, instincts, the mental faculties, and so on. Holding that for such phenomena, which sharply divide living from nonliving substance, the mechanists did not even begin to give satisfactory explanations with reference to physicochemical factors, Rignano proposed instead the hypothesis of a special life force capable of producing them. However, it is an index of the evolution of the vitalist position since La Mettrie's time that, whereas Stahl and his successors had been able to conceive of this life force in terms only of an immaterial soul or an equally intangible *principe vital*, Rignano thought of it as "a new form of energy, always obedient to the general laws of energetics, but endowed with well-defined elementary properties different from those of any form of energy in the inorganic world"[38]—that is, his position was meant to be antimechanistic without being in the least antimaterialistic. Needham's reply to this recognized from the start La Mettrie's relevance to the controversy, and devoted a preliminary essay to his ideas. Like the philosophe, Needham took particular exception to the desire of the vitalist to lay down a hard and fast a priori distinction between organic and inorganic behavior; and he proceeded to show how the attempt to do so is, from the standpoint of theory, more fraught with difficulties than one might at first imagine. In his view, the crux of the vitalist-mechanist debate revolved about the question, not how little or how much of life the mechanist can explain by means of his principles, but whether there exists any other scientific method of explaining it. Indeed, Rignano's "new form of energy" would itself remain an empty abstraction explaining nothing whatever, unless it were somehow measurable in terms of quantities and motions; but if it could be so measured, such an energy would become simply another mechanical principle, even though it remained peculiar to the organic realm. Thus it is in keeping with the spirit of La Mettrie that Needham at once concedes that the mechanistic view of life amounts to a "methodological fiction," but still insists that "in

---

[38] E. Rignano, *Man Not a Machine*, p. 17.

science, man is a machine; or if he is not, then he is nothing at all."[89]

In the last two decades, the question of the *homme machine* has been thrust once more into the foreground of discussion—particularly in the United States, Britain, and France—as a result of the emergence of cybernetics as a special branch of science. If La Mettrie had reached his conclusions with the aid of mechanical analogies so relatively crude as the clock-like automata of Vaucanson, it is easily understandable that the man-machine idea would be raised to a new level of meaning, entering (as it were) on its golden age, with the construction of multipurpose digital computers, logical calculators, and a variety of complex self-regulatory devices embodying the servomechanism principle. The cyberneticians themselves, concerned with the theory of machines which, by receiving, storing and communicating information in suitably controlled fashion, appear actually capable of forms of behavior hitherto thought to characterize only animals and human beings, have lost no time in extending their technical concepts, often with very promising results, to the domains of neurophysiology, psychology, philosophy, and even psychiatry. The literature extant on the subject is already considerable, but unfortunately lack of space does not permit us to go into it here. Suffice it to say that the ghost of La Mettrie, during the past century and a half, has never been so much alive and abroad as he is today.

The most telling impact of cybernetics has been thus far on the vitalist orientation in biology. Among the numerous machines capable of operations peculiar to living creatures, the most impressive have been, perhaps, W. R. Ashby's "Homeostat," which can maintain its equilibrium with astonishing versatility; the various mechanical maze-runners designed by C. E. Shannon and others; Grey Walter's ingenious "tortoise" (the modern descendant of Vaucanson's "canard"!), which attains its goal by overcoming obstacles; and his CORA, which reproduces the mechanical equivalent of conditioned-reflex action. In view of the self-corrective, purposeful comportment of such devices, it has become more difficult than ever for the vitalists to attach to the specific phenomena of life an objective idea that will transcend all mechanistic inter-

---

[89] J. Needham, *Man a Machine*, New York, 1928, pp. 93, 86.

pretation. With the consequent narrowing of the gap between the living and the nonliving, biology has moved proportionately closer to the positive convergence of the organism and the machine.

More than that, however, the devices just described may be said to imitate a series of functions belonging normally to beings endowed with intelligence—such as problem-solving, goal-seeking, learning, memorizing, even thinking (at least along purely mathematical and logical lines). Thus it has seemed natural enough to suppose that analogous operations in animals and in man might be produced by mechanical structures and processes resembling, more or less, those present in their inanimate counterparts. The concept of negative feedback—regarded in cybernetics as the basic principle of mechanical autoregulation—has been assumed to underly generally the functioning of the central nervous system. Such a view has so far been richly suggestive of neurophysiological models and theories, particularly in the area of reflex mechanisms, where the available anatomical knowledge about neural loops has appeared consistent with its application. The cybernetic approach has also proved stimulating, but as yet fairly inconclusive, in the psychological sphere proper. The use of the scansion mechanism as a model in the field of perception, corroborated as it is by the phenomena of brain waves and cortical tension, has been quite valuable; and significant efforts have been made to explain the mechanical basis of memory, together with its peculiarly nonlocalized character, in terms of reverberating circuits of electrochemical nerve impulses. Although the extension of comparable concepts of negative feedback to the higher mental activities has not seemed as rewarding, an attempt has nevertheless been made, by W. S. McCulloch among others, to determine mathematically how the function of reasoning as carried on by the brain could result from arrangements resembling those of a digital computer or a "logical machine." But whatever the final outcome of all this theorizing will be—and there is reason to believe it will not be negligible—one of its more immediate and positive achievements has been to break down much of the rigid traditional dichotomy between mechanism and teleology. Ashby's *Design for a Brain*, and Norbert Wiener, in *Cybernetics: or Control and Communication in the Animal and the Machine*, have in particular sought to make clear what conditions must be satisfied in a physical system in order for it to behave adaptively and, so to speak, with foresight. By showing that self-directive force, far from being contradictory to mechanical causation, is actually in certain cases derivable from it, the cybernetic school has illuminated technically the theme that was found to be so central to *l'Homme machine*, namely, the purposive oscillation of the organism inherent in the irritability principle.

To be sure, the cumulative evidence offered by cybernetics (whatever its more zealous exponents might say) does not prove that a man is literally a machine any more, for that matter, than did La Mettrie's book. Depending on how words are used, machines could well be said to "think" or to "act with purpose." However, unless a dogmatically behavioristic attitude is taken in such matters, it must be duly admitted that machines neither know that they think, nor what the purpose of their thoughts might be; and that precisely these capabilities describe the essence of human, and probably of higher animal, thinking. Seen in this light, the thought or purpose discernible in the operation of a machine is really the property of its creator; for, philosophically speaking, the most cleverly contrived automatic device is no different from the simplest, hand-directed tool. But this does not invalidate the man-machine as a comprehensive and indispensable hypothesis of psychophysiological research. Cybernetics, in opening up new avenues of investigation for mechanistic psychology, has been merely the most recent and, in some ways, the most convincing illustration of the persistent vitality and indefinite promise that were present from the first in the thesis of *l'Homme machine*.

A NOTE ON THE TEXT

As the basis of the present edition, I have chosen the text of *l'Homme machine* in the *Oeuvres philosophiques* of 1751. On that occasion, La Mettrie made a final revision of his book, correcting a number of factual errors and introducing other changes. For the variant readings, I have utilized the three known editions of *l'Homme machine* which antedate the *Oeuvres* of 1751. These, accompanied each by its identifying symbol, are the following:

W   *L'Homme Machine*. A Leyde, De l'Imp. d'Elie Luzac, Fils, 1748. 108 pp.

X   *L'Homme Machine*. A Leyde, De l'Imp. d'Elie Luzac, Fils, 1748. 109 pp.

Y   *L'Homme Machine*. A Leyde, De l'Imp. d'Elie Luzac, Fils, 1748. 148 pp.

W, the authentic first edition, is so exceedingly rare that only Bergmann, to my knowledge, has claimed to have seen it. I succeeded in locating a copy that belongs to the *Bibliothèque nationale et universitaire* of Strasbourg. Although, like X, it bears the year 1748 on its title page, one can readily ascertain that W is the earlier version, because a great many of the typographical errors to be found in it are no longer present in X. W is very likely the edition of *l'Homme machine* that was already in circulation during the last months of 1747. Its scarcity could be explained by supposing that it was also the edition of which the Leyden authorities seized, and presumably destroyed, the available stock in December 1747. The texts of W and X are almost identical, and the slight discrepancy of pagination between the two results merely from differences of page composition. But X, which was long mistaken for the *editio princeps*, has actually been used as the basis of every edition of *l'Homme machine* after 1751.

The text of Y differs at a number of points from that of X, but none of these inconsistencies are encountered in the 1751 version. It is therefore clear that La Mettrie's revisions were made on a copy of X, and that Y was totally ignored for that purpose. This

A NOTE ON THE TEXT

raises the question who is responsible for the variants in Y. Some of these, which make rather dubious sense, might have been the work of the printer. As for the others, which are logically or stylistically plausible, it is possible to attribute them to the author himself. If La Mettrie did make the changes in question, it could be assumed that he neglected to carry them over into the 1751 edition, either because they were not important enough, or because he did not have a copy of Y in his possession at the time. However, the possibility cannot be altogether dismissed that we are dealing in the case of Y with a pirated edition.

In transcribing the 1751 text, I have preserved not only the original spelling and punctuation, but also the variations which these exhibit. I have ventured to retouch only where it seemed obvious that a typographical error had been overlooked. In the variants given, the use of parallel lines as a symbol indicates a substituted or paraphrased passage. Because of the filiation among the texts of *l'Homme machine*, it has seemed simpler to use the letter X to designate the variants that X has in common with both W and Y. Only where one of the latter editions differs from X, have the symbols W or Y been employed instead.

L'HOMME MACHINE

Est-ce là ce Raion de l'Essence suprème,
 Que l'on nous peint si lumineux?
Est-ce là cet Esprit survivant à nous même?
Il naît avec nos sens, croit, s'affoiblit
                    comme eux.
  Helas! il périra de même.
                    —VOLTAIRE[1]

AVERTISSEMENT DE L'IMPRIMEUR[2]

On sera peut-être surpris que j'aie osé mettre mon nom à un livre aussi hardi que celui-ci. Je ne l'aurois certainement pas fait, si je n'avois cru la Religion à l'abri de toutes les tentatives qu'on fait pour la renverser; & si j'eusse pu me persuader, qu'un autre Imprimeur n'eût pas fait très volontiers ce que j'aurois refusé par principe de conscience. Je sai que la Prudence veut qu'on ne donne pas occasion aux Esprits foibles d'être séduits. Mais en les supposant tels, j'ai vu à la première lecture qu'il n'y avoit rien à craindre pour eux. Pourquoi être si attentif, & si alerte à supprimer les Argumens contraires aux Idées de la Divinité & de la Religion? Cela ne peut-il pas faire croire au Peuple qu'on le *leurre*? & dès qu'il commence à douter, adieu la conviction, & par conséquent la Religion! Quel moien, quelle espérance, de confondre jamais les Irréligionnaires, si on semble les redouter? Comment les ramener, si en leur défendant de se servir de leur raison, on se contente de déclamer contre leurs moeurs, à tout hazard, sans s'informer si elles méritent la même censure que leur façon de penser.

Une telle conduite donne gain de cause aux Incrédules; ils se moquent d'une Religion, que notre ignorance voudroit ne pouvoir être conciliée avec la Philosophie: ils chantent victoire dans leurs retranchemens, que notre manière de combattre leur fait croire invincibles. Si la Religion n'est pas victorieuse, c'est la faute des mauvais Auteurs qui la défendent. Que les bons prennent la plume; qu'ils se montrent bien armés; & la Théologie l'emportera de haute lutte sur une aussi foible Rivale. Je compare les Athées à ces Géans qui voulurent escalader les Cieux: ils auront toujours le même sort.

Voilà ce que j'ai cru devoir mettre à la tête de cette petite Brochure, pour prévenir toute inquiétude. Il ne me convient pas de réfuter ce que j'imprime; ni même de dire mon sentiment sur les raisonnemens qu'on trouvera dans cet écrit. Les connoisseurs verront aisément que ce ne sont que des difficultés qui se présentent toutes les fois qu'on veut expliquer l'union de l'Ame avec le Corps. Si les conséquences, que l'Auteur en tire, sont dangereuses, qu'on se souvienne qu'elles n'ont qu'une Hypothèse pour fondement. En faut-il davantage pour les détruire? Mais, s'il m'est permis de supposer ce que je ne crois pas; quand même ces conséquences seroient difficiles à renverser, on n'en auroit qu'une plus belle occasion de briller. *A vaincre sans péril, on triomphe sans gloire.*[a]

[a] X has the additional paragraph: L'Auteur, que je ne connois point, m'a envoïé son Ouvrage de *Berlin*, en me priant seulement d'en envoyer six Exemplaires à l'adresse de Mr. le Marquis D'ARGENS. Assurément on ne peut mieux s'y prendre pour garder l'*incognito*; car je suis persuadé que cette adresse même n'est qu'un persiflage.[8]

A MONSIEUR HALLER,
PROFESSEUR EN MÉDECINE À GOTTINGUE.[4]

Ce n'est point ici une Dédicace; vous êtes fort au-dessus de tous les Eloges que je pourrois vous donner; & je ne connois rien de si inutile, ni de si fade, si ce n'est un Discours Académique. Ce n'est point une Exposition de la nouvelle Méthode que j'ai suivie pour relever un sujet usé & rebattu. Vous lui trouverez du moins ce mérite; & vous jugerez au reste si votre Disciple & votre ami a bien rempli sa carrière. C'est le plaisir que j'ai eu à composer cet ouvrage, dont je veux parler; c'est moi-même, & non mon livre que je vous adresse, pour m'éclairer sur la nature de cette sublime Volupté de l'Etude. Tel est le sujet de ce Discours. Je ne serois[a] pas le premier Ecrivain, qui, n'aiant rien à dire, pour réparer la Stérilité de son Imagination, auroit pris un texte, où il n'y en eut jamais. Dites-moi donc, Double Enfant d'Apollon, Suisse Illustre, Fracastor[5] Moderne, vous qui savez tout à la fois connoître, mesurer la Nature, qui plus est la sentir, qui plus est encore l'exprimer: savant Médecin, encore plus grand Poëte, dites-moi par quels charmes l'Etude peut changer les Heures en momens; quelle est la Nature de ces plaisirs de l'Esprit, si différens des plaisirs vulgaires. . . . Mais la lecture de vos charmantes Poësies m'en a trop pénétré moi-même, pour que je n'essaie pas de dire ce qu'elles m'ont inspiré. L'Homme, consideré dans ce point de vüe, n'a rien d'étranger à mon sujet.

La Volupté des sens, quelque aimable & chérie qu'elle soit, quelques éloges que lui ait donnés la plume apparemment reconnoissante[b] d'un jeune Medecin françois,[6] n'a qu'une seule joüissance qui est son tombeau. Si le plaisir parfait ne la tüe point sans retour, il lui faut un certain tems pour ressusciter. Que les ressources des plaisirs de l'esprit sont différentes! plus on s'approche de la Vérité, plus on la trouve charmante. Non seulement sa joüissance augmente les desirs; mais on joüit ici, dès qu'on cherche à joüir. On joüit long-tems, & cependant plus vîte que l'éclair ne

[a] W: serai   [b] X. aussi reconnoissante que délicate

parcourt. Faut-il s'étonner si la Volupté de l'Esprit est aussi supérieure à celle des sens, que l'Esprit est au-dessus du Corps? L'Esprit n'est-il pas le premier des Sens, & comme le rendez-vous de toutes les sensations? N'y aboutissent-elles pas toutes, comme autant de raions, à un Centre qui les produit? Ne cherchons donc plus par quels invincibles charmes, un coeur que l'Amour de la Vérité enflame, se trouve tout-à-coup transporté, pour ainsi dire, dans un monde plus beau, où il goute des plaisirs dignes des Dieux. De toutes les Attractions de la Nature, la plus forte, du moins pour moi, comme pour vous, cher Haller, est celle de la Philosophie. Quelle gloire plus belle, que d'être conduit à son Temple par la raison & la Sagesse! quelle conquête plus flateuse que de se soumettre tous les Esprits!

Passons en revüe tous les objets de ces plaisirs inconnus aux Ames Vulgaires. De quelle beauté, de quelle étendüe ne sont-ils pas? Le tems, l'espace, l'infini, la terre, la mer, le firmament, tous les Elemens, toutes les sciences, tous les arts, tout entre dans ce genre de Volupté. Trop resserrée dans les bornes du monde, elle en imagine un million. La nature entière est son aliment, & l'imagination son triomphe. Entrons dans quelque détail.

Tantôt c'est la Poësie ou la Peinture; tantôt c'est la Musique ou l'Architecture, le Chant, la Danse &c. qui font gouter aux connoisseurs des plaisirs ravissans. Voiez la Delbar (femme de Piron)[7] dans une loge d'Opera; pâle & rouge tour-à-tour, elle bat la mesure avec Rebel;[8] s'attendrit avec Iphigénie, entre en fureur avec Roland &c. Toutes les impressions de l'Orchestre passent sur son visage, comme sur une toile. Ses yeux s'adoucissent, se pâment, rient, ou s'arment d'un courage guerrier. On la prend pour une folle. Elle ne l'est point, à moins qu'il n'y ait de la folie à sentir le plaisir. Elle n'est que pénétrée de mille beautés qui m'echapent.

Voltaire ne peut refuser des pleurs à sa Merope; c'est qu'il sent le prix, & de l'ouvrage, & de l'Actrice.[9] Vous avez lu ses écrits; & malheureusement pour lui, il n'est point en état de lire les vôtres. Dans les mains, dans la mémoire de qui ne sont-ils pas?[10] & quel coeur assez dur pour ne point en être attendri! Comment tous ses goûts ne se communiqueroient-ils pas? Il en parle avec transport.

Qu'un grand Peintre, je l'ai vu avec plaisir en lisant ces jours passés la Préface de Richardson,[11] parle de la Peinture, quels éloges ne lui donne-t-il pas? Il adore son Art, il le met au-dessus de tout, il doute presque qu'on puisse être heureux sans être Peintre. Tant il est enchanté de sa profession!

Qui n'a pas senti les mêmes transports que Scaliger, ou le Père Mallebranche, en lisant, ou quelques belles Tirades des Poëtes Tragiques, Grecs, Anglois, François; ou certains Ouvrages Philosophiques?[12] Jamais Mme. Dacier n'eût compté sur ce que son Mari lui promettoit; & elle trouva cent fois plus.[13] Si l'on éprouve une sorte d'Enthousiasme à traduire & développer les pensées d'autrui, qu'est-ce donc si l'on pense soi-même? Qu'est-ce que cette génération, cet enfantement d'Idées, que produit le goût de la Nature & la recherche du Vrai? Comment peindre cet Acte de la Volonté, ou de la Mémoire, par lequel l'Ame se reproduit en quelque sorte, en joignant une idée à une autre trace semblable, pour que de leur ressemblance & comme de leur union, il en naisse une troisième: car admirez les productions de la Nature. Telle est son uniformité, qu'elles se font presque toutes de la même manière.

Les plaisirs des sens mal réglés, perdent toute leur vivacité & ne sont plus des plaisirs. Ceux de l'Esprit leur ressemblent jusqu'à un certain point. Il faut les suspendre pour les aiguiser. Enfin l'Etude a ses Extases, comme l'Amour. S'il m'est permis de le dire, c'est une Catalepsie, ou immobilité de l'Esprit, si délicieusement enivré de l'objet qui le fixe & l'enchante, qu'il semble détaché par abstraction de son propre corps & de tout ce qui l'environne, pour être tout entier à ce qu'il poursuit. Il ne sent rien, à force de sentir. Tel est le plaisir qu'on goute, & en cherchant, & en trouvant la Vérité. Jugez de la puissance de ses charmes par l'Extase d'Archimede; vous savez qu'elle lui couta la vie.[14]

Que les autres hommes se jettent dans la foule, pour ne pas se connoître, ou plutôt se haïr; le sage fuit le grand monde & cherche la solitude. Pourquoi ne se plait-il qu'avec lui-même, ou avec ses semblables? C'est que son Ame est un miroir fidèle, dans lequel son juste amour-propre trouve son compte à se regarder. Qui est vertueux, n'a rien à craindre de sa propre connoissance, si ce n'est l'agréable danger de s'aimer.

Comme aux yeux d'un Homme qui regarderoit la terre du haut des Cieux, toute la grandeur des autres Hommes s'évanouïroit, les plus superbes Palais se changeroient en Cabanes, & les plus nombreuses Armées ressembleroient à une troupe de fourmis, combattant pour un grain avec la plus ridicule furie; ainsi paroissent les choses à un sage, tel que vous. Il rit des vaines agitations des Hommes, quand leur multitude embarrasse la Terre & se pousse pour un rien,[a] dont il est juste qu'aucun d'eux ne soit content.

Que Pope débute d'une manière sublime dans son *Essai sur l'Homme*! Que les Grands & les Rois sont petits devant lui! O vous, moins mon Maître, que mon Ami, qui aviez reçu de la Nature la même force de génie que lui, dont vous avez abusé; Ingrat, qui ne méritiez pas d'exceller dans les sciences; vous m'avez appris à rire, comme ce grand Poëte, ou plutôt à gémir des joüets & des bagatelles, qui occupent sérieusement les Monarques. C'est à vous que je dois tout mon bonheur. Non, la conquête du Monde entier ne vaut pas le plaisir qu'un Philosophe goute dans son cabinet, entouré d'Amis müets, qui lui disent cependant tout ce qu'il desire d'entendre. Que Dieu ne m'ôte point le nécessaire & la santé, c'est tout ce que je lui demande. Avec la santé, mon coeur sans dégout aimera la vie. Avec le nécessaire, mon Esprit content cultivera toujours la sagesse.

Oui, l'Etude est un plaisir de tous les âges, de tous les lieux, de toutes les saisons & de tous les momens. A qui Ciceron n'a-t-il pas donné envie d'en faire l'heureuse expérience? Amusement dans la jeunesse, dont il tempère les passions fougueuses; pour le bien goûter, j'ai quelquefois été forcé de me livrer à l'Amour. L'Amour ne fait point de peur à un sage: il sait tout allier & tout faire valoir l'un par l'autre. Les nuages qui offusquent son entendement, ne le rendent point paresseux; ils ne lui indiquent que le remède qui doit les dissiper. Il est vrai que le Soleil n'écarte pas plus vite ceux de l'Atmosphère.

Dans la vieillesse, âge glacé, où on n'est plus propre, ni à donner, ni à recevoir d'autres plaisirs, quelle plus grande ressource que la lecture & la méditation! Quel plaisir de voir *tous les jours, sous ses yeux & par ses mains,* croître & se former un Ouvrage qui charmera les siècles à venir, & même ses contemporains! Je voudrois, me disoit un jour un Homme dont la vanité commençoit à sentir le plaisir d'être Auteur, passer ma vie à aller de chez moi chez l'Im-

[a] X: pour rien

primeur. Avoit-il tort? Et lorsqu'on est applaudi, quelle Mère tendre fut jamais plus charmée d'avoir fait un enfant aimable?

Pourquoi tant vanter les plaisirs de l'Etude? Qui ignore que c'est un bien qui n'apporte point le dégout ou les inquiétudes des autres biens? un trésor inépuisable, le plus sûr contrepoison du cruel ennui; qui se promène & voyage avec nous, & en un mot nous suit partout? Heureux qui a brisé la chaine de tous ses préjugés! Celui-là seul goûtera ce plaisir dans toute sa pureté! Celui-là seul joüira de cette douce tranquillité d'Esprit, de ce parfait contentement d'une ame forte & sans ambition, qui est le Père du bonheur, s'il n'est le bonheur même.

Arrêtons-nous un moment à jetter des fleurs sur les pas de ces grands Hommes que Minerve a, comme vous, couronnés d'un Lierre immortel. Ici c'est Flore qui vous invite avec Linaeus, à monter par de nouveaux sentiers sur le sommet glacé des Alpes, pour y admirer sous une autre Montagne de Neige un Jardin planté par les mains de la Nature: Jardin qui fut jadis tout l'héritage du célébre Professeur Suédois.[15] De-là vous descendez dans ces prairies, dont les fleurs l'attendent pour se ranger dans un ordre, qu'elles sembloient avoir jusqu'alors dédaigné.

Là je vois Maupertuis, l'honneur de la Nation Françoise, dont une autre a merité de joüir.[16] Il sort de la table d'un Prince, qui fait, dirai-je l'admiration, ou l'étonnement de l'Europe?[a] Où va-t-il? dans le Conseil de la Nature, où l'attend Newton.

Que dirois-je du Chymiste, du Geomètre, du Physicien, du Mécanicien, de l'Anatomiste &c? Celui-ci a presqu'autant de plaisir à examiner l'Homme mort, qu'on en a eu à lui donner la vie.

Mais tout cède au grand Art de guérir. Le Médecin est le seul Philosophe qui mérite de sa Patrie[b]; il paroit comme les frères d'Helène dans les tempêtes de la vie.[17] Quelle Magie, quel Enchantement! Sa seule vüe calme le sang, rend la paix à une ame agitée & fait renaître la douce esperance au coeur des malheureux mortels. Il annonce la vie & la mort, comme un Astronome prédit une Eclipse. Chacun a son flambeau qui l'éclaire. Mais si l'Esprit a eu du plaisir à trouver les règles qui le guident, quel triomphe,

[a] X: || d'un ami qui est le plus grand des Rois.
[b] X: Patrie, on l'a dit avant moi;

vous en faites tous les jours l'heureuse expérience; quel triomphe, quand l'évènement en a justifié la hardiesse!

La première utilité des Sciences est donc de les cultiver; c'est déjà un bien réel & solide. Heureux qui a du goût pour l'étude! plus heureux qui réüssit à délivrer par elle son esprit de ses illusions, & son coeur de sa vanité; but désirable, où vous avez été conduit dans un âge encore tendre par les mains de la sagesse; tandis que tant de Pédans, après un demi-siècle de veilles & de travaux, plus courbés sous le faix des préjugés, que sous celui du tems, semblent avoir tout appris, excepté à penser. Science rare à la vérité, surtout dans les savans; & qui cependant devroit être du moins le fruit de toutes les autres. C'est à cette seule Science que je me suis appliqué dès l'enfance. Jugez Mr. si j'ai réüssi: & que cet Hommage de mon Amitié soit éternellement chéri de la vôtre.

L'HOMME MACHINE

Il ne suffit pas à un Sage d'étudier la Nature & la Vérité; il doit oser la dire en faveur du petit nombre de ceux qui veulent & peuvent penser; car pour les autres, qui sont volontairement Esclaves des Préjugés, il ne leur est pas plus possible d'atteindre la Vérité, qu'aux Grenouilles de voler.

Je réduis à deux, les Systêmes des Philosophes sur l'ame de l'Homme. Le premier, & le plus ancien, est le Systême du Matérialisme; le second est celui du Spiritualisme.

Les Métaphisiciens, qui ont insinué que la Matière pourroit bien avoir la faculté de penser, n'ont pas deshonoré leur Raison. Pourquoi? C'est qu'ils ont un avantage (car ici c'en est un,) de s'être mal exprimés. En effet, demander si la Matière peut penser, sans la considérer autrement qu'en elle-même, c'est demander si la Matière peut marquer les heures. On voit d'avance que nous éviterons cet écueil, où Mr. Locke a eu le malheur d'échouer.[18]

Les Leibnitiens, avec leurs *Monades*, ont élevé une hypothèse inintelligible. Ils ont plutôt spiritualisé la Matière, que matérialisé l'Ame. Comment peut-on définir un Etre, dont la nature nous est absolument inconnüe?

Descartes, & tous les Cartésiens, parmi lesquels il y a long-tems qu'on a compté les Mallebranchistes, ont fait la même faute. Ils ont admis deux substances distinctes dans l'Homme, comme s'ils les avoient vües & bien comptées.

Les plus sages ont dit que l'Ame ne pouvoit se connoître, que par les seules lumières de la Foi: cependant en qualité d'Etres raisonnables, ils ont cru pouvoir se réserver le droit d'examiner ce que l'Ecriture a voulu dire par le mot *Esprit*, dont elle se sert, en parlant de l'Ame humaine; & dans leurs recherches, s'ils ne sont pas d'accord sur ce point avec les Théologiens, ceux-ci le sont-ils davantage entr'eux sur tous les autres?

Voici en peu de mots le résultat de toutes leurs réfléxions.

S'il y a un Dieu, il est Auteur de la Nature, comme de la Révélation; il nous a donné l'une, pour expliquer l'autre; & la Raison, pour les accorder ensemble.

Se défier des connoissances qu'on peut puiser dans les Corps animés, c'est regarder la Nature & la Révélation, comme deux contraires qui se détruisent; & par conséquent, c'est oser soutenir cette absurdité: que Dieu se contredit dans ses divers ouvrages, & nous trompe.

S'il y a une Révélation, elle ne peut donc démentir la Nature. Par la Nature seule, on peut découvrir le sens des paroles de l'Evangile, dont l'expérience seule est la véritable Interprète. En effet, les autres Commentateurs jusqu'ici n'ont fait qu'embrouiller la Vérité. Nous allons en juger par l'Auteur du *Spectacle de la Nature*. "Il est étonnant, dit-il (au sujet de Mr. Locke,) qu'un Homme, qui dégrade notre Ame jusqu'à la croire une Ame de boüe, ose établir la Raison pour juge & souveraine Arbitre des Mystères de la Foi; car, ajoute-t-il, quelle idée étonnante auroit-on du Christianisme, si l'on vouloit suivre la Raison?"[19]

Outre que ces réfléxions n'éclaircissent rien par rapport à la Foi, elles forment de si frivoles objections contre la Méthode de ceux qui croient pouvoir interpreter les Livres Saints, que j'ai presque honte de perdre le tems à les réfuter.

1°. L'excellence de la Raison ne dépend pas d'un grand mot vuide de sens (*l'immaterialité*); mais de sa force, de son étendüe, ou de sa Clair-voyance. Ainsi une *Ame de boüe*, qui découvriroit, comme d'un coup d'oeil, les rapports & les suites d'une infinité d'idées, difficiles à saisir, seroit évidemment préférable à une Ame sote & stupide, qui seroit faite des Elémens les plus précieux. Ce n'est pas être Philosophe, que de rougir avec Pline, de la misère de notre origine.[20] Ce qui paroit vil, est ici la chose la plus précieuse, & pour laquelle la Nature semble avoir mis le plus d'art & le plus d'appareil. Mais comme l'Homme, quand même il viendroit d'une Source encore plus vile en apparence, n'en seroit pas moins le plus parfait de tous les Etres; quelle que soit l'origine de son Ame, si elle est pure, noble, sublime, c'est une belle Ame, qui rend respectable quiconque en est doué.[21]

La seconde manière de raisonner de Mr. Pluche, me paroit vicieuse, même dans son système, qui tient un peu du Fanatisme; car si nous avons une idée de la Foi, qui soit contraire aux Principes les plus clairs, aux Vérités les plus incontestables, il faut croire, pour l'honneur de la Révélation & de son Auteur, que cette idée est fausse; & que nous ne connoissons point encore le sens des paroles de l'Evangile.

De deux choses l'une; ou tout est illusion, tant la Nature même, que la Révélation; ou l'expérience seule peut rendre raison de la Foi. Mais quel plus grand ridicule que celui de notre Auteur? Je m'imagine entendre un Péripaticien, qui diroit: "Il ne faut pas croire l'expérience de Toricelli: car si nous la croyions, si nous allions bannir l'horreur du vuide, quelle étonnante Philosophie aurions-nous?"[22]

J'ai fait voir combien le raisonnement de Mr. Pluche est vicieux*, afin de prouver premièrement, que s'il y a une Révélation, elle n'est point suffisamment démontrée par la seule autorité de l'Eglise, & sans aucun examen de la Raison, comme le prétendent tous ceux qui la craignent. Secondement, pour mettre à l'abri de toute attaque la Méthode de ceux qui voudroient suivre la voie que je leur ouvre, d'interpreter les choses surnaturelles, incomprehensibles en soi, par les lumières que chacun a reçues de la Nature.

L'expérience & l'observation doivent donc seules nous guider ici. Elles se trouvent sans nombre dans les Fastes des Médecins, qui ont été Philosophes, & non dans les Philosophes, qui n'ont pas été Médecins. Ceux-ci ont parcouru, ont éclairé le Labyrinthe de l'Homme; ils nous ont seuls dévoilé ces ressorts cachés sous des envelopes, qui dérobent à nos yeux tant de merveilles. Eux seuls, contemplant tranquillement notre Ame, l'ont mille fois surprise, & dans sa misère, & dans sa grandeur, sans plus la mépriser dans l'un de ces états, que l'admirer dans l'autre. Encore une fois, voilà les seuls Physiciens qui aient droit de parler ici. Que nous diroient les autres, & sur-tout les Théologiens? N'est-il pas ridicule de les entendre décider sans pudeur, sur un sujet qu'ils n'ont point été à portée de connoître, dont ils ont été au contraire entièrement détournés par des Etudes obscures, qui les ont conduits à mille préjugés, & pour tout dire en un mot, au Fanatisme, qui ajoute encore à leur ignorance dans le Mécanisme des Corps?

Mais quoique nous aïons choisi les meilleurs Guides, nous trouverons encore beaucoup d'épines & d'obstacles dans cette carrière.

L'Homme est une Machine si composée, qu'il est impossible de s'en faire d'abord une idée claire, & conséquemment de la définir.

---

* *Il péche evidemment par une pétition de Principe.*

C'est pourquoi toutes les recherches que les plus grands Philosophes ont faites *à priori*, c'est à dire, en voulant se servir en quelque sorte des aîles de l'Esprit, ont été vaines. Ainsi ce n'est qu'*à posteriori*, ou en cherchant à demêler l'Ame, comme au travers des Organes du corps, qu'on peut, je ne dis pas, découvrir avec évidence la nature même de l'Homme, mais atteindre le plus grand degré de probabilité possible sur ce sujet.

Prenons donc le bâton de l'expérience,[23] & laissons là l'Histoire de toutes les vaines opinions des Philosophes. Etre Aveugle, & croire pouvoir se passer de ce bâton, c'est le comble de l'aveuglement. Qu'un Moderne a bien raison de dire qu'il n'y a que la vanité seule, qui ne tire pas des causes secondes, le même parti que des premières![24] On peut & on doit même admirer tous ces beaux Génies dans leurs travaux les plus inutiles; les Descartes, les Mallebranches, les Leibnitz, les Wolfs, &c. mais quel fruit, je vous prie, a-t-on retiré de leurs profondes Méditations & de tous leurs Ouvrages? Commençons donc, & voions, non ce qu'on a pensé, mais ce qu'il faut penser pour le repos de la vie.

Autant de tempéramens, autant d'esprits, de caractères & de moeurs différentes. Galien même a connu cette vérité, que Descartes[a] a poussée loin, jusqu'à dire que la Medecine seule pouvoit changer les Esprits & les moeurs avec le Corps.[25] Il est vrai que la Mélancolie, la Bile, le Phlegme, le Sang, &c. suivant la nature, l'abondance & la diverse combinaison de ces humeurs, de chaque Homme font un Homme différent.

Dans les maladies, tantôt l'Ame s'éclipse & ne montre aucun signe d'elle-même; tantôt on diroit qu'elle est double, tant la fureur la transporte; tantôt l'imbécillité se dissipe: & la convalescence, d'un Sot fait un Homme d'esprit. Tantôt le plus beau Génie devenu stupide, ne se reconnoit plus. Adieu toutes ces belles connoissances acquises à si grands frais, & avec tant de peine!

Ici c'est un Paralitique, qui demande si sa jambe est dans son lit: Là c'est un Soldat qui croit avoir le bras qu'on lui a coupé. La mémoire de ses anciennes sensations, & du lieu, où son Ame les rapportoit, fait son illusion, & son espece de délire. Il suffit de lui parler de cette partie qui lui manque, pour lui en rappeller & faire

---

[a] X: Descartes, & non Hippocrate, comme le dit l'Auteur de l'histoire de l'Ame,

sentir tous les mouvemens; ce qui se fait avec je ne sai quel déplaisir d'imagination qu'on ne peut exprimer.

Celui-ci pleure, comme un Enfant, aux approches de la Mort, que celui-là badine. Que falloit-il à Canus Julius, à Séneque, à Pétrone, pour changer leur intrépidité, en pusillanimité, ou en poltronnerie?[26] Une obstruction dans la rate, dans le foie, un embarras dans la veine porte. Pourquoi? Parce que l'imagination se bouche avec les viscères; & de là naissent tous ces singuliers Phénomènes de l'affection hystérique & hypocondriaque.[27]

Que dirois-je de nouveau sur ceux qui s'imaginent être transformés en *Loups-garoux*, en *Coqs*, en *Vampires*, qui croient que les Morts les sucent? Pourquoi m'arrêterois-je à ceux qui croient[a] leur nez, ou autres membres de verre, & à qui il faut conseiller de coucher sur la paille, de peur qu'ils ne se cassent; afin qu'ils en retrouvent l'usage & la véritable chair, lorsque mettant le feu à la paille, on leur fait craindre d'être brûlés: frayeur qui a quelquefois guéri la Paralysie?[28] Je dois légèrement passer sur des choses connues de tout le Monde.

Je ne serai pas plus long sur le détail des effets du Sommeil. Voiez ce Soldat fatigué! Il ronfle dans la tranchée, au bruit de cent pièces de canon! Son Ame n'entend rien, son Sommeil est une parfaite Apoplexie. Une Bombe va l'écraser; il sentira peut-être moins ce coup qu'un Insecte qui se trouve sous le pié.

D'un autre côté, cet Homme que la Jalousie, la Haine, l'Avarice, ou l'Ambition dévore, ne peut trouver aucun repos. Le lieu le plus tranquille, les boissons les plus fraîches & les plus calmantes, tout est inutile à qui n'a pas délivré son coeur du tourment des Passions.

L'Ame & le Corps s'endorment ensemble. A mesure que le mouvement du sang se calme, un doux sentiment de paix & de tranquillité se répand dans toute la Machine; l'Ame se sent mollement s'appésantir avec les paupières & s'affaisser avec les fibres du cerveau: elle devient ainsi peu à peu comme paralitique, avec tous les muscles du corps. Ceux-ci ne peuvent plus porter le poids de la tête; celle-là ne peut plus soutenir le fardeau de la pensée; elle est dans le Sommeil, comme n'étant point.

La circulation se fait-elle avec trop de vitesse? l'Ame ne peut dormir. L'Ame est-elle trop agitée? le Sang ne peut se calmer;

[a] X: voient

il galope dans les veines avec un bruit qu'on entend: telles sont les deux causes réciproques de l'insomnie. Une seule fraieur dans les Songes fait battre le coeur à coups redoublés, & nous arrache à la nécessité, ou à la douceur du repos, comme feroient une vive douleur, ou des besoins urgens. Enfin, comme la seule cessation des fonctions de l'Ame procure le Sommeil, il est, même pendant la veille (qui n'est alors qu'une demie veille) des sortes de petits Sommeils d'Ame très fréquens, des *Rêves à la Suisse,* qui prouvent que l'Ame n'attend pas toujours le corps pour dormir; car si elle ne dort pas tout-à-fait, combien peu s'en faut-il! puisqu'il lui est impossible d'assigner un seul objet auquel elle ait prêté quelque attention, parmi cette foule inombrable d'idées confuses, qui comme autant de nuages, remplissent, pour ainsi dire, l'Atmosphère de notre cerveau.

L'Opium a trop de rapport avec le Sommeil qu'il procure, pour ne pas le placer ici. Ce remede enivre, ainsi que le vin, le caffé &c. chacun à sa manière, & suivant sa dose. Il rend l'Homme heureux dans un état qui sembleroit devoir être le tombeau du sentiment, comme il est l'image de la Mort. Quelle douce Léthargie! L'Ame n'en voudroit jamais sortir. Elle étoit en proie aux plus grandes douleurs; elle ne sent plus que le seul plaisir de ne plus souffrir, & de joüir de la plus charmante tranquillité. L'Opium change jusqu'à la volonté; il force l'Ame qui vouloit veiller & se divertir, d'aller se mettre au Lit malgré elle. Je passe sous silence l'Histoire des Poisons.

C'est en fouëttant l'imagination, que le Caffé, cet Antidote du Vin, dissipe nos maux de tête & nos chagrins, sans nous en ménager, comme cette Liqueur, pour le lendemain.

Contemplons l'Ame dans ses autres besoins.

Le corps humain est une Machine qui monte elle-même ses ressorts; vivante image du mouvement perpétuel. Les alimens entretiennent ce que la fièvre excite. Sans eux l'Ame languit, entre en fureur, & meurt abattüe. C'est une bougie dont la lumière se ranime, au moment de s'éteindre. Mais nourrissez le corps, versez dans ses tuiaux des Sucs vigoureux, des liqueurs fortes; alors l'Ame, généreuse comme elles, s'arme d'un fier courage, & le Soldat que l'eau eût fait fuir, devenu féroce, court gaiement à la mort au bruit des tambours. C'est ainsi que l'eau chaude agite un sang, que l'eau froide eût calmé.

Quelle puissance d'un Repas! La joie renaît dans un coeur triste; elle passe dans l'Ame des Convives qui l'expriment par d'aimables chansons, où le François excelle. Le Mélancolique seul est accablé, & l'Homme d'étude n'y est plus propre.

La viande crue rend les animaux féroces; les hommes le deviendroient par la même nourriture.[a] Cette férocité produit dans l'Ame l'orgueil, la haine, le mépris des autres Nations, l'indocilité & autres sentimens, qui dépravent le caractère, comme des alimens grossiers font un esprit lourd, épais, dont la paresse & l'indolence sont les attributs favoris.

Mr. Pope a bien connu tout l'empire de la gourmandise, lorsqu'il dit: "Le grave Catius parle toujours de vertu, & croit que, qui souffre les Vicieux, est vicieux lui-même. Ces beaux sentimens durent jusqu'à l'heure du diner; alors il préfère un scélerat, qui a une table délicate, à un Saint frugal."

"Considerez, dit-il ailleurs, le même Homme en santé, ou en maladie; possedant une belle charge, ou l'aiant perdue; vous le verrez chérir la vie, ou la détester, Fou à la chasse, Ivrogne dans une Assemblée de Province, Poli au bal, bon Ami en Ville, sans foi à la Cour."[30]

On a vû[b] en Suisse un Baillif, nommé Mr. Steiguer de Wittighofen; il étoit à jeun le plus intègre, & même le plus indulgent des juges; mais malheur au miserable qui se trouvoit sur la Sellette, lorsqu'il avoit fait un grand dîner! Il étoit homme à faire pendre l'innocent, comme le coupable.[32]

Nous pensons, & même nous ne sommes honnêtes Gens, que comme nous sommes gais, ou braves; tout dépend de la manière dont notre Machine est montée. On diroit en certains momens que l'Ame habite dans l'estomac, & que Van Helmont en mettant son siége dans le pylore,[33] ne se seroit trompé, qu'en prenant la partie pour le tout.

[a] X: nourriture; cela est si vrai, que la nation Angloise, qui ne mange pas la chair si cuite que nous, mais rouge & sanglante, paroit participer de cette férocité plus ou moins grande, qui vient en partie de tels Alimens, & d'autres causes, que l'Education peut seule rendre impuissantes.[29]

[b] X: Nous avons eu[31]

A quels excès la faim cruelle peut nous porter! Plus de respect pour les entrailles auxquelles on doit, ou on a donné la vie; on les déchire à belles dents, on s'en fait d'horribles festins; & dans la fureur, dont on est transporté, le plus foible est toujours la proie du plus fort.

La grossesse, cette Emule desirée des pâles couleurs, ne se contente pas d'amener le plus souvent à sa suite les goûts dépravés qui accompagnent ces deux états: elle a quelquefois fait éxécuter à l'Ame les plus affreux complots; effets d'une manie subite, qui étouffe jusqu'à la Loi naturelle. C'est ainsi que le cerveau, cette Matrice de l'esprit, se pervertit à sa manière, avec celle du corps.

Quelle autre fureur d'Homme, ou de Femme, dans ceux que la continence & la santé poursuivent! C'est peu pour cette Fille timide & modeste d'avoir perdu toute honte & toute pudeur; elle ne regarde plus l'Inceste, que comme une femme galante regarde l'Adultère. Si ses besoins ne trouvent pas de promts soulagemens, ils ne se borneront point aux simples accidens d'une passion Utérine, à la Manie, &c. cette malheureuse mourra d'un mal, dont il y a tant de Médecins.

Il ne faut que des yeux pour voir l'Influence nécessaire de l'âge sur la Raison. L'Ame suit les progrès du corps, comme ceux de l'Education. Dans le beau sexe, l'Ame suit encore la délicatesse du tempérament: de là cette tendresse, cette affection, ces sentimens vifs, plutôt fondés sur la passion, que sur la raison; ces préjugés, ces superstitions, dont la forte empreinte peut à peine s'effacer &c. L'Homme, au contraire, dont le cerveau & les nerfs participent de la fermeté de tous les solides, a l'esprit, ainsi que les traits du visage, plus nerveux: l'Education, dont manquent les femmes, ajoute encore de nouveaux degrés de force à son ame. Avec de tels secours de la Nature & de l'art, comment ne seroit-il pas plus reconnoissant, plus généreux, plus constant en amitié, plus ferme dans l'adversité? &c. Mais, suivant à peu près la pensée de l'Auteur des Lettres sur les Physionomies; Qui joint les graces de l'Esprit & du Corps à presque tous les sentimens du coeur les plus tendres & les plus délicats, ne doit point nous envier une double force, qui ne semble avoir été donnée à l'Homme; l'une, que pour se mieux pénétrer des attraits de la beauté; l'autre, que pour mieux servir à ses plaisirs.[34]

Il n'est pas plus nécessaire d'être aussi grand Physionomiste, que cet Auteur, pour deviner la qualité de l'esprit, par la figure, ou la forme des traits, lorsqu'ils sont marqués jusqu'à un certain point; qu'il ne l'est d'être grand Medecin, pour connoitre un mal accompagné de tous ses symptomes évidens. Examinez les Portraits de Locke, de Steele, de Boerhaave, de Maupertuis, &c. vous ne serez point surpris de leur trouver des Physionomies fortes, des yeux d'Aigle.[35] Parcourez-en une infinité d'autres, vous distinguerez toujours le beau du grand Génie, & même souvent l'honnête Homme du Fripon.[a]

L'Histoire nous offre un mémorable exemple de la puissance de l'air. Le fameux Duc de Guise étoit si fort convaincu que Henri III. qui l'avoit eu tant de fois en son pouvoir, n'oseroit jamais l'assassiner, qu'il partit pour Blois. Le Chancelier Chiverni apprenant son départ, s'écria: *voila un Homme perdu.* Lorsque sa fatale prédiction fut justifiée par l'évènement,[37] on lui en demanda la raison. *Il y a vingt ans,* dit-il, *que je connois le Roi; il est naturellement bon & même foible; mais j'ai observé qu'un rien l'impatiente & le met en fureur, lorsqu'il fait froid.*

Tel Peuple a l'esprit lourd & stupide; tel autre l'a vif, léger, pénétrant. D'où cela vient-il, si ce n'est en partie, & de la nourriture qu'il prend, & de la semence de ses Pères,[*] & de ce Cahos de divers élémens qui nagent dans l'immensité de l'air? L'esprit a comme le corps, ses maladies épidémiques & son scorbut.

Tel est l'empire du Climat, qu'un Homme qui en change, se ressent malgré lui de ce changement. C'est une Plante ambulante, qui s'est elle-même transplantée; si le Climat n'est plus le même, il est juste qu'elle dégénère, ou s'améliore.

On prend tout encore de ceux avec qui l'on vit, leurs gestes, leurs accens &c. comme la paupière se baisse à la menace du coup dont on est prévenu, ou par la même raison que le corps du Spectateur imite machinalement, & malgré lui, tous les mouvemens d'un bon Pantomime.

Ce que je viens de dire prouve que la meilleure Compagnie pour

---

[a] X: On a remarqué, par exemple, qu'un Poëte célebre réunit (dans son Portrait) l'air d'un Filou, avec le feu de Prométhée.[36]

[*] L'Histoire des Animaux & des Hommes prouve l'Empire de la semence des Pères sur l'Esprit & le corps des Enfans.[38]

un Homme d'esprit, est la sienne, s'il n'en trouve une semblable. L'Esprit se rouïlle avec ceux qui n'en ont point, faute d'être exercé: à la paume, on renvoie mal la bale, à qui la sert mal. J'aimerois mieux un Homme intelligent, qui n'auroit eu aucune éducation, que s'il en eût eu une mauvaise, pourvû qu'il fût encore assez jeune. Un Esprit mal conduit, est un Acteur que la Province a gâté.

Les divers Etats de l'Ame sont donc toujours corrélatifs à ceux du corps. Mais pour mieux démontrer toute cette dépendance, & ses causes, servons-nous ici de l'Anatomie comparée; Ouvrons les entrailles de l'Homme & des Animaux. Le moien de connoître la Nature humaine, si l'on n'est éclairé par une juste parallèle de la Structure des uns & des autres!

En général la forme & la composition du cerveau des Quadrupèdes est à peu près la même, que dans l'Homme. Même figure, même disposition partout; avec cette difference essentielle, que l'Homme est de tous les Animaux, celui qui a le plus de cerveau, & le cerveau le plus tortueux, en raison de la masse de son corps: Ensuite le Singe, le Castor, l'Eléphant, le Chien, le Renard, le Chat &c. voila les Animaux qui ressemblent le plus à l'Homme; car on remarque aussi chez eux la même Analogie graduée, par rapport au corps calleux, dans lequel Lancisi avoit établi le siége de l'Ame,[39] avant feu M. de la Peyronie, qui cependant a illustré cette opinion par une foule d'expériences.[40]

Après tous les Quadrupèdes, ce sont les Oiseaux qui ont le plus de cerveau. Les Poissons ont la tête grosse; mais elle est vuide de sens, comme celle de bien des Hommes. Ils n'ont point de corps calleux, & fort peu de cerveau, lequel manquent aux Insectes.

Je ne me répandrai point en un plus long détail des variétés de la Nature, ni en conjectures, car les unes & les autres sont infinies; comme on en peut[a] juger, en lisant les seuls Traités de Willis *De Cerebro & de Anima Brutorum*.[41]

Je concluerai seulement ce qui s'ensuit clairement de ces incontestables Observations, 1°. que plus les Animaux sont farouches, moins ils ont de cerveau; 2°. que ce viscère semble s'agrandir en quelque sorte, à proportion de leur docilité; 3°. qu'il y a ici une singulière condition imposée éternellement par la Nature, qui est

[a] Y: peut en

que, plus on gagnera du côté de l'Esprit, plus on perdra du côté de l'instinct. Lequel l'emporte de la perte, ou du gain?

Ne croyez pas au reste que je veuille prétendre par là que le seul volume du cerveau suffise pour faire juger du degré de docilité des Animaux; il faut que la qualité réponde encore à la quantité, & que les solides & les fluides soient dans cet équilibre convenable qui fait la santé.

Si l'imbécile ne manque pas de cerveau, comme on le remarque ordinairement, ce viscère péchera par une mauvaise consistance, par trop de molesse, par exemple. Il en est de même des Fous; les vices de leur cerveau ne se dérobent pas toujours à nos recherches; mais si les causes de l'imbécillité, de la folie &c. ne sont pas sensibles, où aller chercher celles de la variété de tous les Esprits? Elles échaperoient aux yeux des Linx & des Argus. *Un rien, une petite fibre, quelque chose que la plus subtile Anatomie ne peut découvrir*, eût fait deux Sots, d'Erasme, & de Fontenelle, qui le remarque lui-même dans un de ses meilleurs *Dialogues*.[42]

Outre la molesse de la moëlle du cerveau, dans les Enfans, dans les petits Chiens & dans les Oiseaux, Willis a remarqué que les *Corps canelés* sont effacés, & comme décolorés, dans tous ces Animaux; & que leurs *Stries* sont aussi imparfaitement formés que dans les Paralytiques.[43] Il ajoute, ce qui est vrai, que l'Homme a la protubérance annulaire fort grosse; & ensuite toujours diminutivement par degrés, le Singe & les autres Animaux nommés ci-devant, tandis que le Veau, le Boeuf, le Loup, la Brebis, le Cochon, &c. qui ont cette partie d'un très petit volume, ont les *Nates* & *Testes* fort gros.[44]

On a beau être discret & réservé sur les conséquences qu'on peut tirer de ces Observations, & de tant d'autres, sur l'espèce d'inconstance des vaisseaux & des nerfs &c: tant de variétés ne peuvent être des jeux gratuits de la Nature. Elles prouvent du moins la nécessité d'une bonne & abondante organisation, puisque dans tout le Régne Animal l'Ame se raffermissant avec le corps, acquiert de la Sagacité, à mesure qu'il prend des forces.

Arrêtons-nous à contempler la différente docilité des Animaux. Sans doute l'Analogie la mieux entendüe conduit l'Esprit à croire que les causes dont nous avons fait mention, produisent toute la diversité qui se trouve entr'eux & nous, quoiqu'il faille avoüer que notre foible entendement, borné aux observations les plus grossières, ne puisse voir les liens qui régnent entre la cause & les effets. C'est une espèce d'*harmonie* que les Philosophes ne connoîtront jamais.

Parmi les Animaux, les uns apprennent à parler & à chanter; ils retiennent des airs, & prennent tous les tons, aussi exactement qu'un Musicien. Les autres, qui montrent cependant plus d'esprit, tels que le Singe, n'en peuvent venir à bout. Pourquoi cela, si ce n'est par un vice des organes de la parole?

Mais ce vice est-il tellement de conformation, qu'on n'y puisse apporter aucun remède? En un mot seroit-il absolument impossible d'apprendre une Langue à cet Animal? Je ne le croi pas.

Je prendrois le grand Singe préférablement à tout autre, jusqu'à ce que le hazard nous eût fait découvrir quelqu'autre espèce plus semblable à la nôtre, car rien ne répugne qu'il y en ait dans des[a] Régions qui nous sont inconnües. Cet Animal nous ressemble si fort, que les Naturalistes l'ont apellé *Homme Sauvage,* ou *Homme des bois*.[45] Je le prendrois aux mêmes conditions des Ecoliers d'Amman;[46] c'est-à-dire, que je voudrois qu'il ne fût ni trop jeune, ni trop vieux; car ceux qu'on nous apporte en Europe, sont communément trop âgés. Je choisirois celui qui auroit la physionomie la plus spirituelle, & qui tiendroit le mieux dans mille petites opérations, ce qu'elle m'auroit promis. Enfin, ne me trouvant pas digne d'être son Gouverneur, je le mettrois à l'Ecole de l'excellent Maître que je viens de nommer, ou d'un autre aussi habile, s'il en est.

Vous savez par le Livre d'Amman, & par tous ceux[*] qui ont traduit sa Méthode,[47] tous les prodiges qu'il a sû opérer sur les sourds de naissance, dans les yeux desquels il a, comme il le fait entendre lui-même, trouvé des oreilles; & en combien peu de tems enfin il leur a appris à entendre, parler, lire, & écrire. Je veux que les yeux d'un sourd voient plus clair & soient plus intelligens que s'il ne l'étoit pas, par la raison que la perte d'un membre, ou d'un sens, peut augmenter la force, ou la pénétration d'un autre: mais le Singe voit & entend; il comprend ce qu'il entend & ce qu'il voit. Il conçoit si parfaitement les Signes qu'on lui fait, qu'à tout autre

[a] Y: les
[*] *L'Auteur de l'Histoire naturelle de l'Ame &c.*

jeu, ou tout autre exercice, je ne doute point qu'il ne l'emportât sur les disciples d'Amman. Pourquoi donc l'éducation des Singes seroit-elle impossible? Pourquoi ne pourroit-il enfin, à force de soins, imiter, à l'exemple des sourds, les mouvemens nécessaires pour prononcer? Je n'ose décider si les organes de la parole du Singe ne peuvent, quoi qu'on fasse, rien articuler; mais cette impossibilité absolüe me surprendroit, à cause de la grande Analogie du Singe & de l'Homme, & qu'il n'est point d'Animal connu jusqu'à présent, dont le dedans & le dehors lui ressemblent d'une manière si frappante.[48] Mr. Locke, qui certainement n'a jamais été suspect de crédulité, n'a pas fait difficulté de croire l'Histoire que le Chevalier Temple fait dans ses Mémoires, d'un Perroquet, qui répondoit à propos & avoit appris, comme nous, à avoir une espèce de conversation suivie.[49] Je sai qu'on s'est moqué* de ce grand Métaphisicien;[50] mais qui auroit annoncé à l'Univers qu'il y a des générations qui se font sans oeufs & sans Femmes, auroit-il trouvé beaucoup de Partisans? Cependant Mr. Trembley en a découvert, qui se font sans accouplement, & par la seule section.[51] Amman n'eût-il pas aussi passé pour un Fou, s'il se fût vanté, avant que d'en faire l'heureuse expérience, d'instruire, & en aussi peu de tems, des Ecoliers, tels que les siens? Cependant ses succès ont étonné l'Univers, & comme l'Auteur de l'Histoire des Polypes, il a passé de plein vol à l'immortalité. Qui doit à son génie les miracles qu'il opère, l'emporte à mon gré, sur qui doit les siens au hazard. Qui a trouvé l'art d'embellir le plus beau des Règnes, & de lui donner des perfections qu'il n'avoit pas, doit être mis au-dessus d'un Faiseur oisif de systèmes frivoles, ou d'un Auteur laborieux de stériles découvertes. Celles d'Amman sont bien d'un autre prix; il a tiré les Hommes, de l'Instinct auquel ils sembloient condamnés; il leur a donné des idées, de l'Esprit, une Ame en un mot, qu'ils n'eussent jamais eüe. Quel plus grand pouvoir!

Ne bornons point les ressources de la Nature; elles sont infinies, surtout aidées d'un grand Art.

La même Mécanique, qui ouvre le Canal d'Eustachi dans les Sourds, ne pourroit-elle le déboucher dans les Singes? Une heureuse envie d'imiter la prononciation du Maître, ne pourroit-elle mettre en liberté les organes de la parole, dans des Animaux, qui

---

* *L'Auteur de l'Hist. d'Ame.*

imitent tant d'autres Signes, avec tant d'adresse & d'intelligence? Non seulement je défie qu'on me cite aucune expérience vraiment concluante, qui décide mon projet impossible & ridicule; mais la similitude de la structure & des opérations du Singe est telle, que je ne doute presque point, si on exerçoit parfaitement cet Animal, qu'on ne vînt enfin à bout de lui apprendre à prononcer, & par conséquent à savoir une langue. Alors ce ne seroit plus ni un Homme Sauvage, ni un Homme manqué: ce seroit un Homme parfait, un petit Homme de Ville, avec autant d'étoffe ou de muscles que nous-mêmes, pour penser & profiter de son éducation.

Des Animaux à l'Homme, la transition n'est pas violente; les vrais Philosophes en conviendront. Qu'étoit l'Homme, avant l'invention des Mots & la connoissance des Langues? Un Animal de son espèce, qui avec beaucoup moins d'instinct naturel, que les autres, dont alors il ne se croioit pas Roi, n'étoit distingué du Singe & des autres Animaux, que comme le Singe l'est lui-même; je veux dire, par une physionomie qui annonçoit plus de discernement.[52] Réduit à la seule *connoissance intuitive* des Leibnitiens,[53] il ne voioit que des Figures & des Couleurs, sans pouvoir rien distinguer entr'elles; vieux, comme jeune, Enfant à tout âge, il bégaioit ses sensations & ses besoins, comme un chien affamé, ou ennuié du repos,[a] demande à manger, ou à se promener.

Les Mots, les Langues, les Loix, les Sciences, les Beaux Arts sont venus; & par eux enfin le Diamant brut de notre esprit a été poli. On a dressé un Homme, comme un Animal; on est devenu Auteur, comme Porte-faix. Un Geomètre a appris à faire les Démonstrations & les Calculs les plus difficiles, comme un Singe à ôter, ou mettre son petit chapeau, & à monter sur son chien docile. Tout s'est fait par des Signes; chaque espèce a compris ce qu'elle a pu comprendre; & c'est de cette manière que les Hommes ont acquis la *connoissance symbolique,* ainsi nommée encore par nos Philosophes d'Allemagne.

Rien de si simple, comme on voit, que la Mécanique de notre Education! Tout se réduit à des sons, ou à des mots, qui de la bouche de l'un, passent par l'oreille de l'autre, dans le cerveau, qui reçoit en même tems par les yeux la figure des corps, dont ces mots sont les Signes arbitraires.

[a] Y: de son repos,

L'HOMME MACHINE

Mais qui a parlé le premier? Qui a été le premier Précepteur du Genre humain? Qui a inventé les moiens de mettre à profit la docilité de notre organisation? Je n'en sai rien; le nom de ces heureux & premiers Génies a été perdu dans la nuit des tems. Mais l'Art est le fils de la Nature; elle a dû long-tems le précéder.

On doit croire que les Hommes les mieux organisés, ceux pour qui la Nature aura épuisé ses bienfaits, auront instruit les autres. Ils n'auront pû entendre un bruit nouveau, par exemple, éprouver de nouvelles sensations, être frappés de tous ces beaux objets divers qui forment le ravissant Spectacle de la Nature, sans se trouver dans le cas de ce Sourd de Chartres, dont Fontenelle[a] nous a le premier donné l'Histoire, lorsqu'il entendit pour la première fois à quarante ans le bruit étonnant des cloches.[54]

De là seroit-il absurde de croire que ces premiers Mortels essaièrent, à la manière de ce Sourd, ou à celle des Animaux & des Müets, (autre Espece d'Animaux) d'exprimer leurs nouveaux sentimens, par des mouvemens dépendans de l'Economie de leur imagination, & conséquemment ensuite par des sons spontanés propres à chaque Animal; expression naturelle de leur surprise, de leur joie, de leurs transports, ou de leurs besoins? Car sans doute ceux que la Nature a doüés d'un sentiment plus exquis, ont eu aussi plus de facilité pour l'exprimer.[55]

Voilà comme je conçois que les Hommes ont emploié leur sentiment, ou leur instinct, pour avoir de l'esprit, & enfin leur esprit, pour avoir des connoissances. Voilà par quels moiens, autant que je peux[b] les saisir, on s'est rempli le cerveau des idées, pour la reception desquelles la Nature l'avoit formé. On s'est aidé l'un par l'autre; & les plus petits commencemens s'agrandissant peu à peu, toutes les choses de l'Univers ont été aussi facilement distinguées, qu'un Cercle.

Comme une corde de Violon, ou une touche de Clavecin, frémit & rend un son, les cordes du cerveau frappées par les raions sonores, ont été excitées à rendre, ou à redire les mots qui les touchoient. Mais comme telle est la construction de ce viscère, que dès qu'une fois les yeux bien formés pour l'Optique, ont reçu la peinture des objets, le cerveau ne peut pas ne pas voir leurs images & leurs dif-

[a] X: le Grand Fontenelle
[b] W: puis

férences; de même, lorsque les Signes de ces différences ont été marqués, ou gravés dans le cerveau, l'Ame en a nécessairement examiné les rapports; examen qui lui étoit impossible, sans la découverte des Signes, ou l'invention des Langues. Dans ces[a] tems, où l'Univers étoit presque müet, l'Ame étoit à l'égard de tous les objets, comme un Homme, qui, sans avoir aucune idée des proportions, regarderoit un tableau, ou une pièce de Sculpture; il n'y pourroit rien distinguer; ou comme un petit Enfant (car alors l'Ame étoit dans son Enfance) qui tenant dans sa main un certain nombre de petits brins de paille, ou de bois, les voit en général d'une vüe vague & superficielle, sans pouvoir les compter, ni les distinguer. Mais qu'on mette une espèce de Pavillon, ou d'Etendart à cette pièce de bois, par exemple, qu'on appelle Mât: qu'on en mette un autre à un autre pareil corps; que le premier venu se nombre par le Signe 1. & le second par le Signe, ou chiffre 2; alors cet Enfant pourra les compter, & ainsi de suite il apprendra toute l'Arithmetique. Dès qu'une Figure lui paroîtra égale à une autre par son Signe *numératif*, il conclura sans peine que ce sont deux Corps différens; que 1. & 1. font deux, que 2. & 2. font 4.* &c.

C'est cette similitude réelle, ou apparente des Figures, qui est la Base fondamentale de toutes les vérités & de toutes nos connoissances, parmi lesquelles il est évident que celles dont les Signes sont moins simples & moins sensibles, sont plus difficiles à apprendre que les autres; en ce qu'elles demandent plus de Génie pour embrasser & combiner cette immense quantité de mots, par lesquels les Sciences dont je parle expriment les vérités de leur ressort: tandis que les Sciences, qui s'annoncent par des chiffres, ou autres petits Signes, s'apprennent facilement; & c'est sans doute cette facilité qui a fait la fortune des Calculs Algébriques, plus encore que leur évidence.

Tout ce savoir dont le vent enfle le Balon du cerveau de nos Pédans orgueilleux, n'est donc qu'un vaste amas de Mots & de Figures, qui forment dans la tête toutes les traces, par lesquelles nous distinguons & nous nous rapellons les objets. Toutes nos idées se réveillent, comme un Jardinier qui connoît les Plantes,

[a] Y: ce
* Il y a encore aujourd'hui des Peuples, qui faute d'un plus grand nombre de Signes, ne peuvent compter que jusqu'à 20.

se souvient de toutes leurs phrases à leur aspect. Ces Mots & ces Figures qui sont désignées par eux, sont tellement liés ensemble dans le cerveau, qu'il est assez rare qu'on imagine une chose, sans le nom, ou le Signe qui lui est attaché.

Je me sers toujours du mot *imaginer*, parce que je crois que tout s'imagine, & que toutes les parties de l'Ame peuvent être justement réduites à la seule imagination, qui les forme toutes; & qu' ainsi le jugement, le raisonnement, la mémoire ne sont que des parties de l'Ame nullement absolües, mais de véritables modifications de cette espèce de *toile médullaire*, sur laquelle les objets peints dans l'oeil, sont renvoiés, comme d'une Lanterne magique.

Mais si tel est ce merveilleux & incompréhensible résultat de l'Organisation du Cerveau; si tout se conçoit par l'imagination, si tout s'explique par elle; pourquoi diviser le Principe sensitif qui pense dans l'Homme? N'est-ce pas une contradiction manifeste dans les Partisans de la simplicité de l'esprit? Car une chose qu'on divise, ne peut plus être sans absurdité, regardée comme indivisible. Voilà où conduit l'abus des Langues, & l'usage de ces grands Mots, *spiritualité, immatérialité* &c. placés à tout hasard, sans être entendus, même par des gens d'Esprit.

Rien de plus facile que de prouver un Système, fondé comme celui-ci, sur le sentiment intime & l'expérience propre de chaque individu. L'imagination, ou cette partie fantastique du cerveau, dont la nature nous est aussi inconnue, que sa manière d'agir, est-elle naturellement petite, ou foible? Elle aura à peine la force de comparer l'Analogie, ou la ressemblance de ses idées; elle ne pourra voir que ce qui sera vis-à-vis d'elle, ou ce qui l'affectera le plus vivement; & encore de quelle manière! Mais toujours est-il vrai que l'imagination seule aperçoit; que c'est elle qui se représente tous les objets, avec les mots & les figures qui les caractérisent; & qu'ainsi c'est elle encore une fois qui est l'Ame, puisqu'elle en fait tous les Rôles. Par elle, par son pinceau flateur, le froid squélette de la Raison prend des chairs vives & vermeilles; par elle les Sciences fleurissent, les Arts s'embellissent, les Bois parlent, les Echos soupirent, les Rochers pleurent, le Marbre respire, tout prend vie parmi les corps inanimés. C'est elle encore qui ajoute à la tendresse d'un coeur amoureux, le piquant attrait de la volupté. Elle la fait germer dans le Cabinet du Philosophe, & du Pédant poudreux; elle forme enfin les Savans, comme les Orateurs & les Poëtes. Sotement décriée par les uns, vainement distinguée par les autres, qui tous l'ont mal connüe, elle ne marche pas seulement à la suite des Graces & des beaux Arts, elle ne peint pas seulement la Nature, elle peut aussi la mesurer. Elle raisonne, juge, pénètre, compare, approfondit. Pourroit-elle si bien sentir les beautés des tableaux qui lui sont tracés, sans en découvrir les rapports? Non; comme elle ne peut se replier sur les plaisirs des sens, sans en goûter toute la perfection, ou la volupté, elle ne peut réfléchir sur ce qu'elle a mécaniquement conçû, sans être alors le jugement même.

Plus on exerce l'imagination, ou le plus maigre Génie, plus il prend, pour ainsi dire, d'embonpoint; plus il s'agrandit, devient nerveux, robuste, vaste & capable de penser. La meilleure Organisation a besoin de cet exercice.

L'Organisation est le premier mérite de l'Homme; c'est en vain que tous les Auteurs de Morale ne mettent point au rang des qualités estimables, celles qu'on tient de la Nature, mais seulement les talens qui s'acquièrent à force de réflexions & d'industrie: car d'où nous vient, je vous prie, l'habileté, la Science & la vertu, si ce n'est d'une disposition qui nous rend propres à devenir habiles, savans & vertueux? Et d'où nous vient encore cette disposition, si ce n'est de la Nature? Nous n'avons de qualités estimables que par elle; nous lui devons tout ce que nous sommes. Pourquoi donc n'estimerois-je pas autant ceux qui ont des qualités naturelles, que ceux qui brillent par des vertus acquises, & comme d'emprunt? Quel que soit le mérite, de quelque endroit qu'il naisse, il est digne d'estime; il ne s'agit que de savoir la mesurer. L'Esprit, la Beauté, les Richesses, la Noblesse, quoiqu'Enfans du Hazard, ont tous leur prix, comme l'Adresse, le Savoir, la Vertu &c. Ceux que la Nature a comblés de ses dons les plus précieux, doivent plaindre ceux à qui ils ont été refusés; mais ils peuvent sentir leur supériorité sans orgueil, & en connoisseurs. Une belle Femme seroit aussi ridicule de se trouver laide, qu'un Homme d'Esprit, de se croire un Sot. Une modestie outrée (défaut rare à la vérité) est une sorte d'ingratitude envers la Nature. Une honnête fierté au contraire est la marque d'une Ame belle & grande, que décelent des traits mâles, moulés comme par le sentiment.

Si l'organisation est un mérite, & le premier mérite, & la source de tous les autres, l'instruction est le second. Le cerveau le mieux construit, sans elle, le seroit en pure perte; comme sans l'usage du monde, l'Homme le mieux fait ne seroit qu'un paysan grossier. Mais aussi quel seroit le fruit de la plus excellente Ecole, sans une Matrice parfaitement ouverte à l'entrée, ou à la conception des idées ? Il est aussi impossible de donner une seule idée à un Homme, privé de tous les sens, que de faire un Enfant à une Femme, à laquelle la Nature auroit poussé la distraction jusqu'à oublier de faire une Vulve, comme je l'ai vû dans une, qui n'avoit ni Fente, ni Vagin, ni Matrice, & qui pour cette raison fut démariée après dix ans de mariage.[56]

Mais si le cerveau est à la fois bien organisé & bien instruit, c'est une terre féconde parfaitement ensemencée, qui produit le centuple de ce qu'elle a reçu: ou, (pour quitter le stile figuré, souvent nécessaire pour mieux exprimer ce qu'on sent & donner des graces à la Vérité même,) l'imagination élevée par l'art, à la belle & rare dignité de Génie, saisit exactement tous les rapports des idées qu'elle a conçües, embrasse avec facilité une foule étonnante d'objets, pour en tirer enfin une longue chaîne de conséquences, lesquelles ne sont encore que de nouveaux rapports, enfantés par la comparaison des premiers, auxquels l'Ame trouve une parfaite ressemblance. Telle est, selon moi, la génération de l'Esprit. Je dis *trouve*, comme j'ai donné ci-devant l'Epithète d'*Apparente*,[57] à la similitude des objets: Non que je pense que nos sens soient toujours trompeurs, comme l'a prétendu le Père Mallebranche,[58] ou que nos yeux naturellement un peu ivres ne voient pas les objets, tels qu'ils sont en eux-mêmes, quoique les Microscopes nous le prouvent tous les jours; mais pour n'avoir aucune dispute avec les Pyrrhoniens, parmi lesquels Bayle s'est distingué.

Je dis de la Vérité en général ce que Mr. de Fontenelle dit de certaines en particulier, qu'il faut la sacrifier aux agrémens de la Société.[59] Il est de la douceur de mon caractère, d'obvier à toute dispute, lorsqu'il ne s'agit pas d'aiguiser la conversation. Les Cartésiens viendroient ici vainement à la charge avec leurs *idées innées*; je ne me donnerois certainement pas le quart de la peine qu'a prise Mr. Locke pour attaquer de telles chimères. Quelle utilité en effet de faire un gros Livre, pour prouver une doctrine qui étoit érigée en axiome, il y a trois mille ans ?

Suivant les Principes que nous avons posés, & que nous croions vrais, celui qui a le plus d'imagination doit être regardé, comme aiant le plus d'esprit, ou de génie, car tous ces mots sont synonimes; & encore une fois c'est par un abus honteux qu'on croit dire des choses différentes, lorsqu'on ne dit que différens mots ou différens sons, auxquels on n'a attaché aucune idée, ou distinction réelle.

La plus belle, la plus grande, ou la plus forte imagination, est donc la plus propre aux Sciences, comme aux Arts. Je ne décide point s'il faut plus d'esprit pour exceller dans l'Art des Aristotes, ou des Descartes, que dans celui des Euripides, ou des Sophocles; & si la Nature s'est mise en plus grands frais, pour faire Newton, que pour former Corneille, (ce dont je doute fort;) mais il est certain que c'est la seule imagination diversement appliquée, qui a fait leur différent triomphe & leur gloire immortelle.

Si quelqu'un passe pour avoir peu de jugement, avec beaucoup d'imagination; cela veut dire que l'imagination trop abandonnée à elle-même, presque toujours comme occupée à se regarder dans le miroir de ses sensations, n'a pas assez contracté l'habitude de les examiner elles-mêmes avec attention; plus profondément pénétrée des traces, ou des images, que de leur vérité ou de leur ressemblance.

Il est vrai que telle est la vivacité des ressorts de l'imagination, que si l'attention, cette clé ou mère des Sciences, ne s'en mêle, il ne lui est guères permis que de parcourir & d'effleurer les objets.

Voiez cet Oiseau sur la branche, il semble toujours prêt à s'envoler; l'imagination est de même. Toujours emportée par le tourbillon[a] du sang & des Esprits; une onde fait une trace, effacée par celle qui suit; l'Ame court après, souvent en vain: Il faut qu'elle s'attende à regretter ce qu'elle n'a pas assez vîte saisi & fixé: & c'est ainsi que l'imagination, véritable Image du tems, se détruit & se renouvelle sans cesse.

Tel est le cahos & la succession continuelle & rapide de nos idées; elles se chassent, comme un flot pousse l'autre; de sorte que si l'imagination n'emploie, pour ainsi dire, une partie de ses muscles, pour être comme en équilibre sur les cordes du cerveau,

---

[a] Y: les tourbillons

L'HOMME MACHINE

pour se soutenir quelque tems sur un objet qui va fuir, & s'empêcher de tomber sur un autre, qu'il n'est pas encore tems de contempler; jamais elle ne sera digne du beau nom de jugement. Elle exprimera vivement ce qu'elle aura senti de même; elle formera les Orateurs, les Musiciens, les Peintres, les Poëtes, & jamais un seul Philosophe. Au contraire si dès l'enfance on acoutume l'imagination à se brider elle-même; à ne point se laisser emporter à sa propre impétuosité, qui ne fait que de brillans Entousiastes; à arrêter, contenir ses idées, à les retourner dans tous les sens, pour voir toutes les faces d'un objet: alors l'imagination prompte à juger, embrassera par le raisonnement, la plus grande Sphère d'objets, & sa vivacité, toujours de si bon augure dans les Enfans, & qu'il ne s'agit que de regler par l'étude & l'exercice, ne sera plus qu'une pénétration clairvoiante, sans laquelle on fait peu de progrès dans les Sciences.

Tels sont les simples fondemens sur lesquels a été bâti l'édifice de la Logique. La Nature les avoit jettés pour tout le Genre Humain; mais les uns en ont profité, les autres en ont abusé.

Malgré toutes ces prérogatives de l'Homme sur les Animaux, c'est lui faire honneur que de le ranger dans la même classe. Il est vrai que jusqu'à un certain age, il est plus animal qu'eux, parce qu'il apporte moins d'instinct en naissant.

Quel est l'Animal qui mourroit de faim au milieu d'une Rivière de Lait? L'Homme seul. Semblable à ce vieux Enfant dont un Moderne parle d'après Arnobe; il ne connoit ni les alimens qui lui sont propres, ni l'eau qui peut le noyer, ni le feu qui peut le réduire en poudre.[60] Faites briller pour la première fois la lumière d'une bougie aux yeux d'un Enfant, il y portera machinalement le doigt, comme pour savoir quel est le nouveau Phénomène qu'il aperçoit; c'est à ses dépens qu'il en connoîtra le danger, mais il n'y sera pas repris.

Mettez-le encore avec un Animal sur le bord d'un précipice: lui seul y tombera; il se noye, où l'autre se sauve[a] à la nage. A quatorze, ou quinze ans, il entrevoit à peine les grands plaisirs qui l'attendent dans la reproduction de son espèce; déjà adolescent, il ne sait pas trop comment s'y prendre dans un jeu, que la Nature apprend si vite aux Animaux: il se cache, comme s'il étoit honteux

[a] Y: sauvera

d'avoir du plaisir & d'être fait pour être heureux, tandis que les Animaux se font gloire d'être *Cyniques*. Sans éducation, ils sont sans préjugés. Mais voions encore ce Chien & cet Enfant qui ont tous deux perdu leur Maître dans un grand chemin: l'Enfant pleure, il ne sait à quel Saint se voüer; le Chien mieux servi par son odorat, que l'autre par sa raison, l'aura bien-tôt trouvé.

La Nature nous avoit donc faits pour être au-dessous des Animaux, ou du moins pour faire par là même mieux éclater les prodiges de l'Education, qui seule nous tire du niveau & nous élève enfin au-dessus d'eux. Mais accordera-t-on la même distinction aux Sourds, aux Aveugles nés, aux Imbéciles, aux Fous, aux Hommes Sauvages, ou qui ont été élevés dans les Bois avec les Bêtes;[61] à ceux dont l'affection hypocondriaque a perdu l'imagination, enfin à toutes ces Bêtes à figure humaine, qui ne montrent que l'instinct le plus grossier? Non, tous ces Hommes de corps, & non d'esprit, ne méritent pas une classe particulière.

Nous n'avons pas dessein de nous dissimuler les objections qu'on peut faire en faveur de la distinction primitive de l'Homme & des Animaux, contre notre sentiment. Il y a, dit-on, dans l'Homme une Loi naturelle, une connoissance du bien & du mal, qui n'a pas été gravée dans le coeur des Animaux.

Mais cette Objection, ou plutôt cette assertion est-elle fondée sur l'expérience, sans laquelle un Philosophe peut tout rejetter? En avons-nous quelqu'une qui nous convainque que l'Homme seul a été éclairé d'un raion refusé à tous les autres Animaux? S'il n'y en a point, nous ne pouvons pas plus connoître par elle ce qui se passe dans eux, & même dans les Hommes, que ne pas sentir ce qui affecte l'intérieur de notre Etre. Nous savons que nous pensons, & que nous avons des remords; un sentiment intime ne nous force que trop d'en convenir; mais pour juger des remords d'autrui, ce sentiment qui est dans nous est insuffisant: c'est pourquoi il en faut croire les autres Hommes sur leur parole, ou sur les signes sensibles & extérieurs que nous avons remarqués en nous-mêmes, lorsque nous éprouvions la même conscience & les mêmes tourmens.

Mais pour décider si les Animaux qui ne parlent point, ont reçu la Loi Naturelle, il faut s'en rapporter conséquemment à ces signes dont je viens de parler, supposé qu'ils existent. Les faits semblent le prouver. Le Chien qui a mordu son Maître qui l'agaçoit, a paru s'en repentir le moment suivant; on l'a vû triste, fâché, n'osant se montrer, & s'avouer coupable par un air rampant & humilié. L'Histoire nous offre un exemple célèbre d'un Lion qui ne voulut pas déchirer un Homme abandonné à sa fureur, parce qu'il le reconnut pour son Bienfaicteur. Qu'il seroit à souhaiter que l'Homme même montrât toujours la même reconnoissance pour les Bienfaits, & le même respect pour l'humanité! On n'auroit plus à craindre les Ingrats, ni ces Guerres qui sont le fléau du Genre Humain & les vrais Bourreaux de la Loi Naturelle.

Mais un Etre à qui la Nature a donné un instinct si précoce, si éclairé, qui juge, combine, raisonne & délibère, autant que s'étend & lui permet la Sphère de son activité: un Etre qui s'attache par les Bienfaits, qui se détache par les mauvais traitemens, & va essayer un meilleur Maître; un Etre d'une structure semblable à la nôtre, qui fait les mêmes opérations, qui a les mêmes passions, les mêmes douleurs, les mêmes plaisirs, plus ou moins vifs, suivant l'empire de l'imagination & la délicatesse des nerfs; un tel Etre enfin ne montre-t-il pas clairement qu'il sent ses torts & les nôtres; qu'il connoît le bien & le mal, & en un mot a conscience de ce qu'il fait? Son Ame qui marque comme la nôtre, les mêmes joies, les mêmes mortifications, les mêmes déconcertemens, seroit-elle sans aucune répugnance, à la vüe de son semblable déchiré, ou après l'avoir lui-même impitoiablement mis en pièces? Cela posé, le don précieux dont il s'agit, n'auroit point été refusé aux Animaux; car puisqu'ils nous offrent des Signes évidens de leur repentir, comme de leur intelligence, qu'y a-t-il d'absurde à penser que des Etres, des Machines presque aussi parfaites que nous, soient comme nous, faites pour penser, & pour sentir la Nature?

Qu'on ne m'objecte point que les Animaux sont pour la plûpart des Etres féroces, qui ne sont pas capables de sentir les maux qu'ils font; car tous les Hommes distinguent-ils mieux les vices & les vertus? Il est dans notre Espèce de la férocité, comme dans la leur. Les Hommes qui sont dans la barbare habitude d'enfreindre la Loi Naturelle, n'en sont pas si tourmentés, que ceux qui la transgressent pour la première fois, & que la force de l'exemple n'a point endurcis. Il en est de même des Animaux, comme des Hommes; Les uns & les autres peuvent être plus ou moins féroces par tempérament, & ils le deviennent encore plus avec ceux qui le sont. Mais un Animal doux, pacifique, qui vit avec d'autres Animaux semblables, & d'alimens doux, sera ennemi du sang & du carnage; il rougira intérieurement de l'avoir versé; avec cette différence peut-être, que comme chez eux tout est immolé aux besoins, aux plaisirs, & aux commodités de la vie, dont ils joüissent plus que nous, leurs remords ne semblent pas devoir être si vifs que les nôtres, parce que nous ne sommes pas dans la même nécessité qu'eux. La coutume émousse, & peut-être étouffe les remords, comme les plaisirs.

Mais je veux pour un moment supposer que je me trompe, & qu'il n'est pas juste que presque tout l'Univers ait tort à ce sujet, tandis que j'aurois seul raison; j'accorde que les Animaux, même les plus excellens, ne connoissent pas la distinction du bien & du mal moral, qu'ils n'ont aucune mémoire des attentions qu'on a eües pour eux, du bien qu'on leur a fait, aucun sentiment de leurs propres vertus; que ce Lion, par exemple, dont j'ai parlé après tant d'autres, ne se souvienne pas de n'avoir pas voulu ravir la vie à cet Homme qui fut livré à sa furie, dans un Spectacle plus inhumain que tous les Lions, les Tigres & les Ours; tandis que nos Compatriotes se battent, Suisses contre Suisses, Frères contre Frères, se reconnoissent, s'enchaînent, ou se tuent sans remords, parce qu'un Prince paie leurs meurtres: je suppose enfin que la Loi naturelle n'ait pas été donnée aux Animaux, quelles en seront les conséquences? L'Homme n'est pas pétri d'un Limon plus précieux; la Nature n'a emploié qu'une seule & même pâte, dont elle a seulement varié les levains. Si donc l'Animal ne se repent pas d'avoir violé le sentiment interieur dont je parle, ou plutôt s'il en est absolument privé, il faut nécessairement que l'Homme soit dans le même cas: moiennant quoi adieu la Loi Naturelle, & tous ces beaux Traités qu'on a publiés sur elle! Tout le Régne Animal en seroit généralement dépourvû. Mais réciproquement si l'Homme ne peut se dispenser de convenir qu'il distingue toujours, lorsque la santé le laisse joüir de lui-même, ceux qui ont de la probité, de l'humanité, de la vertu, de ceux qui ne sont ni humains, ni vertueux, ni honnêtes gens; qu'il est facile de distinguer ce qui est vice, ou vertu, par l'unique plaisir, ou la propre répugnance, qui en sont comme les effets naturels, il s'ensuit que les Animaux formés de la même matière, à laquelle il n'a peut-être manqué qu'un degré de fermentation, pour égaler les Hommes en tout, doivent participer aux mêmes prérogatives de l'Animalité, & qu'ainsi il n'est point d'Ame, ou de substance sensitive, sans remords. La Réfléxion suivante va fortifier celles-ci.

On ne peut détruire la Loi Naturelle. L'Empreinte en est si forte dans tous les Animaux, que je ne doute nullement que les plus sauvages & les plus féroces n'aient quelques momens de repentir. Je crois que la Fille Sauvage de Châlons en Champagne aura porté la peine de son crime, s'il est vrai qu'elle ait mangé sa soeur.[62] Je pense la même chose de tous ceux qui commettent des crimes, même involontaires, ou de tempérament: de Gaston d'Orléans qui ne pouvoit s'empecher de voler;[63] de certaine femme qui fut sujette au même vice dans la grossesse, & dont ses enfans héritèrent:[64] de celle qui dans le même Etat, mangea son mari;[65] de cette autre qui égorgeoit les enfans, saloit leurs corps, & en mangeoit tous les jours comme du petit salé:[66] de cette fille de Voleur Antropophage, qui la devint à 12 ans, quoiqu'aiant perdu Père & Mère à l'age d'un an, elle eût été élevée par d'honnêtes gens;[67] pour ne rien dire de tant d'autres exemples dont nos observateurs sont remplis; & qui prouvent tous qu'il est mille vices & vertus héréditaires, qui passent des parens aux enfans, comme ceux de la Nourice, à ceux qu'elle allaite. Je dis donc & j'accorde que ces malheureux ne sentent pas pour la plupart sur le champ l'énormité de leur action. La *Boulymie*, par exemple, ou la faim canine peut éteindre tout sentiment; c'est une manie d'estomac qu'on est forcé de satisfaire. Mais revenües à elles-mêmes, & comme désenivrées, quels remords pour ces femmes qui se rappellent le meurtre qu'elles ont commis dans ce qu'elles avoient de plus cher! quelle punition d'un mal involontaire, auquel elles n'ont pu résister, dont elles n'ont eu aucune conscience! Cependant ce n'est point assez apparemment pour les Juges. Parmi les femmes dont je parle, l'une fut roüée, & brulée, l'autre enterrée vive. Je sens tout ce que demande l'intérêt de la société. Mais il seroit sans doute à souhaiter qu'il n'y eût pour Juges, que d'excellens Medecins. Eux seuls pourroient distinguer le criminel innocent, du coupable. Si la raison est esclave d'un sens dépravé, ou en fureur, comment peut-elle le gouverner?⁶⁸

Mais si le crime porte avec soi sa propre punition plus ou moins cruelle; si la plus longue & la plus barbare habitude ne peut tout-à-fait arracher le repentir des coeurs les plus inhumains; s'ils sont déchirés par la mémoire même de leurs actions, pourquoi effraier l'imagination des esprits foibles par un Enfer, par des spectres, & des précipices de feu, moins réels encore que ceux de Pascal*? Qu'est-il besoin de recourir à des fables, comme un Pape de bonne foi l'a dit lui-même, pour tourmenter les malheureux mêmes qu'on fait périr, parce qu'on ne les trouve pas assez punis par leur propre conscience, qui est leur premier Bourreau? Ce n'est pas que je veüille dire que tous les criminels soient injustement punis; je prétens seulement que ceux dont la volonté est dépravée, & la conscience éteinte, le sont assez par leurs remords, quand ils reviennent à eux-mêmes; remords, j'ose encore le dire, dont la Nature auroit dû en ce cas, ce me semble, délivrer des malheureux entraînés par une fatale nécessité.

Les Criminels, les Méchans, les Ingrats, ceux enfin qui ne sentent pas la Nature, Tyrans malheureux & indignes du jour, ont beau se faire un cruel plaisir de leur Barbarie, il est des momens calmes & de réfléxion, où la Conscience vengeresse s'élève, dépose contr'eux, & les condamne à être presque sans cesse déchirés de ses propres mains. Qui tourmente les Hommes, est tourmenté par lui-même; & les maux qu'il sentira, seront la juste mesure^b de ceux qu'il aura faits.

D'un autre côté, il y a tant de plaisir à faire du bien, à sentir, à reconnoître celui qu'on reçoit, tant de contentement à pratiquer la vertu, à être doux, humain, tendre, charitable, compatissant & généreux, (ce seul mot renferme toutes les vertus), que je tiens

---

* *Dans un cercle, ou à table, il lui falloit toujours un rempart de Chaises, ou quelqu'un dans son voisinage du coté gauche, pour l'empêcher de voir des Abimes épouvantables dans lesquels il craignoit quelquefois de tomber, quelque connoissance qu'il eût de ces illusions. Quel effraiant effet de l'Imagination, ou d'une singulière circulation dans un Lobe du cerveau! Grand Homme d'un coté, il étoit à moitié fou de l'autre. La folie & la sagesse avoient chacune leur département, ou leur Lobe, séparé par la faux. De quel coté tenoit-il si fort à Mrs. de Port-Roial?*[a]

[a] X: *J'ai lu ce fait dans un extrait du traité du vertige de Mr. de la Mettrie.*⁶⁹
[b] Y: la mesure

pour assez puni, quiconque a le malheur de n'être pas né Vertueux.

Nous n'avons pas originairement été faits pour être Savans; c'est peut-être par une espèce d'abus de nos facultés organiques, que nous le sommes devenus; & cela à la charge de l'Etat, qui nourrit une multitude de Fainéans, que la vanité a décorés du nom de *Philosophes*. La Nature nous a tous créés uniquement pour être heureux; ouï tous, depuis le ver qui rampe, jusqu'à l'Aigle qui se perd dans la Nüe. C'est pourquoi elle a donné à tous les Animaux quelque portion de la Loi naturelle, portion plus ou moins exquise, selon que le comportent les Organes bien conditionnés de chaque Animal.

A présent comment définirons-nous la Loi naturelle? C'est un sentiment, qui nous apprend ce que nous ne devons pas faire, par ce que nous ne voudrions pas qu'on nous fît.[a] Oserois-je ajouter à cette idée commune, qu'il me semble que ce sentiment n'est qu'une espèce de crainte, ou de fraieur, aussi salutaire à l'espèce, qu'à l'individu; car peut-être ne respectons-nous la bourse & la vie des autres, que pour nous conserver nos Biens, notre honneur & nous-mêmes; semblables à ces *Ixions du Christianisme*, qui n'aiment Dieu & n'embrassent tant de chimériques vertus, que parce qu'ils craignent l'Enfer.[70]

Vous voyez que la Loi naturelle n'est qu'un sentiment intime, qui appartient encore à l'imagination, comme tous les autres, parmi lesquels on compte la pensée. Par conséquent elle ne suppose évidemment ni éducation, ni révélation, ni Législateur, à moins qu'on ne veüille la confondre avec les Loix Civiles, à la maniere ridicule des Théologiens.

Les armes du Fanatisme peuvent détruire ceux qui soutiennent ces vérités; mais elles ne détruiront jamais ces vérités mêmes.

Ce n'est pas que je révoque en doute l'existence d'un Etre suprême; il me semble au contraire que le plus grand degré de Probabilité est pour elle: mais comme cette existence ne prouve pas plus la nécessité d'un culte, que tout autre, c'est une vérité théorique, qui n'est guères d'usage dans la Pratique: de sorte que, comme on peut dire d'après tant d'expériences, que la Re-

[a] X: parce que nous ne voudrions pas qu'on nous le fît.

ligion ne suppose pas l'exacte probité, les mêmes raisons autorisent à penser que l'Atheïsme ne l'exclut pas.

Qui sait d'ailleurs si la raison de l'Existence de l'Homme, ne seroit pas dans son existence même? Peut-être a-t-il été jetté au hazard sur un point de la surface de la Terre, sans qu'on puisse savoir ni comment, ni pourquoi; mais seulement qu'il doit vivre & mourir; semblable à ces champignons, qui paroissent d'un jour à l'autre, ou à ces fleurs qui bordent les fossés & couvrent les murailles.

Ne nous perdons point dans l'infini, nous ne sommes pas faits pour en avoir la moindre idée; il nous est absolument impossible de remonter à l'origine des choses. Il est égal d'ailleurs pour notre repos, que la matière soit éternelle, ou qu'elle ait été créée; qu'il y ait un Dieu, ou qu'il n'y en ait pas. Quelle folie de tant se tourmenter pour ce qu'il est impossible de connoître, & ce qui ne nous rendroit pas plus heureux, quand nous en viendrions à bout.

Mais, dit-on, lisez tous les ouvrages des Fénelons, des Nieuwentits, des Abadies, des Derhams, des Raïs &c.[71] Eh bien! que m'apprendront-ils? ou plutôt que m'ont-ils appris? Ce ne sont que d'ennuieuses répétitions d'Ecrivains zélés, dont l'un n'ajoute à l'autre qu'un verbiage, plus propre à fortifier, qu'à saper les fondemens de l'Atheïsme. Le volume des preuves qu'on tire du spectacle de la nature, ne leur donne pas plus de force. La structure seule d'un doigt, d'une oreille, d'un oeil, *une observation de Malpighi*,[72] prouve tout, & sans doute beaucoup mieux que *Descartes & Mallebranche*; ou tout le reste ne prouve rien.[73] Les Deïstes, & les Chrétiens mêmes devroient donc se contenter de faire observer que dans tout le Régne Animal, les mêmes vües sont exécutées par une infinité de divers moiens, tous cependant exactement géométriques. Car de quelles plus fortes Armes pourroit-on terrasser les Athées? Il est vrai que si ma raison ne me trompe pas, l'Homme & tout l'Univers semblent avoir été destinés à cette unité de vües. Le Soleil, l'Air, l'Eau, l'Organisation, la forme des corps, tout est arrangé dans l'oeil, comme dans un miroir qui présente fidèlement à l'imagination les objets qui y sont peints, suivant les loix qu'exige cette infinie variété de corps qui servent à la vision. Dans l'oreille, nous trouvons partout une diversité frappante, sans que cette diverse fabrique de l'Homme, des Animaux, des Oiseaux, des Poissons, produise differens usages. Toutes les oreilles sont si mathématiquement faites, qu'elles tendent également au seul & même but, qui est d'entendre. Le Hazard, demande le Déiste, seroit-il donc assez grand Géometre, pour varier ainsi à son gré les ouvrages dont on le suppose Auteur, sans que tant de diversité pût l'empêcher d'atteindre la même fin. Il objecte encore ces parties evidemment contenües dans l'Animal pour de futurs usages; le Papillon dans la Chenille; l'Homme dans le Ver spermatique;[74] un Polype entier dans chacune de ses parties;[75] la valvule du trou ovale,[76] le Poumon dans le fetus; les dens dans leurs Alvéoles; les os dans les fluides, qui s'en détachent & se durcissent d'une manière incompréhensible. Et comme les Partisans de ce système, loin de rien négliger pour le faire valoir, ne se lassent jamais d'accumuler preuves sur preuves, ils veulent profiter de tout, & de la foiblesse même de l'Esprit en certains cas. Voiez, disent-ils, les Spinosa, les Vanini, les Desbarreaux, les Boindin, Apôtres qui font plus d'honneur, que de tort au Déisme! La durée de la santé de ces derniers a été la mesure de leur incrédulité:[77] & il est rare en effet, ajoutent-ils, qu'on n'abjure pas l'Athéisme, dès que les passions se sont affoiblies avec le corps qui en est l'instrument.

Voilà certainement tout ce qu'on peut dire de plus favorable à l'existence d'un Dieu, quoique le dernier argument soit frivole, en ce que ces conversions sont courtes, l'Esprit reprenant presque toujours ses anciennes opinions, & se conduisant en conséquence, dès qu'il a recouvré, ou plutôt retrouvé ses forces dans celles du corps. En voilà du moins beaucoup plus que n'en dit le Medecin *Diderot*,[78] dans ses *Pensées Philosophiques*, sublime ouvrage qui ne convaincra pas un Athée. Que répondre en effet à un Homme qui dit: "Nous ne connoissons point la Nature: Des causes cachées dans son sein pourroient avoir tout produit. Voiez à votre tour le Polype de Trembley! Ne contient-il pas en soi les causes qui donnent lieu à sa régénération? Quelle absurdité y auroit-il donc à penser qu'il est des causes physiques pour lesquelles tout a été fait, & auxquelles toute la chaine de ce vaste Univers est si nécessairement liée & assujetie, que rien de ce qui arrive, ne pouvoit ne pas[a] arriver; des causes dont

[a] X: pas ne pas

l'ignorance absolument invincible nous a fait recourir à un Dieu, qui n'est pas même un *Etre de Raison,* suivant certains? Ainsi détruire le Hazard, ce n'est pas prouver l'existence d'un Etre suprême, puisqu'il peut y avoir autre chose qui ne seroit ni Hazard, ni Dieu; je veux dire la Nature, dont l'étude par conséquent ne peut faire que des incrédules; comme le prouve la façon de penser de tous ses plus heureux scrutateurs."[79]

Le *poids de l'Univers* n'ébranle donc pas un véritable Athée, loin de *l'écraser;*[80] & tous ces indices mille & mille fois rebattus d'un Créateur, indices qu'on met fort au-dessus de la façon de penser dans nos semblables, ne sont évidens, quelque loin qu'on pousse cet argument, que pour les Anti-pirrhoniens, ou pour ceux qui ont assés de confiance dans leur raison, pour croire pouvoir juger sur certaines apparences, auxquelles, comme vous voiez, les Athées peuvent en opposer d'autres peut-être aussi fortes, & absolument contraires. Car si nous écoutons encore les Naturalistes; ils nous diront que les mêmes causes qui, dans les mains d'un Chimiste, & par le Hazard de divers mêlanges, ont fait le premier miroir, dans celles de la Nature ont fait l'eau pure, qui en sert à la simple Bergère: que le mouvement qui conserve le monde, a pu le créer; que chaque corps a pris la place que sa Nature lui a assignée; que l'air a dû entourer la terre, par la même raison que le Fer & les autres Métaux sont l'ouvrage de ses entrailles; que le Soleil est une production aussi naturelle, que celle de l'Electricité; qu'il n'a pas plus été fait pour échaufer la Terre, & tous ses Habitans, qu'il brule quelquefois, que la pluie pour faire pousser les grains, qu'elle gâte souvent; que le miroir & l'eau n'ont pas plus été faits pour qu'on pût s'y regarder, que tous les corps polis qui ont la même propriété: que l'oeil est à la vérité une espèce de Trumeau dans lequel l'Ame peut contempler l'image des objets, tels qu'ils lui sont representés par ces corps; mais qu'il n'est pas démontré que cet organe ait été réellement fait exprès pour cette contemplation, ni exprès placé dans l'orbite: qu'enfin il se pourroit bien faire que Lucrèce, le Medecin Lamy, & tous les Epicuriens anciens & modernes, eussent raison, lorsqu'ils avancent que l'oeil ne voit que par ce qu'il se trouve organisé, & placé comme il l'est;[81] que, posées une fois les mêmes régles de mouvement que suit la Nature dans la génération & le dévelopement des corps, il n'étoit pas possible que ce merveilleux organe fût organisé & placé autrement.

Tel est le pour & le contre, & l'abrégé des grandes raisons qui partageront éternellement les Philosophes: je ne prens aucun parti.

Non nostrum inter vos tantas componere lites.[82]

C'est ce que je disois à un François de mes amis, aussi franc Pirrhonien que moi, Homme de beaucoup de mérite, & digne d'un meilleur sort. Il me fit à ce sujet une réponse fort singulière. Il est vrai, me dit-il, que le pour & le contre ne doit point inquiéter l'Ame d'un Philosophe, qui voit que rien n'est démontré avec assez de clarté pour forcer son consentement, & même que les idées indicatives qui s'offrent d'un coté, sont aussitôt détruites par celles qui se montrent de l'autre. Cependant, reprit-il, l'Univers ne sera jamais heureux, à moins qu'il ne soit Athée. Voici quelles étoient les raisons de cet *abominable* Homme. Si l'Athéïsme, disoit-il, étoit généralement répandu, toutes les branches de la Religion seroient alors détruites & coupées par la racine. Plus de guerres théologiques; plus de soldats de Religion; soldats terribles! la Nature infectée d'un poison sacré, reprendroit ses droits & sa pureté. Sourds à toute autre voix, les Mortels tranquilles ne suivroient que les conseils spontanés de leur propre individu; les seuls qu'on ne méprise point impunément, & qui peuvent seuls nous conduire au bonheur par les agréables sentiers de la vertu.

Telle est la Loi Naturelle; quiconque en est rigide observateur, est honnête Homme, & mérite la confiance de tout le genre humain. Quiconque ne la suit pas scrupuleusement, a beau affecter les specieux dehors d'une autre Religion, c'est un fourbe, ou un Hippocrite dont je me défie.

Après cela qu'un vain Peuple pense différemment; qu'il ose affirmer qu'il y va de la probité même, à ne pas croire la Révélation; qu'il faut en un mot une autre Religion, que celle de la Nature, quelle qu'elle soit! quelle misere! quelle pitié! & la bonne[a] opinion que chacun nous donne de celle qu'il a embrassée! Nous ne briguons point ici le suffrage du vulgaire. Qui dresse dans son coeur des Autels à la Superstition, est né pour adorer les Idoles, & non pour sentir la Vertu.

[a] Y: eh, la bonne

Mais puisque toutes les facultés de l'Ame dépendent tellement de la propre Organisation du Cerveau & de tout le Corps, qu'elles ne sont visiblement que cette Organisation même; voilà une Machine bien éclairée! Car enfin quand l'Homme seul auroit reçu en partage la Loi Naturelle, en seroit-il moins une Machine? Des Roües, quelques ressorts de plus que dans les Animaux les plus parfaits, le cerveau proportionnellement plus proche du coeur, & recevant aussi plus de sang, la même raison donnée; que sais-je enfin? des causes inconnües, produiroient toujours cette conscience délicate, si facile à blesser, ces remords qui ne sont pas plus étrangers à la matière, que la pensée, & en un mot toute la différence qu'on suppose ici. L'organisation suffiroit-elle donc à tout? Oüi, encore une fois. Puisque la pensée se développe visiblement avec les organes, pourquoi la matière dont ils sont faits, ne seroit-elle pas aussi susceptible de remords, quand une fois elle a acquis avec le tems la faculté de sentir?

L'Ame n'est donc qu'un vain terme dont on n'a point d'idée, & dont un bon Esprit ne doit se servir que pour nommer la partie qui pense en nous. Posé le moindre principe de mouvement, les corps animés auront tout ce qu'il leur faut pour se mouvoir, sentir, penser, se repentir, & se conduire en un mot dans le Physique, & dans le Moral qui en dépend.

Nous ne supposons rien; ceux qui croiroient que toutes les difficultés ne seroient pas encore levées, vont trouver des expériences, qui acheveront de les satisfaire.

1. Toutes les chairs des Animaux palpitent après la mort, d'autant plus longtems, que l'Animal est plus froid & transpire moins. Les Tortües, les Lézards, les Serpens &c. en font foi.

2. Les muscles séparés du corps, se retirent, lorsqu'on les pique.

3. Les entrailles conservent long-tems leur mouvement péristaltique, ou vermiculaire.

4. Une simple injection d'eau chaude ranime le coeur & les muscles, suivant Cowper.[83]

5. Le coeur de la Grenoüille, surtout exposé au Soleil, encore mieux sur une table, ou une assiette chaude, se remüe pendant une heure & plus, après avoir été arraché du corps. Le mouvement semble-t-il perdu sans ressource? Il n'y a qu'à piquer le coeur, &

ce muscle creux bat encore. Harvey a fait la même observation sur les Crapaux.[84]

6. Le Chancelier Bacon, Auteur du premier ordre, parle, dans son *Histoire de la vie & de la mort*, d'un homme convaincu de trahison qu'on ouvrit vivant, pour en arracher le coeur & le jetter au feu: ce muscle sauta d'abord à la hauteur perpendiculaire d'un pié & demi; mais ensuite perdant ses forces, à chaque reprise, toujours moins haut, pendant 7 ou 8 minutes.[a85]

7. Prenez un petit Poulet encore dans l'oeuf; arrachez-lui le coeur; vous observerez les mêmes Phénomènes, avec à peu près les mêmes circonstances. La seule chaleur de l'haleine ranime un Animal prêt à périr dans la Machine Pneumatique.

Les mêmes Expériences que nous devons à Boyle & à Sténon, se font dans les Pigeons, dans les Chiens, dans les Lapins, dont les morceaux de coeur se remüent, comme les Coeurs entiers.[86] On voit le même mouvement dans les pattes de Taupe arrachées.

8. La Chenille, les Vers, l'Araignée, la Mouche, l'Anguille, offrent les mêmes choses à considerer; & le mouvement des parties coupées augmente dans l'eau chaude, à cause du feu qu'elle contient.

9. Un Soldat yvre emporta d'un coup de sabre la tête d'un Coq d'Inde. Cet Animal resta debout, ensuite il marcha, courut; venant à rencontrer une muraille, il se tourna, battit des ailes, en continuant de courir, & tomba enfin. Etendu par terre, tous les muscles de ce Coq se remuoient encore. Voilà ce que j'ai vu, & il est facile de voir à peu près ces phénomènes dans les petits chats, ou chiens, dont on a coupé la tête.

10. Les Polypes font plus que de se mouvoir, après la Section; ils se reproduisent dans huit jours en autant d'Animaux, qu'il y a de parties coupées. J'en suis fâché pour le système des Naturalistes sur la génération,[87] ou plutôt j'en suis bien aise; car que cette découverte nous apprend bien à ne jamais rien conclure de général, même de toutes les Expériences connües, & les plus décisives!

Voilà beaucoup plus de faits qu'il n'en faut, pour prouver d'une manière incontestable que chaque petite fibre, ou partie des corps

---

[a] X: || 6. Bacon de Verulam, dans son Traité *Sylva-Sylvarum*, parle d'un Homme convaincu de trahison, qu'on ouvrit vivant, & dont le coeur jetté dans l'eau chaude, sauta à plusieurs reprises, toujours moins haut, à la distance perpendiculaire de 2 piés.

organisés, se meut par un principe qui lui est propre, & dont l'action ne dépend point des nerfs, comme les mouvemens volontaires;[88] puisque les mouvemens en question s'exercent, sans que les parties qui les manifestent, aient aucun commerce avec la circulation. Or si cette force se fait remarquer jusques dans des morceaux de fibres, le coeur, qui est un composé de fibres singulièrement entrelacées, doit avoir la même proprieté. L'Histoire de Bacon n'étoit pas nécessaire pour me le persuader. Il m'étoit facile d'en juger, & par la parfaite Analogie de la structure du Coeur de l'Homme & des Animaux; & par la masse même du premier, dans laquelle ce mouvement ne se cache aux yeux, que parce qu'il y est étouffé, & enfin parce que tout est froid & affaissé dans les cadavres. Si les dissections se faisoient sur des Criminels suppliciés, dont les corps sont encore chauds, on verroit dans leur coeur les mêmes mouvemens, qu'on observe dans les muscles du visage des gens décapités.

Tel est ce principe moteur des Corps entiers, ou des parties coupées en morceaux, qu'il produit des mouvemens non déreglés, comme on l'a cru, mais très réguliers, & cela, tant dans les Animaux chauds & parfaits, que dans ceux qui sont froids & imparfaits. Il ne reste donc aucune ressource à nos Adversaires, si ce n'est de nier mille & mille faits que chacun peut facilement vérifier.[89]

Si on me demande à présent quel est le siége de cette force innée dans nos corps; je répons qu'elle réside très clairement dans ce que les Anciens ont appellé *Parenchyme*; c'est-à-dire dans la substance propre des parties, abstraction faite des Veines, des Artères, des Nerfs, en un mot de l'Organisation de tout le corps; & que par conséquent chaque partie contient en soi des ressorts plus ou moins vifs, selon le besoin qu'elles en avoient.

Entrons dans quelque détail de ces ressorts de la Machine humaine. Tous les mouvemens vitaux, animaux, naturels, & automatiques se font par leur action. N'est-ce pas machinalement que le corps se retire, frappé de terreur à l'aspect d'un précipice inattendu ? que les paupières se baissent à la menace d'un coup, comme on l'a dit ? que la *Pupille* s'étrécit au grand jour pour conserver la Rétine, & s'élargit pour voir les objets dans l'obscurité ? N'est-ce pas machinalement que les pores de la peau se ferment en Hyver, pour que le froid ne pénètre pas l'intérieur des vaisseaux ? que l'estomac se soulève, irrité par le poison, par une certaine quantité d'Opium, par tous les Emétiques &c. ? que le Coeur, les Artères, les Muscles se contractent pendant le sommeil, comme pendant la veille ? que le Poumon fait l'office d'un souflet continuellement exercé ? N'est-ce pas machinalement qu'agissent tous les Sphincters de la Vessie, du *Rectum* &c. ? que le Coeur a une contraction plus forte que tout autre muscle ? que les muscles érecteurs font dresser La Verge dans l'Homme, comme dans les Animaux qui s'en battent le ventre; & même dans l'enfant, capable d'érection, pour peu que cette partie soit irritée ?[90] Ce qui prouve, pour le dire en passant, qu'il est un ressort singulier dans ce membre, encore peu connu, & qui produit des effets qu'on n'a point encore bien expliqués, malgré toutes les lumières de l'Anatomie.

Je ne m'étendrai pas davantage sur tous ces petits ressorts subalternes connus de tout le monde. Mais il en est un autre plus subtil, & plus merveilleux, qui les anime tous; il est la source de tous nos sentimens, de tous nos plaisirs, de toutes nos passions, de toutes nos pensées; car le cerveau a ses muscles pour penser, comme les jambes pour marcher. Je veux parler de ce principe incitant, & impétueux, qu'Hippocrate appelle ενορμων (l'Ame). Ce principe existe, & il a son siége dans le cerveau à l'origine des nerfs, par lesquels il exerce son empire sur tout le reste du corps.[91] Par là s'explique tout ce qui peut s'expliquer, jusqu'aux effets surprenans des maladies de l'Imagination.

Mais pour ne pas languir dans une richesse & une fécondité mal entendüe, il faut se borner à un petit nombre de questions & de réfléxions.

Pourquoi la vüe, ou la simple idée d'une belle femme nous cause-t-elle des mouvemens & des désirs singuliers ? Ce qui se passe alors dans certains organes, vient-il de la nature même de ces organes ? Point du tout; mais du commerce & de l'espèce de sympathie[92] de ces muscles avec l'imagination. Il n'y a ici qu'un premier ressort excité par le *beneplacitum* des Anciens, ou par l'image de la beauté, qui en excite un autre, lequel étoit fort assoupi, quand l'imagination l'a éveillé: & comment cela, si ce n'est par le désordre & le tumulte du sang & des esprits,[93] qui galopent avec une promptitude extraordinaire, & vont gonfler les corps caverneux ?

Puisqu'il est des communications évidentes entre la Mère & l'Enfant*, & qu'il est dur de nier des faits rapportés par Tulpius,[94] & par d'autres Ecrivains aussi dignes de foi (il n'y en a point qui le soient plus), nous croirons que c'est par la même voie que le foetus ressent l'impétuosité de l'imagination maternelle, comme une cire molle reçoit toutes sortes d'impressions; & que les mêmes traces, ou Envies de la Mère, peuvent s'imprimer sur le foetus, sans que cela puisse se comprendre, quoi qu'en disent Blondel & tous ses adhérens. Ainsi nous faisons réparation d'honneur au P. Malebranche, beaucoup trop raillé de sa crédulité par des Auteurs qui n'ont point observé d'assez près la Nature, & ont voulu l'assujettir à leurs idées.[95]

Voiez le Portrait de ce fameux Pope, le Voltaire[a] des Anglois. Les Efforts, les Nerfs de son Génie sont peints sur sa Physionomie; Elle est toute en convulsion; ses yeux sortent de l'Orbite, ses sourcils s'élèvent avec les muscles du Front. Pourquoi? C'est que l'origine des Nerfs est en travail, & que tout le corps doit se ressentir d'une espèce d'accouchement aussi laborieux. S'il n'y avoit une corde interne qui tirât ainsi celles du dehors, d'où viendroient tous ces phénomènes? Admettre une *Ame*, pour les expliquer, c'est être réduit à *l'Operation du St. Esprit*.

En effet si ce qui pense en mon Cerveau, n'est pas une partie de ce Viscère, & conséquemment de tout le Corps, pourquoi lorsque tranquille dans mon lit je forme le plan d'un Ouvrage, ou que je poursuis un raisonnement abstrait, pourquoi mon sang s'échaufe-t-il? Pourquoi la fièvre de mon Esprit passe-t-elle dans mes Veines? Demandez-le aux Hommes d'Imagination, aux grands Poëtes, à ceux qu'un sentiment bien rendu ravit, qu'un goût exquis, que les charmes de la Nature, de la Vérité, ou de la Vertu, transportent! Par leur Entousiasme, par ce qu'ils vous diront avoir éprouvé, vous jugerez de la cause par les effets: par cette *Harmonie*, que Borelli, qu'un seul Anatomiste a mieux connüe que tous les Leibnitiens, vous connoitrez l'Unité matérielle de l'Homme.[96] Car enfin si la tension des nerfs qui fait la douleur, cause la fièvre, par laquelle l'Esprit est troublé, & n'a plus de volonté; & que réciproquement l'Esprit trop exercé trouble le corps,

---
* *Au moins par les vaisseaux. Est-il sûr qu'il n'y en a point par les nerfs?*
[a] X: au moins le Voltaire

& allume ce feu de consomption qui a enlevé Bayle dans un âge si peu avancé;[97] si telle titillation me fait vouloir, me force de désirer ardemment ce dont je ne me souciois nullement le moment d'auparavant; si à leur tour certaines traces du Cerveau excitent le même prurit & les mêmes désirs, pourquoi faire double, qui n'est évidemment qu'un? C'est en vain qu'on se récrie sur l'empire de la Volonté. Pour un ordre qu'elle donne, elle subit cent fois le joug. Et quelle merveille que le corps obéisse dans l'état sain, puisqu'un torrent de sang & d'esprits vient l'y forcer; la volonté aiant pour Ministres une légion invisible de fluides plus vifs que l'Eclair, & toujours prêts à la servir! Mais comme c'est par les Nerfs que son pouvoir s'exerce, c'est aussi par eux qu'il est arrêté. La meilleure volonté d'un Amant épuisé, les plus violens désirs lui rendront-ils sa vigueur perdüe? Hélas! non; & elle en sera la première punie, parce que, posées certaines circonstances, il n'est pas dans sa puissance de ne pas vouloir du plaisir. Ce que j'ai dit de la Paralysie &c. revient ici.

La Jaunisse vous surprend! Ne savez-vous pas que la couleur des corps dépend de celle des verres au travers desquels on les regarde! Ignorez-vous que telle est la teinte des humeurs, telle est celle des objets, au moins par rapport à nous, vains joüets de mille illusions. Mais ôtez cette teinte de l'humeur aqueuse de l'oeil; faites couler la Bile par son tamis naturel; alors l'Ame aiant d'autres yeux, ne verra plus jaune. N'est-ce pas encore ainsi qu'en abattant la Cataracte, ou en injectant le Canal d'Eustachi, on rend la Vüe aux Aveugles, & l'Ouïe aux Sourds? Combien de gens qui n'étoient peut-être que d'habiles Charlatans dans des siècles ignorans, ont passé pour faire de grands Miracles! La belle Ame & la puissante Volonté qui ne peut agir, qu'autant que les dispositions du corps le lui permettent, & dont les goûts changent avec l'âge & la fièvre! Faut-il donc s'étonner si les Philosophes ont toujours eu en vüe la santé du corps, pour conserver celle de l'Ame? si Pythagore a aussi soigneusement ordonné la Diète, que Platon a défendu le vin?[98] Le Régime qui convient au corps, est toujours celui par lequel les Medecins sensés prétendent qu'on doit préluder, lorsqu'il s'agit de former l'Esprit, de l'élever à la connoissance de la vérité & de la vertu; vains sons dans le désordre des Maladies & le tumulte des Sens! Sans les Préceptes de l'Hygiène, Epictète, Socrate,

Platon, &c. prêchent en vain: toute morale est infructueuse, pour qui n'a pas la sobriété en partage; c'est la source de toutes les Vertus, comme l'Intempérance est celle de tous les Vices.

En faut-il davantage, (& pourquoi irois-je me perdre dans l'Histoire des passions, qui toutes s'expliquent[a] par l'ενορμων d'Hippocrate,) pour prouver que l'Homme n'est qu'un Animal, ou un Assemblage de ressorts, qui tous se montent les uns par les autres, sans qu'on puisse dire par quel point du cercle humain la Nature a commencé? Si ces ressorts diffèrent entr'eux, ce n'est donc que par leur Siége, & par quelques degrés de force, & jamais par leur Nature; & par consequent l'Ame n'est qu'un principe de mouvement, ou une Partie matérielle sensible du Cerveau, qu'on peut, sans craindre l'erreur, regarder comme un ressort principal de toute la Machine, qui a une influence visible sur tous les autres, & même paroit avoir été fait le premier; en sorte que tous les autres n'en seroient qu'une émanation, comme on le verra par quelques Observations que je rapporterai, & qui ont été faites sur divers Embryons."

Cette oscillation naturelle, ou propre à notre Machine, & dont est douée chaque fibre, &, pour ainsi dire, chaque Elément fibreux, semblable à celle d'une Pendule, ne peut toujours s'exercer. Il faut la renouveller, à mesure qu'elle se perd; lui donner des forces, quand elle languit; l'affoiblir, lorsqu'elle est opprimée par un excès de force & de vigueur. C'est en cela seul que la vraie Médecine consiste.

Le corps n'est qu'une horloge, dont le nouveau chyle est l'horloger. Le premier soin de la Nature, quand il entre dans le sang, c'est d'y exciter une sorte de fièvre, que les Chymistes qui ne rêvent que fourneaux, ont dû prendre pour une fermentation. Cette fièvre procure une plus grande filtration d'esprits, qui machinalement vont animer les Muscles & le Coeur, comme s'ils y étoient envoiés par ordre de la Volonté.

Ce sont donc les causes ou les forces de la vie, qui entretiennent ainsi durant 100 ans le mouvement perpetuel des solides & des fluides, aussi nécessaire aux uns qu'aux autres. Mais qui peut dire si les solides contribuent à ce jeu, plus que les fluides, & *vice versa*? Tout ce qu'on sait, c'est que l'action des premiers seroit bientôt

[a] Y: s'expriment

anéantie, sans le secours des seconds. Ce sont les liqueurs qui par leur choc éveillent & conservent l'élasticité des vaisseaux, de laquelle dépend leur propre circulation. De-là vient qu'après la mort, le ressort naturel de chaque substance est plus ou moins fort encore, suivant les restes de la vie, auxquels il survit, pour expirer le dernier. Tant il est vrai que cette force des parties animales peut bien se conserver & s'augmenter par celle de la Circulation, mais qu'elle n'en dépend point, puisqu'elle se passe même de l'intégrité de chaque Membre, ou Viscère, comme on l'a vû!

Je n'ignore pas que cette opinion n'a pas été goutée de tous les Savans, & que Staahl sur-tout l'a fort dédaignée. Ce grand Chymiste a voulu nous persuader que l'Ame étoit la seule cause de tous nos mouvemens.[100] Mais c'est parler en Fanatique, & non en Philosophe.

Pour détruire l'hypothèse Staahlienne, il ne faut pas faire tant d'efforts que je vois qu'on en a faits avant moi. Il n'y a qu'à jetter les yeux sur un joüeur de violon. Quelle souplesse! Quelle agilité dans les doigts! Les mouvemens sont si prompts, qu'il ne paroît presque pas y avoir de succession. Or je prie, ou plutôt je défie les Staahliens de me dire, eux qui connoissent si bien tout ce que peut notre Ame, comment il seroit possible qu'elle exécutât si vîte tant de mouvemens, des mouvemens qui se passent si loin d'elle, & en tant d'endroits divers. C'est supposer un joüeur de flûte qui pourroit faire de brillantes cadences sur une infinité de trous qu'il ne connoitroit pas, & auxquels il ne pourroit seulement pas appliquer le doigt.

Mais disons avec Mr. Hecquet qu'il n'est pas permis à tout le Monde d'aller à Corinthe.[101] Et pourquoi Staahl n'auroit-il pas été encore plus favorisé de la Nature en qualité d'Homme, qu'en qualité de Chymiste & de Praticien? Il falloit (l'heureux Mortel!) qu'il eût reçu une autre Ame que le reste des Hommes; une Ame souveraine, qui non contente d'avoir quelque empire sur les muscles *volontaires*, tenoit sans peine les rênes de tous les mouvemens du Corps, pouvoit les suspendre, les calmer, ou les exciter à son gré! Avec une Maitresse aussi despotique, dans les mains de laquelle étoient en quelque sorte les battemens du Coeur & les loix de la Circulation, point de fièvre sans doute; point de douleur; point de langueur; ni honteuse impuissance, ni facheux Priapisme. L'Ame veut, & les ressorts joüent, se dressent, ou se débandent.

Comment ceux de la Machine de Staahl se sont-ils si tôt détraqués? Qui a chez soi un si grand Medecin, devroit être immortel.

Staahl au reste n'est pas le seul qui ait rejetté le principe d'Oscillation des corps organisés. De plus grands esprits ne l'ont pas employé, lorsqu'ils ont voulu expliquer l'action du Coeur, l'Erection du *Penis* &c. Il n'y a qu'à lire les Institutions de Medecine de Boerhaave, pour voir quels laborieux & séduisans systêmes, faute d'admettre une force aussi frappante dans le coeur,[a] ce grand Homme a été obligé d'enfanter à la sueur de son puissant génie.[102]

Willis & Perrault, Esprits d'une plus foible trempe, mais Observateurs assidus de la Nature, (que le fameux Professeur de Leyde n'a guères connüe que par autrui, & n'a eüe, presque que de la seconde main,[b]) paroissent avoir mieux aimé supposer une Ame généralement répandüe par tout le corps, que le principe dont nous parlons.[103] Mais dans cette Hypothèse qui fut celle de Virgile,[104] & de tous les Epicuriens, Hypothèse que l'histoire du Polype sembleroit favoriser à la premiere vüe, les mouvemens qui survivent au sujet dans lequel ils sont inhérens, viennent d'un *reste d'Ame*, que conservent encore les parties qui se contractent, sans être désormais irritées par le sang & les esprits.[105] D'où l'on voit que ces Ecrivains, dont les ouvrages solides éclipsent aisément toutes les fables Philosophiques, ne se sont trompés que sur le modèle de ceux qui ont donné à la matière la faculté de penser, je veux dire, pour s'être mal exprimés, en termes obscurs, & qui ne signifient rien. En effet, qu'est-ce que ce *reste d'Ame*, si ce n'est la force motrice des Leibnitiens,[106] mal rendüe par une telle expression, & que cependant Perrault sur-tout a véritablement entrevüe. V. son *Traité de la Mécanique des Animaux*.[107]

A présent qu'il est clairement démontré contre les Cartésiens, les Staahliens, les Mallebranchistes, & les Théologiens peu dignes d'être ici placés, que la matière se meut par elle-même, non seulement lorsqu'elle est organisée, comme dans un Coeur entier, par exemple, mais lors même que cette organisation est détruite; la curiosité de l'Homme voudroit savoir comment un Corps, par cela même qu'il est originairement doué d'un soufle de Vie, se

[a] X: dans tous les corps,
[b] X: n'a connüe que par autrui, & n'a eüe, pour ainsi dire, que de la seconde main,

trouve en conséquence orné de la faculté de sentir, & enfin par celle-ci de la Pensée. Et pour en venir à bout, ô bon Dieu, quels efforts n'ont pas faits certains Philosophes! Et quel galimathias j'ai eu la patience de lire à ce sujet!

Tout ce que l'Expérience nous apprend, c'est que tant que le mouvement subsiste, si petit qu'il soit, dans une ou plusieurs fibres; il n'y a qu'à les piquer, pour réveiller, animer ce mouvement presque éteint, comme on l'a vû dans cette foule d'Expériences dont j'ai voulu accabler les Systèmes. Il est donc constant que le mouvement & le sentiment s'excitent tour à tour, & dans les Corps entiers, & dans les mêmes Corps, dont la structure est détruite, pour ne rien dire ce certaines Plantes qui semblent nous offrir les mêmes phénomènes de la réunion du sentiment & du mouvement.

Mais de plus, combien d'excellens Philosophes ont démontré que la pensée n'est qu'une faculté de sentir; & que l'Ame raisonnable, n'est que l'Ame sensitive appliquée à contempler les idées, & à raisonner! Ce qui seroit prouvé par cela seul que, lorsque le sentiment est éteint, la pensée l'est aussi, comme dans l'Apoplexie, la Léthargie, la Catalepsie &c. Car ceux qui ont avancé que l'Ame n'avoit pas moins pensé dans les maladies soporeuses, quoiqu'elle ne se souvînt pas des idées qu'elle avoit eües, ont soutenu une chose ridicule.

Pour ce qui est de ce dévelopement, c'est une folie de perdre le tems à en rechercher le mécanisme. La Nature du mouvement nous est aussi inconnüe que celle de la matière. Le moien de découvrir comment il s'y produit, à moins que de ressusciter avec l'Auteur de *l'Histoire de l'Ame* l'ancienne & inintelligible Doctrine des *formes substantielles*![108] Je suis donc tout aussi consolé d'ignorer comment la Matière, d'inerte & simple, devient active & composée d'organes, que de ne pouvoir regarder le Soleil sans verre rouge. Et je suis d'aussi bonne composition sur les autres Merveilles incompréhensibles de la Nature, sur la production du Sentiment & de la Pensée dans un Etre qui ne paroissoit autrefois à nos yeux bornés qu'un peu de boüe.

Qu'on m'accorde seulement que la Matière organisée est douée d'un principe moteur, qui seul la différencie de celle qui ne l'est pas (eh! peut-on rien refuser à l'Observation la plus incontestable?) & que tout dépend dans les Animaux de la diversité de cette Organisation, comme je l'ai assez prouvé; c'en est assez pour deviner l'Enigme des Substances & celle de l'Homme. On voit qu'il n'y en a qu'une dans l'Univers, & que l'Homme est la plus parfaite. Il est au Singe, aux Animaux les plus spirituels, ce que la Pendule Planétaire de Huygens, est à une Montre de Julien le Roi.[109] S'il a fallu plus d'instrumens, plus de Roüages, plus de ressorts pour marquer les mouvemens des Planètes, que pour marquer les Heures, ou les répéter; s'il a fallu plus d'art à Vaucanson pour faire son *Fluteur*, que pour son *Canard*,[110] il eût dû en emploier encore davantage pour faire un *Parleur*; Machine qui ne peut plus être regardée comme impossible, surtout entre les mains d'un nouveau Prométhée. Il étoit donc de même nécessaire que la Nature emploiât plus d'art & d'appareil pour faire & entretenir une Machine, qui pendant un siècle entier pût marquer tous les battemens du coeur & de l'esprit; car si on n'en voit pas au pouls les heures,[a] c'est du moins le Baromètre de la chaleur & de la vivacité, par laquelle on peut juger de la nature de l'Ame. Je ne me trompe point; le corps humain est une horloge, mais immense, & construite avec tant d'artifice & d'habileté, que si la roüe qui sert à marquer les secondes, vient à s'arrêter; celle des minutes tourne & va toujours son train; comme la roüe des Quarts continüe de se mouvoir: & ainsi des autres, quand les premieres, roüillées, ou dérangées par quelque cause que ce soit, ont interrompu leur marche. Car n'est-ce pas ainsi que l'obstruction de quelques Vaisseaux ne suffit pas pour détruire, ou suspendre le fort des mouvemens, qui est dans le coeur, comme dans la pièce ouvrière de la Machine; puisqu'au contraire les fluides dont le volume est diminué, aiant moins de chemin à faire, le parcourent d'autant plus vîte, emportés comme par un nouveau courant, que la force du coeur s'augmente, en raison de la résistance qu'il trouve à l'extrémité des vaisseaux? Lorsque le nerf optique seul comprimé ne laisse plus passer l'image des Objets, n'est-ce pas ainsi que la privation de la Vüe n'empêche pas plus l'usage de l'Oüie, que la privation de ce sens, lorsque les fonctions de la *Portion Molle*[111] sont interdites, ne suppose celle de l'autre? N'est-ce pas ainsi encore que l'un entend, sans pouvoir dire qu'il entend, (si ce n'est

[a] Y: les heures au pouls,

après l'attaque du mal,) & que l'autre qui n'entend rien, mais dont les nerfs linguaux sont libres dans le cerveau, dit machinalement tous les rêves qui lui passent par la tête? Phénomènes qui ne surprennent point les Medecins éclairés. Ils savent à quoi s'en tenir sur la Nature de l'Homme: & pour le dire en passant, de deux Medecins, le meilleur, celui qui mérite le plus de confiance, c'est toujours, à mon avis, celui qui est le plus versé dans la Physique, ou la Mécanique du corps humain, & qui laissant l'Ame, & toutes les inquiétudes que cette chimère donne aux sots & aux ignorans, n'est occupé sérieusement que du pur Naturalisme.

Laissons donc le prétendu Mr. Charp se mocquer des Philosophes qui ont regardé les Animaux, comme des Machines.[112] Que je pense differemment! Je crois que Descartes seroit un Homme respectable à tous égards, si né dans un siècle qu'il n'eût pas dû éclairer, il eût connu le prix de l'Expérience & de l'Observation, & le danger de s'en écarter. Mais il n'est pas moins juste que je fasse ici une autentique réparation à ce grand Homme, pour tous ces petits Philosophes, mauvais plaisans, & mauvais Singes de Locke, qui au lieu de rire impudemment[a] au nés de Descartes, feroient mieux de sentir que sans lui le champ de la Philosophie, comme celui du bon Esprit sans Newton, seroit peut-être encore en friche.

Il est vrai que ce célèbre Philosophe s'est beaucoup trompé, & personne n'en disconvient. Mais enfin il a connu la Nature Animale; il a le premier parfaitement démontré que les Animaux étoient de pures Machines. Or après une découverte de cette importance, & qui suppose autant de sagacité, le moien sans ingratitude, de ne pas faire grace à toutes ses erreurs!

Elles sont à mes yeux toutes réparées par ce grand aveu. Car enfin, quoi qu'il chante sur la distinction des deux substances; il est visible que ce n'est qu'un tour d'adresse, une ruse de stile, pour faire avaler aux Théologiens un poison caché à l'ombre d'une Analogie qui frappe tout le Monde, & qu'eux seuls ne voient pas. Car c'est elle, c'est cette forte Analogie, qui force tous les Savans & les vrais juges d'avouër que ces êtres fiers & vains, plus distingués par leur orgueil, que par le nom d'Hommes, quelque envie qu'ils aient de s'élever, ne sont au fond que des Animaux, &

[a] Y: imprudemment

des Machines perpendiculairement rampantes. Elles ont toutes ce merveilleux Instinct, dont l'Education fait de l'Esprit, & qui a toujours son siége dans le Cerveau, & à son défaut, comme lorsqu'il manque, ou est ossifié, dans la Moëlle allongée, & jamais dans le Cervelet; car je l'ai vu considerablement blessé; d'autres* l'ont trouvé schirreux, sans que l'Ame cessât de faire ses fonctions.¹¹³

Etre Machine, sentir, penser, savoir distinguer le bien du mal, comme le bleu du jaune, en un mot être né avec de l'Intelligence, & un Instinct sûr de Morale, & n'être qu'un Animal, sont donc des choses qui ne sont pas plus contradictoires, qu'être un Singe, ou un Perroquet, & savoir se donner du plaisir. Car puisque l'occasion se présente de le dire, qui eût jamais deviné *à priori*, qu'une goute de la liqueur qui se lance dans l'accouplement, fît ressentir des plaisirs divins, & qu'il en naîtroit une petite créature, qui pourroit un jour, posées certaines loix, joüir des mêmes délices? Je crois la pensée si peu incompatible avec la matière organisée, qu'elle semble en être une propriété, telle que l'Electricité, la Faculté motrice, l'Impénétrabilité, l'Etendüe, &c.

Voulez-vous de nouvelles observations? En voici qui sont sans réplique, & qui prouvent toutes que l'Homme ressemble parfaitement aux Animaux dans son origine, comme dans tout ce que nous avons déjà cru essentiel de comparer.

J'en appelle à la bonne foi de nos Observateurs. Qu'ils nous disent s'il n'est pas vrai que l'Homme dans son Principe n'est qu'un Ver, qui devient Homme, comme la Chenille, Papillon.¹¹⁴ Les plus graves* Auteurs nous ont appris comment il faut s'y prendre pour voir cet Animalcule. Tous les Curieux l'ont vû, comme Hartsoeker,¹¹⁶ dans la semence de l'Homme, & non dans celle de la Femme; il n'y a que les sots qui s'en soient fait scrupule. Comme chaque goute de sperme contient une infinité de ces petits vers, lorsqu'ils sont lancés à l'Ovaire, il n'y a que le plus adroit, ou le plus vigoureux qui ait la force de s'insinüer & de s'implanter dans l'oeuf que fournit la femme, & qui lui donne sa première nourriture. Cet oeuf, quelquefois surpris dans les Trompes de Fallope, est porté par ces canaux à la Matrice, où il prend racine, comme un grain de blé dans la terre. Mais

---

* *Haller dans les* Transact. Philosoph.
* *Boerh.* Inst. Med.,¹¹⁵ *& tant d'autres.*

quoiqu'il y devienne monstrueux par sa croissance de 9 mois, il ne diffère point des oeufs des autres femelles, si ce n'est que sa peau (l'*Amnios*) ne se durcit jamais, & se dilate prodigieusement, comme on en peut juger, en comparant le foetus trouvé en situation & prêt d'éclore, (ce que j'ai eu le plaisir d'observer dans une femme, morte un moment avant l'Accouchement,) avec d'autres petits Embryons très proches de leur origine: car alors c'est toujours l'oeuf dans sa Coque, & l'Animal dans l'oeuf, qui gêné dans ses mouvemens, cherche machinalement à voir le jour; & pour y réüssir, il commence par rompre avec la tête cette membrane, d'où il sort, comme le Poulet, l'Oiseau &c. de la leur. J'ajouterai une observation que je ne trouve nulle part; c'est que l'*Amnios* n'en est pas plus mince, pour s'être prodigieusement étendu; semblable en cela à la Matrice, dont la substance même se gonfle de sucs infiltrés, indépendamment de la réplétion & du déploiement de tous ses Coudes Vasculeux.

Voions l'Homme dans & hors de sa Coque; examinons avec un Microscope les plus jeunes Embryons, de 4, de 6, de 8 ou de 15 jours; après ce tems les yeux suffisent. Que voit-on? La tête seule; un petit oeuf rond avec deux points noirs qui marquent les yeux. Avant ce tems, tout étant plus informe, on n'aperçoit qu'une pulpe médullaire, qui est le Cerveau, dans lequel se forme d'abord l'origine des Nerfs, ou le principe du sentiment, & le coeur qui a déjà par lui-même dans cette pulpe la faculté de battre: c'est le *Punctum saliens* de Malpighi,[117] qui doit peut-être déjà une partie de sa vivacité à l'influence des nerfs. Ensuite peu-à-peu on voit la Tête allonger le Col, qui en se dilatant forme d'abord le *Thorax*, où le coeur a déjà descendu, pour s'y fixer; après quoi vient le bas ventre, qu'une cloison (le diafragme) sépare. Ces dilatations donnent l'une, les bras, les mains, les doigts, les ongles, & les poils; l'autre les cuisses, les jambes, les pieds &c. avec la seule différence de situation qu'on leur connoit, qui fait l'appui & le balancier du corps. C'est une Végétation frappante. Ici ce sont des cheveux qui couvrent le sommet de nos têtes; là ce sont des feuilles & des fleurs. Par-tout brille le même Luxe de la Nature; & enfin l'Esprit Recteur[118] des Plantes est placé, où nous avons notre ame, cette autre Quintessence de l'Homme.

Telle est l'Uniformité de la Nature qu'on commence à sentir,

& l'Analogie du régne Animal & Végétal, de l'Homme à la Plante. Peut-être même y a-t-il des Plantes Animales, c'est-à-dire, qui en végétant, ou se battent comme les Polypes, ou font d'autres fonctions propres aux Animaux?

Voilà à peu près tout ce qu'on sait de la génération. Que les parties qui s'attirent, qui sont faites pour s'unir ensemble, & pour occuper telle, ou telle place, se réünissent toutes suivant leur Nature; & qu'ainsi se forment les yeux, le coeur, l'estomac, & enfin tout le corps, comme de grands Hommes l'ont écrit, cela est possible. Mais comme l'expérience nous abandonne au milieu de ces subtilités, je ne supposerai rien, regardant tout ce qui ne frappe pas mes sens, comme un mystère impénétrable. Il est si rare que les deux semences se rencontrent dans le Congrés, que je serois tenté de croire que la semence de la femme est inutile à la génération.[119]

Mais comment en expliquer les phénomènes, sans ce commode rapport de parties, qui rend si bien raison des ressemblances des enfans, tantôt au Père, & tantôt à la Mère? D'un autre coté l'embarras d'une explication doit-elle contrebalancer un fait? Il me paroît que c'est le Mâle qui fait tout, dans une femme qui dort, comme dans la plus lubrique. L'arrangement des parties seroit donc fait de toute éternité dans le germe, ou dans le Ver même de l'Homme. Mais tout ceci est fort au-dessus de la portée des plus excellens Observateurs. Comme ils n'y peuvent rien saisir, ils ne peuvent pas plus juger de la mécanique de la formation & du dévelopement des Corps, qu'une Taupe, du chemin qu'un Cerf peut parcourir.

Nous sommes de vraies Taupes dans le champ de la Nature; nous n'y faisons guères que le trajet de cet Animal; & c'est notre orgueil qui donne des bornes à ce qui n'en a point. Nous sommes dans le cas d'une Montre qui diroit: (un Fabuliste en feroit un Personnage de conséquence dans un Ouvrage frivole;) "quoi! c'est ce sot ouvrier qui m'a faite, moi qui divise le tems! moi qui marque si exactement le cours du Soleil; moi qui répète à haute voix les heures que j'indique! Non, cela ne se peut pas." Nous dédaignons de même, Ingrats que nous sommes, cette mère commune de tous les *Règnes*, comme parlent les Chymistes.[120] Nous imaginons, ou plutôt supposons, une cause supérieure à celle à qui nous devons tout, & qui a véritablement tout fait d'une manière inconcevable. Non, la matière n'a rien de vil, qu'aux yeux grossiers qui la méconnoissent dans ses plus brillans Ouvrages; & la Nature n'est point une Ouvrière bornée. Elle produit des millions d'Hommes avec plus de facilité & de plaisir, qu'un Horloger n'a de peine à faire la montre la plus composée. Sa puissance éclate également, & dans la production du plus vil Insecte, & dans celle de l'Homme le plus superbe; le régne Animal ne lui coute pas plus que le Végétal, ni le plus beau Génie, qu'un Epi de blé. Jugeons donc par ce que nous voyons, de ce qui se dérobe à la curiosité de nos yeux & de nos recherches, & n'imaginons rien au delà. Suivons le Singe, le Castor, l'Eléphant &c. dans leurs Operations. S'il est évident qu'elles ne peuvent se faire sans intelligence, pourquoi la refuser à ces Animaux? & si vous leur accordez une Ame, Fanatiques, vous êtes perdus; vous aurez beau dire que vous ne décidez point sur sa Nature, tandis que vous lui ôtez l'immortalité; qui ne voit que c'est une assertion gratuite? Qui ne voit qu'elle doit être, ou mortelle, ou immortelle, comme la nôtre, dont[a] elle doit subir le même sort, quel qu'il soit; & qu'ainsi c'est *tomber dans Scilla, pour vouloir éviter Caribde?*

Brisez la chaîne de vos préjugés; armez-vous du flambeau de l'Expérience, & vous ferez à la Nature l'Honneur qu'elle mérite; au lieu de rien conclure à son désavantage, de l'ignorance, où elle vous a laissés. Ouvrez les yeux seulement, & laissez là ce que vous ne pouvez comprendre; & vous verrez que ce Laboureur dont l'Esprit & les lumières ne s'étendent pas plus loin que les bords de son sillon, ne diffère point essentiellement du plus grand Génie, comme l'eût prouvé la dissection des cerveaux de Descartes & de Newton: vous serez persuadé que l'imbécille, ou le stupide, sont des Bêtes à figure Humaine, comme le Singe plein d'Esprit, est un petit Homme sous une autre forme; & qu'enfin tout dépendant absolument de la diversité de l'organisation, un Animal bien construit, à qui on a appris l'Astronomie, peut prédire une Eclipse, comme la guérison, ou la mort, lorsqu'il a porté quelque tems du génie & de bons yeux à l'Ecole d'Hippocrate & au lit des Malades. C'est par cette file d'observations & de vérités qu'on par-

[a] X: donc

vient à lier à la matière l'admirable proprieté de penser, sans qu'on en puisse voir les liens, parce que le sujet de cet attribut nous est essentiellement inconnu.

Ne disons point que toute Machine, ou tout Animal, périt tout-à-fait, ou prend une autre forme, après la mort; car nous n'en savons absolument rien. Mais assurer qu'une Machine immortelle est une chimère, ou un *être de raison*, c'est faire un raisonnement aussi absurde, que celui que feroient des Chenilles, qui voyant les dépouïlles de leurs semblables, déploreroient amèrement le sort de leur espèce qui leur sembleroit s'anéantir. L'Ame de ces Insectes, (car chaque Animal a la sienne,) est trop bornée pour comprendre les Métamorphoses de la Nature. Jamais un seul des plus rusés d'entr'eux n'eût imaginé qu'il dût devenir Papillon. Il en est de même de nous. Que savons-nous plus de notre destinée, que de notre origine? Soumettons-nous donc à une ignorance invincible, de laquelle notre bonheur dépend.

Qui pensera ainsi, sera sage, juste, tranquille sur son sort, & par conséquent heureux. Il attendra la mort, sans la craindre, ni la désirer; & chérissant la vie, comprenant à peine comment le dégoût vient corrompre un coeur dans ce lieu plein de délices; plein de respect pour la Nature; plein de reconnoissance, d'attachement, & de tendresse, à proportion du sentiment, & des bienfaits qu'il en a reçus, heureux enfin de la sentir, & d'être au charmant Spectacle de l'Univers, il ne la détruira certainement jamais dans soi, ni dans les autres. Que dis-je! plein d'humanité, il en aimera le caractère jusques dans ses ennemis. Jugez comme il traitera les autres. Il plaindra les vicieux, sans les haïr; ce ne seront à ses yeux que des Hommes contrefaits. Mais en faisant grace aux défauts de la conformation de l'Esprit & du corps, il n'en admirera pas moins leurs beautés, & leurs vertus. Ceux que la Nature aura favorisés, lui paroîtront mériter plus d'égards, que ceux qu'elle aura traités en Marâtre. C'est ainsi qu'on a vû que les dons naturels, la source de tout ce qui s'acquiert, trouvent dans la bouche & le coeur du Matérialiste, des hommages que tout autre leur refuse injustement. Enfin le Matérialiste convaincu, quoi que murmure sa propre vanité, qu'il n'est qu'une Machine, ou qu'un Animal, ne maltraitera point ses semblables;

trop instruit sur la Nature de ces actions, dont l'inhumanité[a] est toujours proportionnée au degré d'Analogie prouvée ci-devant; & ne voulant pas en un mot, suivant la Loi Naturelle donnée à tous les Animaux, faire à autrui, ce qu'il ne voudroit pas qu'on lui fît.

Concluons donc hardiment que l'Homme est une Machine; & qu'il n'y a dans tout l'Univers qu'une seule substance diversement modifiée. Ce n'est point ici une Hypothese élevée à force de demandes & de suppositions: ce n'est point l'ouvrage du Préjugé, ni même de ma Raison seule; j'eusse dédaigné un Guide que je crois si peu sûr, si mes sens portant, pour ainsi dire, le flambeau, ne m'eussent engagé à la suivre, en l'éclairant. L'Expérience m'a donc parlé pour la Raison; c'est ainsi que je les ai jointes ensemble.

Mais on a dû voir que je ne me suis permis le raisonnement le plus rigoureux[b] & le plus immédiatement tiré, qu'à la suite d'une multitude d'Observations Physiques qu'aucun Savant ne contestera; & c'est encore eux seuls que je reconnois pour Juges des conséquences que j'en tire; recusant ici tout Homme à préjugés, & qui n'est ni Anatomiste, ni au fait de la seule Philosophie qui est ici de mise, celle du corps humain. Que pourroient contre un Chêne aussi ferme & solide, ces foibles Roseaux de la Théologie, de la Métaphysique & des Ecoles; Armes puériles, semblables aux fleurets de nos salles, qui peuvent bien donner le plaisir de l'Escrime, mais jamais entamer son Adversaire. Faut-il dire que je parle de ces idées creuses & triviales, de ces raisonnemens rebattus & pitoiables, qu'on fera sur la prétendüe incompatibilité de deux substances, qui se touchent & se remüent sans cesse l'une & l'autre, tant qu'il restera l'ombre du préjugé, ou de la superstition sur la Terre? Voilà mon Système, ou plutôt la Vérité, si je ne me trompe fort. Elle est courte & simple. Dispute à présent qui voudra!

[a] Y: ses actions, dont l'humanité
[b] X: vigoureux

NOTES

1. These verses, given on the title pages of editions W, X, and Y (see above, "A Note on the Text"), but no longer present in the *Oeuvres philosophiques* of 1751, are from Voltaire's "Epître à Monsieur de Genonville" (*Oeuvres*, Moland, x, 246). La Mettrie saw fit to change the final verse from an interrogation—"Hélas! périrait-il de même?"—to an affirmation. The omission of these lines and a number of other revisions in the 1751 text reflect La Mettrie's desire not to embarrass Voltaire, with whom he had since become friendly in Berlin, and on whose aid he was counting to obtain permission to return to France.

2. Contrary to Assézat and Valkhoff, who took the "Avertissement" to be by the publisher Luzac, Lemée has attributed it to La Mettrie, without, however, giving any good reason for going against the prima-facie evidence. The reprinting of the "Avertissement" in the *Oeuvres philosophiques* of 1751 lends some, but insufficient, support to Lemée's view. Although there is no way of proving that La Mettrie was *not* the author, it is pointless to insist that he was, for the "Avertissement" is altogether typical of Luzac's known attitude about the freedom of the press.

3. This paragraph, meant to camouflage the author of the book, had lost its purpose by 1751, and was removed. The skeptical tone of Luzac's remark did not prevent some readers from leaping to a false conclusion. Thus the English edition of 1749 claimed to be "translated from the French of the Marquiss d'Argens," and went on to relate quite fancifully that the work, "by the orders of a certain foreign court ... would have been sentenced to the flames, had it not been whispered into the ears of the leading men, that it had for its author no less a person than ... D'Argens, the known favourite of the court, the darling of the ladies, the terror of bigots, and the delight of men of sense."

4. This Dedication, springing from a complex of motives, is the first of several episodes in the war of satire waged between La Mettrie and the group around Albrecht von Haller. Bergmann has described the main events leading up to it (*Satiren des Herrn Maschine*, pp. 12ff.). Haller had first reviewed, in the *Göttingische Zeitungen von gelehrten Sachen* (June 1745, pp. 377-78), La Mettrie's translation of

his own annotated edition of Boerhaave's *Institutiones rei medicae*. The title page of the translation, from which Haller's name was inexplicably absent (though he was duly given credit in the Introduction), had been so worded as to leave an unsuspecting reader with the impression that La Mettrie himself was the sole author of the commentary. This, and some other circumstances, had brought from Haller an indignant charge of plagiarism, which was quite justified even though the action of La Mettrie (or of his publisher) cannot be judged—in an age when the sense of literary property was rather vague—with the severity of present-day standards.

But Haller's feelings must have continued to rankle, for when he had a chance to review La Mettrie's *Histoire naturelle de l'âme* in the same journal (June 1747, pp. 413-15), he renewed the same accusation in stronger terms and added a list of plagiarized passages. This time his protests were exaggerated and unfair; for if La Mettrie had used some illustrative material taken from Haller's edition of the *Institutiones*, he had done so with respect only to questions of technical detail, while the major arguments of the *Histoire de l'âme* remained definitely his own. The dedication of *l'Homme machine* to Haller was La Mettrie's revenge for this second review. To discomfit his accuser, La Mettrie seemingly concurred in the charge of plagiarism to the point of publicly acclaiming Haller as the source of inspiration for his own "scandalous" ideas. Moreover, the text itself of the "Dédicace" is actually a parody, adorned with erotic innuendos, of a well-known poem by Haller, the "Vergnügen an den Wissenschaften" (or "Ode an Gessner"). The stolid professor of Göttingen, who had made the error of recording the amorous sentiments of his youth with perhaps too much enthusiasm, was thereby also to prove vulnerable more than once to La Mettrie's mockery (see Bergmann's account of the later phases of the quarrel).

Haller, who was quite lacking in a sense of humor, failed apparently to recognize at the outset the sarcastic nature of the praises heaped on him in the Dedication; nor did he realize that the sly hand of La Mettrie was behind it all. Instead, his review of *l'Homme machine* (*Gött. Zeit.*, December 1747) solemnly made known the extreme distaste he felt at finding himself linked in any way to the doctrines expressed in the anonymous volume. On that occasion, as on subsequent ones, Haller's serious-minded response to La Mettrie's jests caused him to be regarded by an amused public, despite his being the morally injured party, as in some measure deserving of the ridicule he met with. But once the author of *l'Homme machine* was discovered, Haller, it seems, grew more and more anxious about the possible harm to his good name in being associated with so unsavory a figure, until finally he made a belated public statement. In a letter to Réaumur dated March 12, 1749 (and printed in the May issue of the *Journal des savants*), he swore that he had never known or corresponded with La Mettrie, had never been his teacher, and shared none of his philosophical opinions. Actually, La Mettrie's posing in the "Dédicace" as Haller's "friend and disciple" had been sheer irony, for the two had in fact never met, nor is there any evidence of an exchange of letters between them.

Despite Haller's protests—or rather because of them—La Mettrie did not remove the Dedication from the 1751 edition of the *Oeuvres philosophiques*. Instead, obviously still savouring the incident, he gave his reasons for republishing it: "C'est la nécessité de me cacher, qui m'a fait imaginer la *dédicace à M. Haller*. Je sens que c'est une double extravagance de dédier amicalement un livre aussi hardi que *l'Homme Machine*, à un savant que je n'ai jamais vu, & que 50 ans n'ont pu délivrer de tous les préjugés de l'enfance; mais je ne croyois pas que mon style m'eût trahi. Je devrois peut-être suprimer une pièce qui a fait tant crier, gémir, renier celui à qui elle est adressée, mais elle a reçu de si grands éloges publics d'écrivains, dont le suffrage est infiniment flatteur, que je n'ai pas eu ce courage. Je prends la liberté de la faire reparoître, telle qu'on l'a déjà vue dans toutes les éditions de *l'Homme machine, cum bonâ veniâ celeberrimi,* SAVANTISSIMI, PEDANTISSIMI *professoris*" (*Oeuvres*, I, 62). The need for secrecy mentioned here by La Mettrie must also be counted among his original reasons for inscribing *l'Homme machine* to Haller. He had indeed wished to remain anonymous, and it must have been keenly amusing to him to think that the stratagem of the Dedication would at once punish Haller and conceal his own identity.

The "Dédicace" may be said to have sprung from still another and subtler motive, as yet unnoticed by scholars, which probably was operative on a less conscious level of La Mettrie's mind. It is difficult to see nothing more than a coincidence in the remarkable fact that the person to whom La Mettrie dedicated *l'Homme machine* was the very same one to whom he was indebted for the scientific *pièce de résistance* of his materialist philosophy, namely, the principle of muscular irritability. Thus when La Mettrie described himself as Haller's disciple, he was being ironic in one sense, but quite sincere in another. If the text of *l'Homme machine* nowhere mentioned the fact, clearly known to its author, that Haller had been the immediate source for its theory of irritability, the Dedication represented a devious act of restitution for that oversight. Fortunately there is a little more support for such a supposition than mere psychological intuition. Haller himself later came to see La Mettrie in the guise of an "adversary-disciple." In the *Mémoires sur la nature sensible et irritable des parties du corps animal* (I, 90), he stated: "Feu M. de La Mettrie a fait de l'Irritabilité, la base du sisteme qu'il a proposé contre la spiritualité de l'ame; après avoir dit, que Stahl & Boerhaave ne l'avoient pas connue, il a le front de s'en dire l'inventeur; mais je sais par des voyes sûres, qu'il tenoit tout ce qu'il pouvoit savoir là-dessus, d'un jeune Suisse qui, sans être médecin, & sans m'avoir jamais connu, avoit lu mes ouvrages, & vu les expériences de l'illustre M. Albinus; c'est là-dessus que La Mettrie a fondé ce sisteme impie. . . ." Perhaps it was only Haller's old and stubborn estimate of La Mettrie as a plagiarist that prevented him from perceiving what was hidden behind the latter's ambiguous gesture of dedicating *l'Homme machine* to him. But the meaning of this gesture did not go wholly unnoticed by their contemporaries. To quote one example, we read in Condorcet's "Eloge de Haller": "Ces découvertes sur l'irritabilité furent pour M. de Haller l'occasion d'un chagrin très-vif. Lamétrie fit de cette propriété de la matière animée le fondement d'un système de matérialisme; et il trouva plaisant de dédier son livre à M. de Haller, et de dire que c'était à lui qu'il devait la connaissance des grandes vérités que ce livre contenait" (*Oeuvres de Condorcet*, Paris, 1847, II, 302).

5. The Italian humanist Hieronymus Fracastor (1483-1553) was, like Haller, outstanding in both medicine and poetry. He owed his reputation as a poet to a work, still highly esteemed in the eighteenth century, on the subject of syphilis (from which the disease got its name): *Syphilidis, sive morbi gallici libri tres* (1530). One of La Mettrie's literary aims was, apparently, to render it into French verse (cf. *Ouvrage de Pénélope*, II, 48).

6. A reference to La Mettrie's own *La Volupté* (1745).

7. Mlle de Bar (1688-1751), born Marie-Thérèse Quenaudon, and Alexis Piron (1689-1773), a minor writer best known for his comedy, *La Métromanie*, were married in 1741 after a liaison of some twenty years' standing. La Mettrie's remarks about her are curious, in view of the fact that in 1749 she suffered from a severe nervous disorder that left her paralyzed and insane until her death.

8. François Rebel (1701-1775), "surintendant de la musique du roi," held jointly with his friend Francoeur the post of director of the

Opéra from 1737 to 1747. He composed, in collaboration with the latter, a number of operas, ballets, and *divertissements*.

9. Voltaire's *Mérope*, which had a brilliant success on its performance in 1743, illustrated well the change that its author sought to effect in literary taste by stressing the element of pathos in tragedy. The leading part was played by Mlle Dumesnil, who scored a great personal triumph.

10. *i.e.*, the works of Voltaire.

11. Vide, Jonathan Richardson, *An Essay on the Theory of Painting*, London, 1715, pp. 3-38, passim. The work was translated into French in 1728.

12. La Mettrie probably has in mind Joseph-Juste Scaliger (1540-1609), the French classical scholar and philologist, rather than his father, Jules-César, whose name is better known in the same field. It was the son who habitually voiced his admiration for ancient authors with an excess of superlatives (cf. G. W. Robinson, "Joseph Scaliger's Estimates of Greek and Latin Authors," *Harvard Studies in Classical Philology*, XXIX (1918), pp. 133-76, passim).

The "transports" felt by Malebranche are no doubt an allusion to the story of his first encounter with Descartes's philosophy, at the age of twenty-six, when the *Traité de l'homme* came into his hands. Fontenelle had publicized the event in his "Eloge du P. Malebranche": "Il acheta le Livre, le lut avec empressement, &, ce qu'on aura peut-être peine à croire, avec un tel transport, qu'il lui en prenoit des battemens de coeur, qui l'obligeoient quelques fois d'interrompre sa lecture" (*Oeuvres de Fontenelle*, 1766, v, 392).

13. Anne-Lefèvre Dacier (1651-1720) had married in 1683 the classicist André Dacier, not only out of love, but also in the hope of collaborating with him on translations of Greek and Latin authors. As a translator, Mme Dacier eventually surpassed her husband with her own versions of the *Iliad* and *Odyssey*, Aristophanes, Terence, Plautus, Anacreon, Sappho, and others.

14. Archimedes was massacred by mistake—while he was busy drawing mathematical figures on the sand—during the violence that followed the capture of Syracuse in 212 B.C. by the Roman general, Marcellus.

15. Haller, an early devotee of mountain climbing, had found in that pastime both a source of poetic inspiration and a means of making vast studies of Alpine plants. In the belabored comparison given here by La Mettrie, Haller's investigations of mountain flora are likened to Linnaeus' botanical researches in Lapland (published in 1737 as

NOTES

the *Flora laponica*), which of course were part of a much wider system of classification. The final phrase means that the inheritance of Linnaeus, who was desperately poor as a young man, had been merely the plants of the earth.

16. Maupertuis had finally accepted Frederick's offer to settle in Berlin, where in 1746 he was made president of the newly reorganized Prussian Academy of Sciences.

17. The "frères d'Hélène" are Castor and Pollux, who were believed, when appearing in the form of St. Elmo's fire during storms, to give protection to sailors.

18. The passage on the basis of which materialism was imputed to Locke occurs in the *Essay concerning Human Understanding*, Bk. IV, Chap. iii, #6: "We have the ideas of *matter* and *thinking*, but possibly shall never be able to know whether any mere material being thinks or no; it being impossible for us, by the contemplation of our own ideas, without revelation, to discover whether Omnipotency has not given to some systems of matter, fitly disposed, a power to perceive and think, or else joined and fixed to matter, so disposed, a thinking immaterial substance: it being, in respect of our notions, not much more remote from our comprehension to conceive that GOD can, if he pleases, superadd to matter *a faculty of thinking*, than that he should superadd to it *another substance with a faculty of thinking*; since we know not wherein thinking consists, nor to what sort of substances the Almighty has been pleased to give that power, which cannot be in any created being, but merely by the good pleasure and bounty of the Creator" (Fraser edn., II, 192-93). By this Locke had meant simply to say that the metaphysical possibility of "thinking matter" could not be excluded a priori, even though he had no epistemological use for this proposition. While he held that the materiality of the mind was not demonstrable, he believed the existence of an immaterial soul to be at least "very probable." The whole metaphysical tradition involved in such problems was, of course, deeply alien to the spirit and method of Locke's theory of knowledge, a basic feature of which was the ambition to analyze the contents of the mind without having to make any presupposition about its substantial nature. Nevertheless, Locke's text was given a materialist meaning during the French Enlightenment, particularly by Voltaire. In the *Histoire naturelle de l'âme*, La Mettrie employed the current misinterpretation of Locke as an argument in support of his own position: "Et comment concevoir que la matière puisse sentir & penser? J'avoue que je ne le conçois pas; mais, outre qu'il est impie de borner la toute-

puissance du Créateur, en soutenant qu'il n'a pu faire penser la matière, lui qui d'un mot a fait la lumière, dois-je dépouiller un être des propriétés qui frappent mes sens, parce que l'essence de cet être m'est inconnue?" (I, 122-23).

If in 1748 La Mettrie's mistaken notion of what Locke had meant to say was not changed, he at least criticized it as a badly conceived version of materialism. While, on the one hand, Locke was now supposed to have said that thought is a general *metaphysical* property of matter, and, owing to its theological origin, an unintelligible property besides; *l'Homme machine*, on the other hand, regarded thought as a specifically *mechanical* property of matter, hence as the object of scientific explanation. La Mettrie's divergence here from Locke's presumed materialism is made clearer by the following passage of the *Essay* (IV, x, 10), in which, despite the metaphysical possibility of thinking matter, the very conceivability of a mechanistic theory of mind is categorically denied: "Matter, *incogitative* matter and motion, whatever changes it might produce of figure and bulk, could never produce thought. . . . Divide matter into as many parts as you will (which we are apt to imagine a sort of spiritualizing, or making a thinking thing of it), vary the figure and motion of it as much as you please—a globe, cube, cone, prism, cylinder, &c., whose diameters are but 100,000th part of a *gry*, will operate no otherwise upon other bodies of proportionable bulk, than those of an inch or foot diameter. . . . They knock, impel, and resist one another, just as the greater do; and that is all they can do."

19. The abbé Noël Pluche's popularization of science, *Le Spectacle de la nature, ou Entretiens sur les particularités de l'histoire naturelle* (Tome v, 1746, pp. 176-77), had quite typically echoed, in a passage here paraphrased by La Mettrie, the misrepresentation of Locke as a materialist: "[il] nous croit bornés au point de ne savoir pas encore si un amas de matière, un bloc de marbre, un potiron, surtout un corps rangé par manière de cerveau (quoiqu'il connoisse un cerveau beaucoup moins qu'un potiron) ne pourroit pas avoir la puissance de penser, d'appercevoir, de juger, & de raisonner. . . . On est après cela fort surpris qu'un homme qui exténue & matérialise la raison jusqu'à la confondre avec une masse de boue, ou avec un tourbillonnet de poussière, ose placer cette raison sur un Tribunal souverain pour juger en dernier ressort de la foi, & pour décider de ce que Dieu a dû ou non nous proposer à croire." The same volume contained a statement (cf. pp. 135-40) about the futility of the scientist's aim to understand human nature via the organic functions, which, probably taken

by La Mettrie as a retort to his newly published *Histoire de l'âme*, might well have led him in *l'Homme machine* to single out the mediocre Pluche for attack.

20. See, for example, Pliny's *Natural History* (vii, 1), where various reflections on the physical inferiority with which man, as compared to the animals, enters the world, induce a mood of pagan pessimism about the "human condition": "Heu dementiam ab iis initiis existimantium ad superbiam se genetos"; and: "Itaque multi exstitere, qui non nasci optimum censerent, aut quam ocissime aboleri."

21. Compare with Voltaire's *Lettres philosophiques* (éd. Naves, p. 66): "Il importe peu à la Religion de quelle substance soit l'âme, pourvu qu'elle soit vertueuse."

22. Evangelista Torricelli (1608-47), a disciple of Galileo, was professor of mathematics in the Florentine Academy. His famous experiment of 1643 proved that the column of mercury in a "Torricelli tube" rose in relation to atmospheric pressure and its own specific gravity. The discovery of this principle was one of the turning points in seventeenth-century science, because, by discrediting the notion of a *horror vacui*, it helped to overthrow Aristotelian "occultism" in favor of the experimental-mathematical method of modern physics.

23. The simile comes from Mme Du Châtelet, whom La Mettrie regarded as a leading exponent of the experimental method: "Souvenez-vous . . . que l'Expérience est le bâton que la nature a donné à nous autres aveugles, pour nous conduire dans nos recherches; nous ne laissons pas avec son secours de faire bien du chemin, mais nous ne pouvons manquer de tomber si nous cessons de nous en servir" (*Institutions de physique*, Paris, 1740, p. 10).

24. La Mettrie himself, in the *Histoire naturelle de l'âme* (i, 174).

25. The Hippocratic humoral doctrines had been greatly emphasized in the works of Galen (born c. 130 A.D.), with the result that his opinions about the dependence of the temperament on the physical constitution seemed often like an ancient foreshadowing of La Mettrie's philosophy.

Descartes took up the same theme as part of his ambitious, but still immature plan to found a system of scientific medicine on the general principles of mechanics. By such a step he had intended not only to replace the hit-or-miss practice of the *empyriques*, but to utilize concrete knowledge about the interdependence of mind and body in order to extend the competence of medicine into the psychological and ethical realms. Accordingly, the Sixth Book of the *Discours de la méthode* stressed, among the blessings to humanity of the new physics, "la conservation de la santé, laquelle est sans doute le premier bien et le fondement de tous les autres biens de cette vie; car même l'esprit dépend si fort du tempérament, et de la disposition des organes du corps que, s'il est possible de trouver quelque moyen qui rende communément les hommes plus sages et plus habiles qu'ils n'ont été jusques ici, je crois que c'est dans la médecine qu'on doit le chercher" (éd. Gilson, p. 62). It was almost the same ideal, with its twin features of a scientific medicine based on the certainty of mechanics and its aim of merging psychiatry and ethics, that inspired *l'Homme machine*. La Mettrie, however, presented the ideal in a new philosophical context and with the advantage of a more advanced physiology than Descartes had known. Thanks to La Mettrie, Descartes's visionary hopes about the destiny of medicine were at last taking root.

26. Canus Julius, sentenced on a charge of conspiracy under Caligula, is reputed to have calmly played chess with a friend while the moment of execution drew near. Regarding death as a sort of philosophic adventure, he spent his last minutes in assuring his friends that after he had learned about the state of the soul in the next life, he would return to enlighten them. The story of Canus Julius was admiringly told in Seneca's *De tranquillitate animi* (Chap. 14). However, La Mettrie's allusion was suggested by Gaubius (*De regimine mentis*, 1747, pp. 31-32), who had already explained the Roman's courage on purely physiological grounds.

Seneca, the Stoic philosopher and tragedian, was commanded by Nero, whose tutor he had formerly been, to commit suicide as the penalty for his involvement in the conspiracy of Piso. From the moment of receiving this order until his death, Seneca's conduct was a model of Stoic fortitude and self-mastery.

The Roman satirist Petronius, who was in all probability Nero's *arbiter elegantiae* of the same name, committed suicide after his arrest for having incurred the Emperor's wrath. Causing the blood to drain leisurely from his veins, he is said to have devoted his last hours to literary and gastronomic pleasures.

27. The role of the liver and spleen in the etiology of the numerous physical and neurotic complaints classed formerly under the heading of hypochondria, goes back of course to the humoral teachings of the Hippocratic and Galenic schools. It was still universally accepted in the eighteenth century that dysfunction of those viscera produced the "hysterico-hypochondriacal affections," although many different explanations were given about the exact manner in which this took

place. La Mettrie echoes here the wide-spread belief that hypochondria resulted from an obstruction of the flow of blood in the spleen and liver, supposedly causing distension and a "stagnation of humors" in those organs. That congestion of the portal vein could also produce the same type of disorder was suggested by its position in the hypochondrium and its close anatomical links with the spleen and liver. This particular notion owed much of its vogue in the eighteenth century to Stahl's *De venae portae porta malorum hypochondriaco-splenetico-suffocativo-hysterico-haemorrhoïdariorum* (1698).

28. The therapeutic effect of shock with regard to nervous and mental disorders was generally known to the eighteenth century, and was even used occasionally as a successful method of treatment. Concerning specifically the fear of fire in the cure of hysterical paralysis, La Mettrie might have remembered, among other sources, a passage in Stahl's *Theoria medica vera*: "Quant à nous, nous avons été témoin de deux cas de ce genre dans un incendie. C'étaient deux femmes atteintes de douleurs *arthritico-goutteuses*, qui ne pouvaient absolument faire aucun usage de leurs membres; effrayées à la vue du péril, frappées de terreur et comme affligées de ne pouvoir sauver le poids trop lourd de leurs membres, oubliant aussitôt et leurs douleurs et leur extrême faiblesse, elles firent un violent et suprême effort pour se soulever; le double résultat de cette vive volonté énergique fut non-seulement la guérison complète de leur double affection *goutteuse* et *arthritique*, mais encore la libre et facile exécution ultérieure de tous leurs mouvements" (G. E. Stahl, *Oeuvres médico-philosophiques et pratiques*, traduites et commentées par T. Blondin, Paris, 1859-64, III, 471).

29. La Mettrie removed this passage probably out of deference for the land of philosophic liberty. The notion that the "ferocity" of the English came from their consumption of meat was fairly current in eighteenth-century France. Rousseau, for example, remarks in *La Nouvelle Héloïse* (IV, x): "Vous autres Anglais, grands mangeurs de viande, avez dans vos inflexibles vertus quelque chose de dur qui tient de la barbarie."

30. Cf. Alexander Pope, *Moral Essays*, Epistle 1 (1733), ll. 71-76, 77-80.

31. The wording was changed here because La Mettrie's original plan to disguise himself by pretending to be a friend and compatriot of Haller's, who was Swiss by birth, had lost its purpose.

32. The origin and truth of this anecdote remain unverified. Hans-Ludwig Steiger (1688-1745), proprietor of Wittigkofen, who belonged to an old, noble, and highly ramified family of Berne, held the rank

of bailiff of Schenkenberg from 1737 to 1743. He was mentioned again in *Le petit homme à longue queue,* where it was prankishly related that Haller had introduced his "disciple" La Mettrie "chez ce célèbre Mr. Steiguer de Wittighoffen, si excellent Juge avant-Diner, & qui tenoit un véritable Hôtel de Rambouillet; avec cette heureuse différence, qu'au lieu d'un précieux Bel Esprit, la Philosophie levant hardiment la tête, les plus grandes questions y étoient agitées avec cette liberté de penser, sans laquelle l'homme dégénère. . . . C'est là sans doute, que mené par la main au Temple de l'incrédulité . . . l'Auteur de *l'Homme machine* aura puisé les Principes de son Ouvrage, aura trouvé les saints débris, sur lesquels il s'est fièrement élevé."

33. La Mettrie's reference here is slightly in error, for Van Helmont had actually placed the seat of the soul in the upper opening of the stomach, or the cardiac orifice. The confusion was caused no doubt by the fact that Van Helmont had also attributed to the pylorus, or the lower opening, a fantastic importance, making it the over-all regulator of the digestive process and the source of a great many pathological conditions. However, his locating the soul in the epigastric region was part of a tradition that went back to antiquity, the basis for which was the physical sensation commonly experienced there as the result of emotion. For Van Helmont's exposition of his doctrine, see *Opera omnia,* Frankfurt, 1682, pp. 272-78. Envisaging things in the context of a mystical vitalism inherited mainly from Paracelsus, he described the *Archaeus* (or soul) lodged in the cardiac orifice as an offshoot of the *anima mundi,* and as the agent that controlled the various subordinate "archaei" activating each of the bodily organs. Van Helmont's entire viewpoint was thus in reality quite remote from that of La Mettrie.

34. These lines are paraphrased from the abbé Jacques Pernetti's *Lettres philosophiques sur les physionomies,* La Haye, 1746, pp. 109-10.

35. These physiognomic interpretations are La Mettrie's own, although in his coupling of "eagle-eyes" with genius he has apparently followed the advice of Pernetti, who, believing that the eyes reveal the inner man, had said: "Je me contente de vous mettre sur les voies: c'est à vous d'aller au-delà, & d'en tirer les inductions que vous croïez pouvoir vous convenir" (*op.cit.,* p. 242). Concerning the broader reasons for La Mettrie's interest in Pernetti, see above, Chapter iv.

36. The allusion here is to Voltaire. La Mettrie is supposed to have confessed that his remark "n'était vraie qu'à demi."

37. Henri, duc de Guise, whose power as head of the Catholic party in the Wars of the League had come to overshadow that of the King,

was murdered at Blois on December 23, 1588, by order of Henri III. Actually, Philippe Hurault (1528-99), comte de Chiverny and *Chancelier de France*, was not alone in foreseeing this event, for the Duke had in fact gone to Blois despite strong warnings by many of his friends.

38. For La Mettrie's views on heredity, see note 119.

39. The Italian physician Giovanni Lancisi (1654-1720) is perhaps best known for his contributions to the study of malaria and aneurysms. His theory about the location of the *sensorium commune* was offered in the *Dissertatio altera de sede cogitantis animae* (1712) (*Opera*, Geneva, 1718, II, 302-18). In choosing the *corpus callosum* as the seat of the soul, Lancisi was guided essentially by such anatomical evidence as its medial position in the brain, its fibrous composition, its non-geminate structure, and so forth.

40. François Gigot de La Peyronie (1678-1747) was appointed in 1736 to the post of *premier chirurgien du roi*. Using his influence with Louis XV to secure for the corps of surgeons a more favored position in France, he obtained royal permission for the establishment of the Académie de chirurgie in 1731.

While La Peyronie had as early as 1709 (in a memoir read to the Société des Sciences de Montpellier) regarded the *corpus callosum* as the seat of the soul, a fuller treatment of the subject was given in his "Observations par lesquelles on tâche de découvrir la partie du cerveau où l'âme exerce ses fonctions," published in the *Mémoires de l'académie royale des sciences* for 1741 (ed. in-4°, pp. 199-218). The article described how autopsies of patients who had suffered losses of consciousness or sensation invariably showed injury to the *corpus callosum*, and came to the conclusion that the *sensorium commune* is lodged in that part of the brain. If La Peyronie, in contrast to Lancisi's anatomical approach, relied almost wholly on neurological data, this of course did not render his theory less erroneous. However, his efforts represented at least a significant advance in methodology over most of the earlier theorizing in the field, as La Peyronie himself was well aware: "Il faut certainement suivre une route différente pour nous conduire avec quelque sureté dans la recherche du siège de l'Ame: c'est d'observations en observations que nous devons remonter jusqu'à ce premier organe; ce n'est que par un enchaînement de faits puisés dans la Nature qu'on peut développer un pareil mystère" (*ibid.*, p. 201).

41. Thomas Willis (1621-1675), the English anatomist and physician, was named in 1660 to the Sedleian chair of natural philosophy at Oxford. His several treatises on the anatomy and pathology of the nervous

system—*De cerebri anatome, cui accessit nervorum descriptio et usus* (1664), *Pathologiae cerebri et nervosi generis specimen* (1667), *Affectionum quae dicuntur hystericae et hypocondriacae pathologia spasmodica vindicata* (1670), *De anima brutorum, quae hominis vitalis et sensitiva est* (1672)—assure to Willis a place of honor among the early pioneers of neurophysiology and neuropsychiatry. His writings proved to be a rich mine of facts and theories on which La Mettrie was able to draw for confirmation and illustration of the man-machine philosophy. Particularly in *De cerebri anatome*, which was the most influential of Willis' works and remained an authoritative treatment of the subject well into the eighteenth century, a remarkably accurate description was given of the human brain which, moreover, it was the author's method to compare repeatedly with the brains of a variety of animals —sheep, dog, cat, fox, calf, horse, fowl, fish, etc. Willis thereby laid the foundations of a comparative anatomy of the nervous system. He employed the same comparative method to frame hypotheses concerning the set of problems that perhaps interested him most of all, namely, the cerebral localizations of the intellectual, sensory, motor, and emotive functions. In the elaborate topography—frequently erroneous in detail but extremely promising in outline—which he worked out, the medullar substance of the main hemispheres was made the organ of volition, memory, imagination, etc., while the cerebellum and midbrain were assigned the responsibility for sensation and involuntary actions. If Willis resisted the temptation to draw materialist consequences from his neurological opinions, he nonetheless consistently traced all vital, motor, and psychic phenomena to physiological factors, which he sought moreover to define concretely. His works were also full of clinical observations which allowed him to explain mental and nervous maladies exclusively in terms of alterations of the central nervous system. But while Willis ostensibly regarded the brain and the whole organism as a machine, the mechanistic aspect of his theorizing was very much blurred both by an incipient animism and by his strong predilection for iatrochemical concepts.

42. Cf., Fontenelle, *Dialogues des morts*, "Charles V et Erasme": "Quoi! l'esprit ne consiste-t-il pas dans une certaine conformation du cerveau, & le hasard est-il moindre, de naître avec un cerveau bien disposé, que de naître d'un père qui soit Roi? Vous étiez un grand génie: mais demandez à tous les Philosophes à quoi il tenoit que vous ne fussiez stupide & hébété; presque à rien, à une petite disposition de fibres; enfin, à quelque chose que l'anatomie la plus délicate ne sauroit jamais appercevoir." The theme of this particular dialogue, as indi-

cated by Charles V's remark, is that a person's mental capacity is a matter not of choice, but of chance, "pourvu qu'on donne ce nom à un ordre que l'on ne connoît point."

43. Willis (*De cerebri anatome*, xiii) had placed the *sensorium commune* in the *corpora striata* (*corps cannelés*) mainly because of their anatomically central position on the pathways of communication between the upper brain, the cerebellum, and the medulla oblongata: "These bodies, placed between the Brain and its Appendix, are the great and common diverting places of either; to wit, which receive whatsoever impulses or forces of the Animal Spirits are sent from either, and communicate them presently to the other; Or that I may speak more plainly, this part is the common Sensory . . . that receives the strokes of all sensible things, dilated from the Nerves of every Organ, and so causes the perception of every sense." However, for the important role assigned to the *corpus striatum*, Willis had also utilized his own clinical experience: "Further, that these bodies . . . perform the offices of the first Sensory, besides the fabrick of their parts, and the Analogy to be collected thence of their use, it seems yet more certainly to appear from some Observations concerning these chamfered bodies, after what manner they are affected in Paralytick diseases. For as often as I have opened the bodies of those who dyed of a long Palsie, and most grievous resolution of the Nerves, I always found these bodies less firm than others in the Brain, discoloured like filth or dirt, and many chamferings obliterated. Further, in Whelps newly littered, that want their sight, and hardly perform the other faculties of motion and sense, these streaks or chamferings, being scarce wholly formed, appear only rude" (*Dr. Willis's Practice of Physick*, trans. S. Pordage, London, 1683-84; *The Anatomy of the Brain*, p. 84). La Mettrie's reference, by the way, is a bit inexact, for Willis said nothing about the state of the *corpora striata* in children or birds. Also, the first clause of La Mettrie's sentence should be read independently of the allusion to Willis.

44. The *protubérance annulaire* is the *Pons Varolii*. The nates and testes compose together the corpora quadrigemina, the former being the superior colliculi, the latter the inferior colliculi. The actual functions of these bodies, which constitute respectively optic and auditory reflex centers and relays in the midbrain, were wholly unknown in the period of Willis and La Mettrie.

Willis' researches in comparative brain anatomy had disclosed an inverse ratio between the size of the annulary protuberance and that of the nates and testes; so that, in the different species compared by him, when the former was observed to be large, the latter tended to be small, and vice versa. As an interpretation of these facts, Willis assumed (rather fancifully, as it turned out) that the *Pons Varolii*, considered to be the instrument of the passions, was well-formed in those animals (such as man, dog, cat, and fox) that required strong motivation in order to act, but in whom the deficiency of instinct was compensated by a greater aptitude for learning; whereas the corpora quadrigemina, regarded as the organic seat of the instincts, was supposed to be well developed in animals like the calf, sheep, and hog, which showed more perfect instinctual behavior, but less docility. Thus, according to Willis, the inverse relationship between these two cerebral organs was the physiological basis of the inverse ratio, beyond a given point, between instinct and intelligence in both man and the animals (see *De cerebri anatome*, xviii).

45. "Homme des bois" and "Homme sauvage" are both literal translations of the term orangutan, which in the eighteenth century was still commonly used in a generic way to designate the anthropoid apes. An important source of La Mettrie's knowledge about the latter was the work of Nicolas Tulpius (see note 94): *Observationes medicae* (Amsterdam, 1641, Bk. III, Chap. 56), which contained the oldest authentic description of the chimpanzee. The author had mistakenly referred the live Angolan chimpanzee examined by him to the same species as the orangutan of Borneo and Sumatra, naming it, furthermore, *satyre indien* in the belief that it was descended from the satyrs of antiquity. Tulpius' error of classification had not been corrected yet in the time of La Mettrie, whose "grand Singe" would consequently include both the chimpanzee and the orangutan—the gorilla being, of course, still unknown. Already in the *Histoire de l'âme*, La Mettrie had entertained the notion of linguistic experimentation with the anthropoids, complaining that Tulpius' account was deficient particularly in regard to the ape's mentality: "Cet auteur ne parle du satyre qu'il a vu, que comme d'un animal: il n'est occupé qu'à décrire les parties de son corps, sans faire mention s'il parloit & s'il avoit des idées. Mais cette parfaite ressemblance qu'il reconnoît entre le corps du satyre & celui des autres hommes, me fait croire que le cerveau de ce prétendu animal est originairement fait pour sentir & penser comme les nôtres" (I, 224-25). An overestimation such as this was owing at least in part to the fact that, around 1750, anthropoid apes, specially live ones, were still rarities in Europe, and that scientifically reliable information about their behavior was not available.

46. Johann Conrad Amman (1669-1730), a physician of Swiss birth who had settled in Amsterdam, made pioneering advances in the *oral*

method of instructing deaf-mutes. The technique developed by him, based on original investigations in phonetics and in voice physiology, was set forth at length in his *Surdus loquens* (1692). His purpose was to enable the deaf-mute to articulate the different speech sounds after having first ascertained, by means of touch and sight, the corresponding dispositions of the vocal apparatus. When La Mettrie wrote, there was as yet no proved or established system of deaf-mute education, and the occasionally successful instruction that did take place was regarded still with a good deal of amazement. See, for example, an article in the *Journal des savans* for December 1747 (pp. 513-20), which described the training of a deaf-mute by the oral method. Buffon said of this particular case that the results were so impressive as to warrant bringing the pupil to a session of the Académie des sciences, in order that its members might observe him (*Histoire naturelle de l'homme*, "Du sens de l'ouïe").

47. The *Histoire de l'âme* had given a detailed account of Amman's methods (I, 209-18), because these seemed to attest the physiological basis of language and, consequently, of the formation of ideas. La Mettrie was all the more eager to give a mechanistic explanation of the origin of language, because the ability to speak had long since been put forth, mainly by the Cartesian school, as the crucial trait that distinguished man from the mere *bête machine*. The effort to break down this distinction, vitiated here by La Mettrie's ambiguous use of "speech" and "language" as equivalent concepts, pursues two lines of argument which converge without quite meeting. It is claimed, in the first place, that speech is not necessarily innate to man, and can be developed in some cases by purely mechanical means (i.e. Amman's method). Secondly, it is conjectured that apes, if similarly instructed, would acquire the same faculty.

48. Concerning the comparative anatomy of anthropoids, La Mettrie might have had some knowledge of Edward Tyson's *Orang-outang, sive homo sylvestris; or, the anatomy of a Pygmie compared with that of a Monkey, an Ape, and a Man* (1699), which described (pp. 51-52, 54-57) the conformity between the speech organs and brain of man and the chimpanzee in such a manner as to bolster the hope of some day teaching the latter to speak. For his insistence on these analogies and on the educability of the ape, La Mettrie has been hailed by some critics as an early exponent of evolutionism. Actually, the context here is not concerned with the theme of biological evolution, which, however, will be exploited later in the *Système d'Epicure*. In his search for parallels between the linguistic and mental capabilities of man and the

ape, La Mettrie is interested mainly in finding experimental proof of the man-machine thesis. For if the physical organization of the two species was indeed similar—and the eighteenth century tended to exaggerate the similarity—then it followed from the *homme machine* theory that apes and human beings would have to think and act in much the same fashion, which of course was not the case. The background of this dilemma, which La Mettrie could not escape, may be seen in the pioneering contributions to comparative anatomy published by Claude Perrault some seventy-five years earlier. Perrault and his co-workers at the Académie royale des sciences, impressed in particular by the close resemblance between the vocal apparatus of homo sapiens and that of some monkeys dissected by them, had been led to reject any simply mechanistic theory of speech: "Les Muscles de l'Os Hyoïde, de la Langue, du Larynx, & du Pharynx, qui servent la pluspart à articuler la parole, estoient entièrement semblables à ceux de l'Homme, & beaucoup plus que ceux de la Main; dont néanmoins le Singe, qui ne parle point, se sert presque avec autant de perfection que l'Homme: ce qui fait voir que la parole est une action plus particulière à l'Homme, & qui le distingue davantage des Brutes que la Main. . . . Car le Singe se trouve pourveû par la Nature de tous ces Organes merveilleux de la parole avec tant d'exactitude, que mesme les trois petits Muscles qui prennent leur origine de l'Apophyse Styloïde, ne luy manquent pas, quoy-que cette Apophyse soit extrêmement petite. Cette particularité fait encore voir que ceux-là n'ont pas raison, qui tiennent que les agens exercent leurs actions, parce qu'il se rencontre qu'ils ont des Organes pour cela: car selon ces Philosophes les Singes devroient parler, puisqu'ils ont les instrumens nécessaires à la parole" (*Mémoires pour servir à l'histoire naturelle des animaux*, Paris, 1676, p. 126). These remarks reveal the meaning of La Mettrie's desire to educate the ape—a project that is further explained by the following words of Buffon, which, while reflecting the logic of the passage just quoted, obviously allude to *l'Homme machine*: "L'âme, la pensée, la parole ne dépendent donc pas de la forme ou de l'organisation du corps; rien ne prouve mieux que c'est un don particulier et fait à l'homme seul, puisque l'orang-outang, qui ne parle ni ne pense, a néanmoins le corps, les membres, les sens, le cerveau et la langue entièrement semblables à l'homme, puisqu'il peut faire ou contrefaire tous les mouvements, toutes les actions humaines, et que cependant il ne fait aucun acte de l'homme. C'est peut-être faute d'éducation? c'est encore faute d'équité dans votre jugement" (*Histoire des animaux*, "Nomenclature des singes"). La Mettrie himself would seem to have realized the cogency of such objections; because, if on some occasions the plan of educating the ape was proposed by him "for the sake of the argument," at other times he could not mention the scheme without a note of wry humor: "Un philosophe eût parlé de l'adresse, de l'air vif, de l'esprit du singe, de sa facilité à être instruit &c. & nous eût, comme l'auteur de *l'Homme machine, Singifiés* avec tout l'agrément dont cet étrange *Paradoxe* est susceptible" (*Ouvrage de Pénélope*, II, 72).

49. This delightful tale, told in Sir William Temple's *Memoirs of what passed in Christendom from 1672 to 1679*, was quoted as follows in Locke's *Essay concerning Human Understanding* (II, xxvii, 9): " 'I had a mind to know, from Prince Maurice's own mouth, the account of a common, but much credited, story, that I had heard so often from many others, of an old parrot he had in Brazil, during his government there, that spoke, and asked, and answered common questions, like a reasonable creature: so that those of his train there generally concluded it to be witchery or possession; and one of his chaplains, who lived long afterwards in Holland, would never from that time endure a parrot, but said they all had a devil in them. I had heard many particulars of this story, and assevered by people hard to be discredited, which made me ask Prince Maurice what there was of it. He said, with his usual plainness and dryness in talk, there was something true, but a great deal false of what had been reported. I desired to know of him what there was of the first. He told me short and coldly, that he had heard of such an old parrot when he had been at Brazil; and though he believed nothing of it, and it was a good way off, yet he had so much curiosity as to send for it: that it was a very great and a very old one; and when it came first into the room where the prince was, with a great many Dutchmen about him, it said presently, *What a company of white men are here!* They asked it, what it thought that man was, pointing to the prince. It answered, *Some General or other*. When they brought it close to him, he asked it, *D'où venez-vous?* It answered, *De Marinnan*. The Prince asked, *A qui estes-vous?* The parrot, *A un Portugais*. The Prince, *Que fais-tu là?* Parrot, *Je garde les poulles*. The Prince laughed, and said, *Vous gardez les poulles?* The parrot answered, *Oui, moi; et je sçai bien faire*; and made the chuck four or five times that people use to make to chickens when they call them. I set down the words of this worthy dialogue in French, just as Prince Maurice said them to me. I asked him in what language the parrot spoke, and he said in Brazilian. I asked whether he under-

stood Brazilian; he said No, but he had taken care to have two interpreters by him'" (Fraser edn., 1, 446-47).

Incidentally, La Mettrie's interest in the "talking parrot" has little to do with the reason for which the anecdote figured in the *Essay*. Locke used it in connection with the problem of identity, and concluded therefrom that even if a parrot were thought to be capable of discoursing rationally, we would still follow Temple in regarding it as a parrot rather than a human being, because our idea of the latter implies more than just the ability to speak. La Mettrie is unfair to Locke in assuming that he accepted Temple's story at face value, for the philosophical end it served did not at all require that Locke himself should consider it true, but merely that someone should.

50. The 1745 edition of the *Histoire de l'âme* (p. 389) contained the following remark (deleted in 1751): "Pour ce qui est du Perroquet raisonnable de M. Locke, c'est un mauvais Conte qu'un aussi bon esprit devoit rejetter." If in *l'Homme machine* La Mettrie seems less scornful of the talking parrot, this is not because he has grown credulous; he merely wishes now to insist that it is sometimes necessary, in the interests of science, to go rashly against common experience and to assume the "impossible." But in *Les animaux plus que machines* he will again become cautious: "[les animaux] n'ont point les organes de la parole: & quand ils les auroient, quel parti pourroient-ils en tirer, puisque les plus spirituels d'entr'eux & les mieux élevés ne prononcent que des sons qu'ils ne comprennent en aucune manière, & parlent toujours, comme nous parlons souvent, sans s'entendre, à moins que vous ne vouliez excepter le perroquet du chevalier Temple, que je ne puis voir sans rire aggrégé à l'humanité, par un métaphysicien qui croyoit à peine en Dieu" (II, 83-84).

51. Abraham Trembley (1700-84), the Genevese naturalist, made one of the most startling discoveries of eighteenth-century biology when, in 1739, he observed that a variety of fresh-water polyp (*Chlorohydra viridissima*), despite its animal characteristics, could reproduce asexually by budding and multiply by artificial division. His investigations of this phenomenon, published as the *Mémoires pour servir à l'histoire d'un genre de polypes d'eau douce, à bras en forme de cornes* (Leyden & Paris, 1744), had a strong impact on some of the leading scientists of the day. Besides La Mettrie, such figures as Réaumur, Bonnet, Maupertuis, Jussieu, Needham, and Buffon found variously in the polyp's anomalous behavior fresh motives for biological speculation, which resulted in the framing of several new theories concerning, in particular, the causes of generation, the differentiae between vegeta-

tive and animal life, the problem of "animal soul," and the nature of the vital principle itself. For a thorough account of Trembley's discovery and of its importance in the history of science, consult John R. Baker, *Abraham Trembley of Geneva: Scientist and Philosopher*, London, 1952.

52. La Mettrie's optimism in this section about the educability of the ape is largely explained by the fact that the eighteenth century, owing to the vagueness of its anthropological knowledge, believed that some primitive peoples led mental lives which were hardly above the anthropoid level. Such an assimilation of the savage to the ape may be found, for example, in Montesquieu's *Lettres persanes* (CVI): "Il y a encore des peuples sur la terre, chez lesquels un singe passablement instruit pourroit vivre avec honneur; il s'y trouveroit, à peu près, à la portée des autres habitants; on ne lui trouveroit point l'esprit singulier, ni le caractère bizarre; il passeroit tout comme un autre, et seroit même distingué par sa gentillesse" (*Oeuvres complètes*, éd. Laboulaye, Paris, 1875, I, 334).

La Mettrie's views about the affinity between man and the anthropoids were to be echoed some years later in Rousseau's *Discours sur l'origine de l'inégalité* (footnote K). From descriptions of the ape available at the time, Rousseau was led to wonder "si divers animaux semblables aux hommes, pris par les voyageurs pour des bêtes sans beaucoup d'examen, ou à cause de quelques différences qu'ils remarquaient dans la conformation extérieure, ou seulement parce que ces animaux ne parlaient pas, ne seraient point en effet de véritables hommes sauvages, dont la race dispersée anciennement dans les bois n'avait eu occasion de développer aucune de ses facultés virtuelles, n'avait acquis aucun degré de perfection, et se trouvait encore dans l'état primitif de nature" (*Oeuvres complètes*, éd. Musset-Pathay, 1823, I, 337). At this juncture, La Mettrie's ideas happened to coincide so well with Rousseau's hypothesis of the *état de nature*, that the latter went on to treat the problem of linguistic capability in a manner which is clearly reminiscent of *l'Homme machine*: "On ne voit point . . . les raisons sur lesquelles les auteurs se fondent pour refuser aux animaux en question le nom d'hommes sauvages: mais il est aisé de conjecturer que c'est à cause de leur stupidité, et aussi parce qu'ils ne parlaient pas; raisons faibles pour ceux qui savent que, quoique l'organe de la parole soit naturel à l'homme, la parole elle-même ne lui est pourtant pas naturelle, et qui connaissent jusqu'à quel point sa perfectibilité peut avoir élevé l'homme civil au-dessus de son état originel" (*ibid.*, 339).

53. La Mettrie here misapplies to the philosophy of Leibniz the term

"intuitive knowledge," which, according to the latter's hierarchy of cognitive categories, denoted the most perfect form of the idea, as exemplified by mathematical or purely logical concepts. La Mettrie would appear to have in mind what Leibniz described as "clear knowledge of the indistinct type," placing it at the bottom of his epistemological ladder (cf. "Meditationes de Cognitione, Veritate et Ideis," *Die philosophischen Schriften von Leibniz*, herausgeg. v. C. J. Gerhardt, Berlin, 1875-90, IV, 422).

54. In the *Histoire naturelle de l'âme*, La Mettrie had quoted almost the complete text of the account of the "sourd de Chartres" given in the *Histoire de l'Académie royale des sciences* (1703, in-4°, pp. 18-19): "M. Felibien, de l'Académie des Inscriptions, fit sçavoir à l'Académie des Sciences un événement singulier, peut-être inoui, qui venoit d'arriver à Chartres. Un jeune Homme de 23 à 24 ans, fils d'un Artisan, sourd & muet de naissance, commença tout d'un coup à parler, au grand étonnement de toute la Ville. On sçut de lui que quelques trois ou quatre mois auparavant il avoit entendu le son des Cloches, & avoit été extrêmement surpris de cette sensation nouvelle & inconnue. Ensuite il lui étoit sorti une espèce d'eau de l'oreille gauche, & il avoit entendu parfaitement des deux oreilles. Il fut ces trois ou quatre mois à écouter sans rien dire, s'accoutumant à répéter tout-bas les paroles qu'il entendoient, & s'affermissant dans la prononciation & dans les idées attachées aux mots. Enfin il se crut en état de rompre le silence, & il déclara qu'il parloit, quoique ce ne fût encore qu'imparfaitement. Aussi-tôt des Théologiens habiles l'interrogèrent sur son état passé, & leurs principales questions roulèrent sur Dieu, sur l'Ame, sur la bonté ou la malice morale des actions. Il ne parut pas avoir poussé ses pensées jusques-là. Quoiqu'il fût né de parents Catholiques, qu'il assistât à la Messe, qu'il fût instruit à faire le signe de la Croix, & à se mettre à genoux dans la contenance d'un homme qui prie, il n'avoit jamais joint à tout cela aucune intention, ni compris celle que les autres y joignoient. Il ne sçavoit pas bien distinctement ce que c'étoit que la mort, & il n'y pensoit jamais. Il menoit une vie purement animale, tout occupé des objets sensibles & présens, & du peu d'idées qu'il recevoit par les yeux. Il ne tiroit pas même de la comparaison de ces idées tout ce qu'il semble qu'il en auroit pû tirer. Ce n'est pas qu'il n'eût naturellement de l'esprit; mais l'esprit d'un homme privé du commerce des autres est si peu exercé, & si peu cultivé, qu'il ne pense qu'autant qu'il y est indispensablement forcé par les objets extérieurs. Le plus grand fonds des idées des hommes est dans leur commerce réciproque."

Condillac, incidentally, discussed this case in his *Essai sur l'origine des connaissances humaines* of 1746 (I, 4, ii), and expressed the view that the deaf-mute in question, before having learned to speak and communicate with others, must have been devoid of all ideas as such, even though he had lacked neither sensations nor instincts.

55. The immediate source of this opinion on the evolution of language was Condillac's *Origine des connaissances humaines* (II, 1, i). The idea that the "cri de la nature" once formed the basis of linguistic expression—which as a psychological theory will soon have an important role both in Rousseau's "Second Discourse" and in Diderot's esthetics—is stated more fully by La Mettrie in *Les Animaux plus que machines*: "Si les hommes parlent, ils doivent songer qu'ils n'ont pas toujours parlé. Tant qu'ils n'ont été qu'à l'école de la nature, des sons inarticulés, tels que ceux des animaux, ont été leur premier langage. Antérieur à l'art & à la parole, c'est celui de la machine, il n'appartient qu'à elle. Par combien d'ailleurs de gestes & de signes, le langage le plus muet peut-il se faire entendre! quelle expression naïve & ingénue! quelle énergie, dont tout le monde est frappé, que tout le monde comprend . . . quoi, faut-il donc parler, pour paroître sentir & réfléchir? parle assez, qui montre du sentiment" (II, 32). It is worth mentioning that Diderot's *Lettre sur les sourds et muets*, which derived a new conception of poetry from assumptions similar to those of the above passage, appeared in 1751, only one year after *Les Animaux plus que machines*.

56. A detailed description of this case may be found in the *Système d'Epicure* (III, 221-22): "J'ai vu cette femme sans sexe, animal indéfinissable, tout à fait châtré dans le sein maternel. Elle n'avoit ni motte, ni clitoris, ni tettons, ni vulve, ni grandes levres, ni vagin, ni matrice, ni regles; & en voici la preuve. On touchoit par l'anus la sonde introduite par l'uretre; le bistouri profondément introduit à l'endroit où est toujours la grande fente dans les femmes, ne perçoit que des graisses & des chairs peu vasculeuses, qui donnoient peu de sang; il fallut renoncer au projet de lui faire une vulve, & la démarier après dix ans de mariage avec un paysan aussi imbécille qu'elle, qui n'étant point au fait, n'avoit eu garde d'instruire sa femme de ce qui lui manquoit. Il croyoit bonnement que la voie des selles étoit celle de la génération, & il agissoit en conséquence, aimant fort sa femme qui l'aimoit aussi beaucoup, & étoit très fâchée que son secret eût été découvert. Mr. le comte d'Erouville, lieutenant-général, tous les médecins & chirurgiens de Gand, ont vu cette femme manquée, & en ont dressé un procès verbal. Elle étoit absolument dépourvue de tout sentiment du plaisir

vénérien; on avoit beau chatouiller le siege du clitoris absent, il n'en résultoit aucune sensation agréable. Sa gorge ne s'enfloit en aucun tems." In the *Système d'Epicure*, this striking example of congenital malformation was related to La Mettrie's belief in organic evolution, which found concrete support in the occasional recurrence of such vestigial forms, despite their general elimination by a process of natural selection.

57. See above, p. 164.

58. Cf. especially Malebranche's *De la recherche de la vérité*, I, v-xx.

59. This attitude was expressed, for instance, in the *Dialogues des morts* ("Homère & Esope"): "Si vous avez la vérité à dire, vous ferez fort bien de l'envelopper dans des fables; elle en plaira beaucoup plus. . . . Ainsi, le vrai a besoin d'emprunter la figure du faux, pour être agréablement reçu dans l'esprit humain." Similarly in the *Dialogues sur la pluralité des mondes*, Fontenelle remarked about the idea that "each star might well be a world": "Selon moi, il n'y a pas jusqu'aux vérités à qui l'agrément ne soit nécessaire."

60. The "moderne" is La Mettrie himself, whose *Histoire de l'âme* had summarized as follows the text of Arnobius (*Adversus Gentes*, II, 20-25): "Faisons, dit-il, un trou en forme de lit dans la terre; qu'il soit entouré de murs, couvert d'un toit; que ce lieu ne soit ni trop chaud, ni trop froid: qu'on n'y entende absolument aucun bruit: imaginons les moyens de n'y faire entrer qu'une pâle lueur entrecoupée de ténèbres. Qu'on mette un enfant nouveau-né dans ce souterrain: que ses sens ne soient frappés d'aucuns objets, qu'une nourrice nue, en silence, lui donne son lait & ses soins. A-t-il besoin d'alimens plus solides? qu'ils lui soient portés par la même femme: qu'ils soient toujours de la même nature, tels que le pain & l'eau froide, bue dans le creux de la main. Que cet enfant, sorti de la race de Platon ou de Pithagore, quitte enfin sa solitude à l'âge de vingt, trente, ou quarante ans; qu'il paroisse dans l'assemblée des mortels! Qu'on lui demande, avant qu'il ait appris à penser & à parler, ce qu'il est lui-même, quel est son père, ce qu'il a fait, ce qu'il a pensé, comment il a été nourri & élevé jusqu'à ce tems. Plus stupide qu'une bête, il n'aura pas plus de sentiment que le bois ou le caillou; il ne connoîtra ni la terre, ni la mer, ni les astres, ni les météores, ni les plantes, ni les animaux. S'il a faim, faute de sa nourriture ordinaire, ou plutôt faute de connoître tout ce qui peut y suppléer, il se laissera mourir. Entouré de feu, ou de bêtes venimeuses, il se jettera au milieu du danger, parce qu'il ne sait encore ce que c'est que la crainte. S'il est forcé de parler, par l'impression de tous ces objets nouveaux, dont il est frappé; il ne sortira de sa

bouche béante, que des sons inarticulés. . . . Demandez-lui, non les idées abstraites & difficiles de métaphysique, de morale ou de géométrie; mais seulement la plus simple question d'arithmétique, il ne comprend pas ce qu'il entend, ni que votre voix puisse signifier quelque chose, ni même si c'est à lui, ou à d'autres que vous parlez. Où est donc cette portion immortelle de la divinité? Où est cette Ame, qui entre dans le corps, si docte & si éclairée, & qui par le secours de l'instruction ne fait que se rappeller les connoissances qu'elle avoit infuses? Est-ce donc là cet être si raisonnable & si fort au-dessus des autres êtres? Hélas! oui, voilà l'homme" (I, 229-31).

Although La Mettrie cited this passage as an early and eloquent defense of the sensationalist position, Arnobius himself, with a theological instead of an epistemological purpose in mind, had used the "fiction of the cave" (originally devised by Plato) as an argument against the Platonic-Pythagorean doctrines of the incorruptibility of the soul and of metempsychosis. La Mettrie's interest in Arnobius may be attributed to the fact that the latter was one of the Church Fathers who had denied the natural immortality of the soul. Afraid that human beings would be encouraged to indulge in every sort of vice if they were not threatened with the total annihilation of their being, Arnobius had described eternal life, not as the normal destiny of an indestructible soul, but as a pure gift of God. Thus, by a curious circuit, a text designed as Christian apologetics around 300 A.D. became a part of La Mettrie's exposition of materialism!

61. La Mettrie no doubt has in mind a case of this sort reported by Bernard Connor (*Evangelium medici, seu medicina mystica*, 1699, pp. 133-34), which he himself summarized in the *Histoire de l'âme* (I, 220-21). It had to do with a ten-year-old child supposedly found in Lithuania in 1694, living with a troop of bears and behaving generally like his companions. At the same time La Mettrie related a similar story which, with some others, served to confirm the Lockean theory of knowledge: "Toute la Hollande a eu le plaisant spectacle d'un enfant, abandonné dans je ne sais quel désert, élevé & trouvé enfin parmi des chevres sauvages. Il se traînoit & vivoit comme ces animaux; il avoit les mêmes goûts, les mêmes inclinations, les mêmes sons de voix: la même imbécillité étoit peinte sur sa physionomie" (I, 227). Many accounts of this type were current in the eighteenth century, and were frequently accepted at face value.

62. The earliest description of the *fille sauvage* was given in the *Mercure de France* for December 1731 (pp. 2983-91). Besides this source, La Mettrie obtained many particulars concerning her from the

NOTES

Maréchal de Saxe. The entire subject was finally discussed at length in 1755 in a work attributed to the geographer and explorer, La Condamine: *Histoire d'une jeune fille sauvage trouvée dans les bois à l'âge de dix ans* (which purported to be by a certain Mme Hecquet). The facts of the story may be summed up briefly. The *fille sauvage* was found—or rather "trapped"—in the forest of Songi (belonging to the Vicomte d'Epinay), near Châlons, in September 1731. Her mode of existence was that of a wild animal. When first observed, she fed on roots, raw fish, frogs, and rabbits; she would catch fish by leaping in rivers or ponds, and was able to overtake and seize game in the field. Of unknown origin and extremely shy of human society, she spoke no language, but expressed her feelings by frightful screeches and howls. For a while she was kept on the estate of M. d'Epinay, where, allowed to live in her accustomed manner, she was exhibited as a curiosity. But thereafter the *fille sauvage* was taken to the Hôpital général de St. Maur in Châlons, to be "tamed" and educated. She was baptized on June 16, 1732, and given the name of Marie Angélique Memmie, to which "Le Blanc" was subsequently added. The civilizing process would seem to have been slow and painful, for the changes in her diet and regimen were accompanied by long illness. In 1744 the Duc d'Orléans saw her at the Couvent des Régentes in Châlons, and took her under his protection. The story about her having eaten her sister was, in all likelihood, a popular embroidery on certain other facts in the case. Once Mlle Le Blanc had learned to speak French, she told of having traveled together with another girl who was slightly older than herself, and from whom she had separated, shortly before her capture, following a quarrel in which the companion had been seriously wounded by a blow on the head. This account was partly borne out by eyewitnesses who had seen the pair together; and since the other girl had later vanished completely, it was assumed that she had succumbed to her injury. Concerning the background of the *fille sauvage*, La Condamine conjectured from the available evidence that she must have been an Eskimo of the Labrador region, taken into slavery and transported to the French West Indies; that, from there, she had been brought with her companion to Europe and placed under a French mistress, from whom the two had fled and taken to the woods some twelve to fifteen days before turning up near Châlons. It was further assumed that no one had ever come to claim the girl because, in view of her savage ways, the mistress had probably been glad to be rid of her.

The subject of the *fille sauvage* proved to be of interest, for various reasons, to a number of eighteenth-century thinkers. In the *Histoire de l'âme*, La Mettrie had already referred to her as one of several cases tending to support Lockean psychology. Voltaire regarded her, in the Preface of the *Poème sur la loi naturelle* (1756), as illustrating the natural basis of remorse; and though in this respect he merely echoed the comment of *l'Homme machine*, Voltaire's poem sprang from a deep disagreement with the *Anti-Sénèque* of La Mettrie, whose views on the naturalness of remorse had in the meanwhile changed radically. Buffon's *Histoire naturelle de l'homme* saw in the girl a personification of the "sauvage absolument sauvage," in whom the endowment of nature was supposed to be still unaffected by the *apport* of civilization (*Oeuvres*, Paris, 1842, III, 308). Finally Herder, in the *Philosophie der Geschichte der Menschheit* (1784-91, III, 6), viewed the *fille sauvage* as an example of the adjustability of the human body to an animal mode of life, that is, as a proof of his theory of organic adaptation.

63. Jean-Baptiste Gaston, duc d'Orléans (1608-60), was the third son of Henri IV and a brother of Louis XIII.

64. La Mettrie found this case in Gaubius (*De regimine mentis*, pp. 93-94): "It was learned by reliable observation in a town near [Leyden] that a certain lady became subject in pregnancy to an irresistible desire to steal. So that, though she was not in need of anything, she could not withstand the urge to pilfer whatever was at hand, even the silver plates of her friends while she was being entertained by them. After childbirth the impulse went off, but came back whenever she became pregnant again, and was even handed down as a most unfortunate inheritance to some of her offspring."

65. For this gruesome example of "pregnancy mania" La Mettrie was again indebted to Gaubius (*op.cit.*, p. 94), who had in turn taken it from Johann Schenk (*Observationum medicarum rariorum libri VII*, Lyon, 1644, p. 546): "In the year 1553, a certain pregnant woman of Prettenburg, while making a pie, was completely overpowered by the unhappy and inhuman desire to eat her husband. Therefore when night had fallen, she placed a sharp knife against her dear spouse's throat and, with abominable daring, slashed it open. While her dead husband's body was still warm, she avidly chewed and consumed his left arm and, indeed, the left side as far as the wind-pipe. What was left of the rest of the body, after she had disposed of the inwards and the severed head, was salted down and put aside for another feast. In the meanwhile, the time of her delivery came and, fate being kind, she gave birth to three sons in a row. While the midwives, suspecting no evil, were making haste (as is customary) to bring the glad tidings

to the husband, they were suddenly called back by the mother of the children, who, having confessed her grievous crime with many groans, gave them an account of the deed. Furthermore, from the precise moment of her confinement she voluntarily demanded of the magistrate that she be punished accordingly. Wherefore she was condemned to imprisonment for life."

66. This case of cannibalism was first related in Gasparo Bugati's *Historia universale, nella quale si racconta tutto quel ch'è successo dal principio del mondo sino all'anno 1569* (Venice, 1570, pp. 754-55): "During the same year [1519] in Milan, a certain female artisan named Elisabetta, a ferocious beast rather than a woman, was put to death on the wheel and burned. Prompted by gluttony or hunger, or perhaps by her native cruelty, she would entice children of tender years who passed her house, and, having led them inside, would kill them, salt their flesh, and devour it day by day. Her savagery was disclosed thanks to a cat that carried away a child's hand to a nearby house, in the vicinity of which a search was being made for a missing little girl named Catterina, who belonged to the Serona family. When what the cat had found was traced back to its source, that voracious beast of a woman was discovered, and next to her there was seen still intact the corpse of the same Catterina, who was buried in the Church of Santa Maria Secreta with an epitaph describing that strange event." This story was retold by Donati (*De medica historia mirabili*, IV, i), and later by Gaubius (*op.cit.*, p. 95), before appearing in *l'Homme machine*.

67. The original version of this incident is found in Hector Boece's *Scotorum historiae a prima gentis origine* (1527). It was repeated by Donati (*op.cit.*, IV, i); but La Mettrie's immediate source was once again Gaubius (*op.cit.*, p. 96). Boece's account is as follows: "[In 1460] there was a certeine theefe, that with his familie lived apart from the companie of men, remaining secretlie within a Den in Angus called Frenisden, who used to kill young persons, and to feed on their flesh, for the which abominable offense, being apprehended with his wife and all his familie, they were burnt to death. One of his daughters that was scarse twelve moneths of age, onelie excepted, the which being preserved and brought up in Dundee, before she came to the age of twelve yeeres, she was taken in the like crime for the which hir Father died, whereupon she was judged to be buried quicke: and going to execution, when people in great multitudes followed hir, in wondering at so horrible an offense committed by one of hir age and sexe, she turned to them that thus detested hir wicked doing,

and with a contenance representing hir cruell inclination, said to them: What need you thus to raile upon me, as if I had done an heinous act contrairie to the nature of man? I tell you, that if you knew how pleasant mans flesh is in taste, there would none of you all forbeare to eat it. And thus with an impenitent and stubborne minde she suffered the appointed execution (*Historie of Scotland*, trans. R. Hollinshed, 1585, p. 278).

68. For La Mettrie's anticipation of the psychiatric contribution to modern penology, see Hans von Hentig, "La Mettrie als Kriminalanthropologe," *Archiv für Kriminalanthropologie und Kriminalistik*, LI (1913), 53-59.

69. This sentence was removed in 1751 because Pascal had actually not been mentioned in the *Traité du vertige*. La Mettrie's slip of memory resulted from the fact that he had referred to Pascal's illness in the *Histoire de l'âme* (I, 131).

70. Ixion, according to mythology, had been pardoned by Zeus for the murder of his father-in-law, Deïoneos, and graciously invited to Olympus. When he repaid this kindness by trying to seduce Hera, Zeus cast him into hell, bound hand and foot to a flaming wheel that revolved endlessly. By "Ixions du Christianisme" La Mettrie means those who accept the Christian faith because they fear that, if they did not, an offended God would punish them with a similar fate.

71. François de Salignac de la Mothe-Fénelon (1651-1715), archbishop of Cambrai, is known chiefly as the author of *Télémaque*, and as a leader of the Quietist movement in the Gallican Church. With respect to the passage that follows, La Mettrie has in mind his *Démonstration de l'existence de Dieu, tirée de la connaissance de la nature, et proportionnée à la faible intelligence des plus simples* (1713).

Bernard Nieuwentijd (1654-1718), Dutch mathematician, published in 1715 an apologetic work that enjoyed a considerable vogue and was eventually translated into French under the title: *l'Existence de Dieu démontrée par les merveilles de la nature*.

Jacques Abbadie (1654-1727), a French Protestant theologian, lived as an exile in England from 1688 on. Among his prolific writings, La Mettrie is most likely referring to the *Traité de la vérité de la religion chrétienne* (1684).

William Derham (1657-1735), the English divine, had a deep interest in natural science and was a member of the Royal Society. La Mettrie is thinking mainly of his well-known *Physico-Theology, or a Demonstration of the Being and Attributes of God from his Works of Creation* (1713).

NOTES

John Ray (1627-1705), perhaps the foremost botanist of his time and an important forerunner of Linnaeus and Jussieu, made valuable contributions in his *Historia plantarum* (1686-1704) toward establishing a system of natural classification, not to mention his original researches in the histology and physiology of plants. Ray's chief excursion into the field of apologetics was *The Wisdom of God manifested in the Works of the Creation* (1691).

72. Marcello Malpighi (1628-94), famous Italian biologist, played a crucial role in the development of microanatomy. Among the mysteries laid bare by his microscope, the most notable were the capillary circulation of the blood, the vesicular composition of the lung, the structure of secreting glands, the mucous layer of the epidermis, and the follicular bodies in the spleen. Malpighi made important observations also in the fields of plant histology and animal embryology.

73. This sentence alludes to the standpoint of Diderot's *Pensées philosophiques* (1746): "Ce n'est pas de la main du Métaphysicien que sont partis les grands coups que l'Athéisme a reçus. Les méditations sublimes de Mallebranche & de Descartes étoient moins propres à ébranler le matérialisme, qu'une observation de Malpighi. Si cette dangereuse hypothèse chancelle de nos jours, c'est à la Physique expérimentale que l'honneur en est dû. Ce n'est que dans les ouvrages de Newton, de Muschenbroek, d'Hartzoeker, & de Nieuwentit qu'on a trouvé des preuves satisfaisantes de l'existence d'un Etre souverainement intelligent" (éd. R. Niklaus, Genève, 1950, pp. 12-13). In the following paragraphs, La Mettrie considers the general case for a "theology of nature" as it was stated above all in the *Pensées philosophiques*—a work which seemed to him to be a particularly forceful defense of deistic teleology. It is a curious fact that the *Pensées philosophiques* was at this very time being attributed to La Mettrie himself, who later made a formal repudiation (cf. *Ouvrage de Pénélope*, III, 355ff.).

74. Concerning the spermatist theory of reproduction, see below, note 114.

75. See above, note 51. One explanation—proposed by Trembley himself—for the polyp's amazing powers of regeneration was that countless pre-existent polyps were scattered *en germe* throughout the body of the parent zoophyte. This hypothesis found favor with many people because it seemed able to reconcile the fresh-water hydra's apparently spontaneous self-production with the more familiar and conservative premises of preformationist biology.

76. This is the valve of the *foramen ovale*, through which in foetal circulation blood is allowed to pass from the right to the left auricle of the heart. The valve normally closes soon after birth, and the *foramen ovale* is presently replaced by a solid membrane between the atria, which keeps venous blood from entering directly into the arterial system.

77. As regards Spinoza, it is not known that any illness or the fear of death caused him to renounce his "atheism." La Mettrie doubtless owed this mistaken belief to the common practice during the eighteenth century of fabricating pious tales about the deathbed conversions of famous *incrédules*. Actually, La Mettrie here anticipates and discounts in advance the rumors which, circulating after his own death, were to result in what Voltaire described as "une grande dispute pour savoir s'il est mort en chrétien ou en médecin."

Lucilio Vanini, born around 1585 in the Kingdom of Naples, was convicted of atheism and burned at the stake in Toulouse in 1619. Of a restless temperament, he had traveled in France, Germany, Bohemia, The Netherlands, Switzerland and England, earning his livelihood as a teacher of medicine, theology, and philosophy, and acquiring in the process a reputation for secretly spreading atheism among his students and acquaintances. It was to protect himself against denunciation that Vanini published his *Amphitheatrum aeternae providentiae* (1615), in which he ostensibly refuted naturalism. However, a less guarded expression of his views may be found in *De admirandis naturae reginae deaeque mortalium arcanis* (1616), a work which tended more or less surreptitiously toward a vague pantheism and a skeptical treatment of the questions of providence and the immortality of the soul. The reference of La Mettrie to his conversion has to do, very likely, with Vanini's recantations while on trial for his life in Toulouse. But this—if accounts by biased contemporaries are true—was more a case of prudent hypocrisy than of a change of heart, for when his "conversion" failed to move the judges, he is supposed to have died uttering blasphemies. Following Bayle's attempt to rehabilitate his reputation in the *Pensées diverses sur la comète*, Vanini came to be regarded in the Enlightenment as a "martyr of free thought."

Jacques Vallée Des Barreaux (1599-1673), a "conseiller" at the Parlement of Paris, had been in youth a follower and friend of the voluptuary poet, Théophile de Viau, before becoming notorious in his own right as a *libertin*. On falling ill in 1641, he experienced a temporary conversion, which was followed by another in 1666 when, stricken more seriously, he wrote the well-known sonnet beginning: "Grand Dieu! tes jugemens sont remplis d'équité." He became penitent once again on his deathbed, and asked God for three favors: "oubli pour le passé, patience pour le présent, et miséricorde pour l'avenir" (cf. Frédéric Lachèvre, *Le prince des libertins du XVIIe siècle: Jacques Vallée Des Barreaux, sa vie et ses poésies*, Paris, 1907, pp. 83-84, 95-96, 102-03, 173-74).

Nicolas Boindin (1676-1751), a minor author of theatrical pieces and of scholarly studies on language and poetry, was received in 1706 into the *Académie des inscriptions et belles-lettres*. Despite his open profession of incredulity, which caused the doors of the French Academy to be closed to him, he was unusually lucky in escaping persecution—a fact that he explained to a puzzled *confrère* with one of his best quips: "On vous tourmente, parce que vous êtes un athée janséniste; mais on me laisse en paix, parce que je suis un athée moliniste." Boindin was, along with Fontenelle, Duclos and Marmontel, a frequenter of the Café Procope, where La Mettrie probably had made his acquaintance. I have not been able to learn to what incident in his life La Mettrie alludes.

78. La Mettrie here mistakes Diderot for a physician because of the latter's part in the French translation of Robert James's *Medicinal Dictionary; including physic, surgery, anatomy, chymistry, and botany* (London, 1743-45). The same error is repeated in the *Ouvrage de Pénélope* (III, 35). It is therefore obvious that La Mettrie did not know Diderot personally.

79. On the relationship of the polyp to naturalistic thought in the Enlightenment, see my "Trembley's Polyp, La Mettrie, and Eighteenth-century French Materialism," *Journal of the History of Ideas*, XI (1950), 259-86.

80. Cf. *Pensées philosophiques*, p. 16, where Diderot argued that design in nature implied an Intelligent Creator as surely as coherent speech implied intelligence in a human being, and concluded with the remark: "Songez donc que je ne vous objectois qu'une aile de papillon, qu'un oeil de ciron, quand je pouvois vous écraser du poids de l'univers."

81. The reference in Lucretius is to *De rerum natura*, IV, 829-39:

> Caetera de genere hoc inter quaecumque pretantur
> Omnia perversa praepostera sunt ratione.
> Nil ideo quoniam natumst in corpore, ut uti
> Possemus; sed quod natumst, id procreat usum.

NOTES

> Nec fuit ante videre oculorum lumina nata,
> Nec dictis orare prius quam lingua creatast,
> Sed potius longe linguae praecessit origo
> Sermonem, multoque creatae sunt prius aures
> Quam sonus est auditus, et omnia denique membra
> Ante fuere (ut opinor) eorum quam foret usus.
> Haud igitur potuere utendi crescere causa.

Guillaume Lamy, a professor of the Paris Medical Faculty, was a seventeenth-century exponent of Epicurean philosophy, which, in his treatment of the problem of final cause, he combined with certain features of Cartesianism. By asserting that God was the creator of matter and of the laws of motion, he was able not only to avoid the atheism that attached to Epicurean physics, but also to infer the futility of all finalistic reasoning, on the grounds that the purpose of the universe, as of each of its parts, must remain ultimately knowable to God alone. This Epicuro-Cartesian complex of ideas, which had a special importance among the sources of La Mettrie's materialism, found expression in Lamy's *Discours anatomiques* (2e édn., Paris, 1685, pp. 45-48): "Considérons l'Auteur de la nature comme un ouvrier qui a tout fait pour soy-mesme. . . . Il a produit la matiere avec des mouvemens dans ses differentes particules, par la necessité desquels tous les corps que nous voyons, & une infinité d'autres qui nous sont inconnus, ont esté formés. . . . Dieu a donc fait ses ouvrages pour soy . . . et il n'est point constant que les usages des parties soient la fin qu'il s'est proposée, parce qu'il a pû s'en proposer d'autres, qui nous sont inconnues. Il y a mesme des occasions, où il n'y a point d'apparence de le dire, & d'autres où ce seroit un crime de le penser. Sans donc s'embarasser, en raisonnant de la sorte, & sans asseurer que les yeux sont faits pour voir, les pieds pour marcher, les aisles pour voler; il suffit de connoistre qu'entre les differens animaux que Dieu a faits, il en a voulu faire avec des yeux, des pieds, des aisles: & qu'il a bien connû que ceux qui auroient des yeux verroient; ceux qui auroient des pieds marcheroient. . . . Suivant ces principes tres-simples, & tres-vray-semblables, un Physicien peut dire en un mot, que la partie est apparemment faite pour composer le tout; & le tout est sans doute fait pour l'ouvrier, qui a travaillé pour soy-mesme. Ensuite il employera son esprit à démesler les ressorts des machines qu'il connoist, à chercher l'usage de leurs parties, & à expliquer leurs fonctions, qu'il prendra comme des suites du nombre, de la structure, & de la situation de ces parties, sans inferer que c'en soit la fin, & que les choses ne pouvoient estre mieux, à l'égard de l'animal à qui elles servent."

NOTES

82. Virgil, *Bucolics*, Eclogue III, l. 108.

83. William Cowper (1666-1709) was the author of a work highly regarded in its field, the *Anatomy of humane bodies* (1698), which gave the results of many original observations. In 1702 he published a description of the glands that are still known by his name. La Mettrie's reference is to his *Myotomia reformata: or, A new administration of all the muscles of humane bodies* (London, 1694, p. 11): "The Experiments I have made ... seem to intimate, that the Bloud, barely as a Fluid, is an Assistant in the Contraction of a *Muscle*: and this did not only appear by making a Ligature on the Descending Trunck of the *Aorta* of the living Animal, whereby all the Inferior Parts became Destitute of Motion, which they again recovered by loosing that Ligature, and admitting the Bloud to flow again into the Muscles; But even after the cessation of motion in the same Animal it was surprising to Observe the Muscles of the Legs renew their Contractions, upon the injection of Water only into the Crural Artery; which Experiment I have frequently repeated with the like success." Cowper further stated that, by the same method, the muscles of animals could be stimulated to motion even after death, although nothing was said, contrary to La Mettrie's recollection, about the performance of this experiment specifically on the heart. In a second edition of the *Myotomia reformata* (London, 1724, Introduction, p. lxxi), Cowper sought to explain the facts he had observed by means of a theory that fell short of the concept of irritability. He assumed that the effect of the injected water, which acted as a substitute for blood, was merely to keep the muscle tissue warm enough to favor the contracting influence of the "subtle substance" which, identified by him with the Newtonian ether, was supposed to communicate impulses through the nervous system.

84. The reference here to Harvey is slightly inaccurate. La Mettrie would seem to have in mind the following passage from *De motu cordis et sanguinis in animalibus* (1628), Chap. ii: "The heart of an eel taken out of the body of the animal and placed upon the table or the hand [beats], but the same things are manifested in the heart of small fishes and of those colder animals where the organ is more conical or elongated" (*The Works of William Harvey*, trans. R. Willis, London, 1847, p. 21). With respect to the phenomenon of irritability, Harvey's classic work had cited other examples which could have been of even greater use to La Mettrie, among them the following: "The heart of an eel, of several fishes, and even of some animals taken out of the body, beats without auricles; nay, if it be cut in pieces the

several parts may still be seen contracting and relaxing; so that in these creatures the body of the heart may be seen pulsating, palpitating, after the cessation of all motion in the auricle. . . . Experimenting with a pigeon upon one occasion, after the heart had wholly ceased to pulsate, and the auricles too had become motionless, I kept my finger wetted with saliva and warm for a short time upon the heart, and observed, that under the influence of this fomentation it recovered new strength and life, so that both ventricles and auricles pulsated, contracting and relaxing alternately, recalled as it were from death to life" (*ibid.*, p. 28). Although in these observations no specific mention had been made of the toad, it should be remembered that in the time of *l'Homme machine* the frog was already entering on its career as the "martyr of science," and that the experiment on its excised heart, to which La Mettrie refers, was well known. He must have been familiar also with Swammerdam's researches concerning the mechanical stimulation of various isolated muscles of the frog, as described in the *Biblia Naturae*, which was translated from the Dutch in 1737-38 by Gaubius, and prefaced by Boerhaave (cf. II, 835-60: "Experimenta circa particularem musculorum in rana motum").

85. Cf. *Historia vitae et mortis* (1623); *Works of Francis Bacon*, eds. Spedding, Ellis, Heath, London, 1870, v, 316. Some less uncommon examples of autonomous muscle action were given in the same place: "Eels, serpents, and insects move a good while in all their parts after being cut in pieces. . . . Birds likewise flutter for a little after their heads are cut off; and the hearts of animals beat for a long time after being torn out." However, Bacon was far from suspecting in these simple observations the meaning they were later to have for muscle physiology. This is best seen from a description of what appeared to him to be another occurrence of the same type, concerning "a man who, having undergone the said punishment for high treason, when his heart had been torn out and was in the hands of the executioner, was heard to utter three or four words of prayer." La Mettrie revised his original reference to Bacon because it was incorrect. The *Sylva Sylvarum* did contain a passage describing the motions of decerebrated birds, as well as of dismembered eels, snakes, worms and insects, but it made no mention of the observation on the human heart.

86. Cf., Robert Boyle, *Some considerations touching the usefulness of experimental natural philosophy* (Oxford, 1663, "Second Part," pp. 13-14), which reported an observation similar to those mentioned here by La Mettrie: "I have sometimes taken the Heart of a Flownder, and having cut it transversly into two parts, and press'd out, and

with a Linnen cloth wip'd off the Blood contain'd in each of them, I observed, that for a considerable space of time, the sever'd and bloodless parts held on their former contraction and relaxation. And once I remember that I observ'd, not without Wonder, that the sever'd portions of a Flownder's Heart, did not onley, after their Blood was drain'd, move as before, but the whole Heart observ'd for a pretty while such a succession of motion in its divided and exsangious pieces, as I have taken notice of in them whilst they were coherent, and as you may with pleasure both see and feel in the intire Heart of the same Fish." Boyle described a number of other experiments, performed on the hearts of frogs, unhatched chicks, and serpents, which likewise deserve a place in the background of La Mettrie's notion of irritability.

Nicholas Steno (1638-86), Danish anatomist and physiologist, made a series of experiments around 1662 which dealt with both spontaneous and artificially induced motion in the cardiac muscle of a variety of animals, including the dog, rabbit, hen, raven, and pigeon. The results were described principally in his memoir: "Ex variorum animalium sectionibus hinc inde factis excerptae observationes circa motum cordis, auricularumque et venae cavae" (cf. *Bibliotheca anatomica*, ed. Le Clerc & Manget, Geneva, 1685, II, 116-18). As an example of what La Mettrie here has in mind, Steno gave the following observation among others: "I noticed that the resected apex of a dog's heart, placed on my fingers, contracted when pricked with either a finger-nail or a knife, so that the retraction of its walls caused it, in fact, to fall from my hand. I saw the same apex, when turned upside down, move in a like fashion." There was present in the same place an account of an experiment made on the heart of the foetal chick, which closely resembles the one mentioned just above by La Mettrie: "Having freed from all its blood-vessels the heart of a chick taken from the shell on the seventh day after incubation, it beat for a long time in my hand; when it thereafter became motionless and seemed to be dead, by breathing on it with my mouth, it was called back again to life; and this was repeated many times with that heart." For additional data of the same kind, see also Steno's "Observationes anatomicae in avibus & cuniculis" (*N. Stenonis opera philosophica*, Copenhagen, 1910, I, 115-20).

87. This refers to the preformationist theory, which was almost universally accepted by scientists from the latter part of the seventeenth century until shortly prior to *l'Homme machine*. Based on the supposition that all living things exist *preformed* in the seed of either

the male or female parent, the theory was often expanded into the doctrine known as "emboîtement des germes," which, in order to explain generation in accordance with theological demands, pictured the history of each animal species as the successive emergence into life of countless pre-existent creatures which God had created, *ab initio*, incapsulated one within the other. Trembley's polyp, with its strangely spontaneous powers of regeneration and reproduction, dealt a serious blow to the belief that preformation represented a general law of nature. Plainly favoring a naturalistic, rather than a theological, approach to the entire problem of generation, it became an important factor in the revival, between 1745 and 1750, of theories of epigenesis (Maupertuis, Buffon) and of abiogenesis (J. T. Needham).

88. Actually, some of the examples adduced above do not bear out experimentally the principle of muscular irritability, which (as La Mettrie defines it) would presuppose the complete isolation of the muscle fiber from the nervous apparatus. Those that most clearly fail to meet this condition are, of course, numbers 1, 3, 8, 9, and 10, which illustrate reflex action rather than contractility. Concerning the reasons for this confusion, see below, note 90.

89. La Mettrie was much better acquainted with the medical literature on the subject of irritability than would appear from the few references given by him in the preceding section. After Harvey, one of the earliest utilizations of the phenomenon in question had come from Richard Lower in 1669: "Finally, the movement of the Heart is shown to be independent of any ebullition of blood by the fact that a Heart taken from a living animal and entirely emptied of blood does not cease to move, even if it is cut into small pieces. It is a matter of common knowledge that the Hearts of fairly young animals, long after they have been cut out of the thorax, pick up their pulsations at once, and continue them for a long time, if they are gently stimulated with a small pin. Eels' Hearts, similarly stimulated with a needle several hours after they have been taken out, are seen to pulsate once more" (*Tractatus de corde, item de motu & colore sanguinis*, Facs. edn., with an Introduction and Translation by K. J. Franklin, Oxford, 1932, p. 66). Besides Lower's famous work, La Mettrie also knew Francis Glisson's *Tractatus de natura substantiae energetica* (1672), and, what is more important, his *Tractatus de ventriculo et intestinis* (1677), which showed that the intestines and other muscles could be stimulated to motion, soon after death and even when removed from the body, by means of corrosive fluids. Some years later, Johann Conrad Peyer described how the hearts of various

animals could be made to contract after death by stimulation with either warm water or air (cf. *Parerga anatomica et medica septem*, Leyden, 1750, vii: "Miraculum anatomicum in cordibus resuscitatis," pp. 259-61). Much the same evidence was cited by Johann Wepfer, who enriched the subject, however, with further observations of his own (cf. *Cicutae acquaticae historia et noxae*, Basel, 1679, pp. 89-90, 155-56, 223). Before long, Stahl conceived of a "tonic movement" that belonged theoretically between the notions of muscle tone and contractility proper. In *De motu tonico vitali* (1692), he discussed this property with the intention of explaining thereby the variability of arterial pressure in the body and its effect on the distribution of blood (*Oeuvres médico-philosophiques*, vi, 518-19). Elsewhere, Stahl viewed "tonic force" in a manner sufficiently generalized to suggest the idea of irritability: "Il ne nous reste plus maintenant qu'à faire une seule et dernière observation: c'est que tous les principaux mouvements vulgairement appelés *vitaux*, bien qu'involontaires, qui s'exécutent dans toute l'étendue du corps, n'ont cependant qu'un seul et même genre d'instrument, c'est-à-dire la *contractilité de la fibre musculaire*, spécialement destinée à produire cet effet" (in *Theoria medica vera, op.cit.*, iii, 474-75). Around 1700, Giorgio Baglivi made some interesting observations of autonomous muscle action, from which he drew the conclusion that the fundamental factor in contraction must inhere in the fabric of the muscle itself. La Mettrie undoubtedly knew the following text: "And indeed, having often and carefully examined the structure of the muscles . . . I began to assert that the principal, not to say the whole power of motion, or the force moving the muscles, resides in the muscles themselves, that is, in the special fabric of the fibers . . . and that the spirits flowing through the nerves serve no purpose other than to regulate their motions. . . . It is most remarkable that, if you observe the ablated heart of a frog newly taken from the water in summer, you will see it move for half an hour; likewise, if it is cut up, each of the severed parts will itself exhibit repeated motions of systole and diastole. And since no force could be communicated by the spirits or the brain to a heart that has been removed and sectioned, I am of the opinion that the entire moving force is produced by the fibers alone. . . . Consequently, if the heart is a muscle and moves by virtue of a certain contraction, tension and continual oscillation of its fibers . . . what prevents us from explaining the movements of all muscles by the laws of cardiac motion?" (cf. *Dissertationes variae*, i, *Opera omnia medico-practica et anatomica*, Antwerp, 1715, pp. 401-02). See, in addition, Baglivi's *De fibra motrice et morbosa* (*op.cit.*, pp. 317, 319ff.). It was noted also by Alexander Stuart that muscle fibers retained their irritable properties after being separated from the related nerves (*Dissertatio de structura et motu musculari*, Leyden, 1711, p. 13). Closer in time to *l'Homme machine*, Johann de Gorter not only attributed contractility to nerve fibers in order to explain the automatic functioning of the vital organs, but recognized in the latter an autonomous source of energy: "It has been demonstrated that the vital organ is constructed in such a fashion as to contract rhythmically by the uniform influx of spirits; and thereupon we have also deduced that the cause of this alternating vital motion is to be sought neither in the cerebellum, nor its covering tissues, nor in the nerve itself, nor in the alternating flow of the spirits, but must arise from the structure itself of the vital organ" (*Exercitationes medicae quatuor*, Amsterdam, 1737, "De motu vitali," §LXIII, p. 44). It is possible, though not likely, that during the writing of *l'Homme machine* La Mettrie was already acquainted with Haller's *Primae lineae physiologiae* (1747), which contained a fuller statement of his *Irritabilitätslehre* than had previously been published.

90. Among the various involuntary actions cited in this paragraph as examples of muscular irritability, only the heartbeat may be regarded as basically related to that cause. Most of the other automatisms represent different types of reflex behavior: the familiar palpebral, pupillary, and vomiting reflexes; the more special mechanisms controling the erection of the penis and the contractions of the bladder and rectum; and the conditioned reflex that results in recoiling before a precipice. In La Mettrie's time, moreover, nothing was known as yet of the respiratory center in the medulla oblongata, the automatic activity of which is not easily classifiable in terms either of irritability or of reflex action.

The inclusion by La Mettrie of reflex mechanisms under the general heading of irritability is typical of the state of physiology around 1750. Although as early as 1670 Willis had expressed the reflex idea in a rudimentary form, and Astruc in 1736 had given it a significant development, reflex theory was still in its infancy when *l'Homme machine* appeared. Despite the crucial advances made later by Whytt (1751), Unzer (1771), and Prochaska (1784), the concept of the reflex continued, in fact, to occupy a rather modest place in the physiological thought of the eighteenth century. There were two main reasons for this. First, the recognition of irritability as an underlying cause of motion in the organism preceded chronologically the clarification of the reflex process; and this advantage was all the greater because

Haller, who expounded and championed the doctrine of irritability, held a position of overwhelming authority among physiologists at the time. It is therefore not surprising to find La Mettrie under Hallerian influence in his attempt to discover the basis of neuromuscular automatism. Secondly, the reflex could not assume its proper importance as a physiological factor so long as there remained a strong tendency—encouraged by the animal-spirits hypothesis—to regard all local movement as resulting from the indivisible activity of the central nervous system. Such phenomena as the persistence of life in excised organs and in decapitated animals, which were referred (as seen by the case of La Mettrie) to the irritability of the muscles, could not be correctly attributed to reflex action until the time when, thanks to Prochaska, the functions that the *medulla spinalis* can perform independently of the brain became generally known. But even so, it was in the course of the nineteenth century that the structure and behavior of the autonomic nervous system—of the ganglion, plexus, and reflex arc—were at last understood well enough to permit the experimental demonstration of the various types of reflex mechanism. For a detailed history of the reflex problem in the eighteenth century, consult Georges Canguilhem, *La formation du concept de réflexe aux XVIIe et XVIIIe siècles*, Paris, 1955, especially pp. 89-131.

91. The ἐνορμῶν, a notion proper to Hippocratic medicine, signified the elemental force—one might now say the *élan vital*—that is supposed to set the organism in motion and to conserve its life. By *origine des nerfs* La Mettrie means the terminal branches of the nerve fibers in the cerebral cortex. In using the term ἐνορμῶν to indicate the energetic basis of motor, sensory, and intellectual activity, as well as in the promising identification of this actuating power with the cortical substance of the cerebrum, La Mettrie was indebted to more than one contemporary. His original source was Haller, who, in commenting on Boerhaave's *Institutiones rei medicae* ("De sensibus internis," §568), had called attention to the important, but until then largely neglected, functions of the cerebral cortex, wherein he chose in fact to place the *sensorium commune*. La Mettrie was sufficiently impressed by Haller's farsighted opinion to adopt it in the *Histoire de l'âme* (1, 116-17), and to draw from it his own conclusions about the extensibility, and hence materiality, of the soul. At about the same time, interest in the ancient concept of the ἐνορμῶν had been revived as a result of a work by Abraham Kaau-Boerhaave (Boerhaave's nephew), entitled *Impetum faciens dictum Hippocrati per corpus consentiens, philologice & physiologice illustratum* (1745). La Mettrie was directly influenced, how-

ever, not so much by Kaau-Boerhaave's somewhat vapid speculations, as by certain remarks of Gaubius, who had been inclined to locate the ἐνορμῶν at the *origines nervorum*, and to regard it as the organic principle that coordinated the spheres of physical and mental behavior by serving as the source of energy common to both (cf. *De regimine mentis*, pp. 40-41, 45-46).

92. The theory of sympathies, deriving from Hippocratic tradition, was employed regularly in the eighteenth century as a means of explaining the correspondence of various physiological events, or pathological symptoms, in different parts of the body which appeared to have no direct anatomical connection. In the paragraphs that follow, La Mettrie will apply the same theory to comparable phenomena of a psychosomatic character. His attempt to attribute these, in a more concrete way, to the influence of the animal spirits, represented the type of hypothesis that was most popular at the time. But its scientific value was greatly impaired by the relative ignorance of the eighteenth century concerning the autonomic—i.e. sympathetic—nervous system, as well as the endocrine and other pertinent biochemical factors involved in the production of "sympathies."

93. It is to be noted that the basic roles assigned by La Mettrie to irritability and reflex action have not weakened his faith in the *esprits animaux*. The use in *l'Homme machine* of this seemingly obsolete hypothesis has sometimes been regarded as a serious defect, but, in our opinion, unjustifiably so. The notion of animal spirits, which had dominated physiological inquiry since the middle of the seventeenth century, was by 1750 far from being understood in the naïvely erroneous fashion of its chief promulgators, Descartes and Malebranche. Like most of his contemporaries, La Mettrie realized that the nerves were not exactly hollow tubes, and that the fluid believed to convey cerebral impulses through them had, until then, defied all efforts of detection. But despite this, it was assumed that contraction normally resulted from the influx of some nerve substance, however imperceptible, into the muscle mass. As a physiological idea, the animal spirits referred experimentally to this unknown factor, the electrochemical properties of which the eighteenth century was in no position to describe, but the existence of which was rightly thought to be as certain as its nature and mode of operation remained obscure. Thus La Mettrie was correct enough in supposing that the automatic activity of the organism sprang from the stimulus exerted by an indeterminate nerve impulse (*esprits animaux*) on the "ressort inné de chaque fibre."

NOTES

94. Nicolas Tulp (1593-1674) was in 1628 appointed Praelector of Anatomy at the *Chirurgijns-Gild* of Amsterdam—the role in which Rembrandt portrayed him in the famous "Anatomy Lesson." Tulp was elected Burgermeister of Amsterdam in 1654, a post to which he was re-elected in 1655, 1666, and 1671. The facts reported by him which La Mettrie has in mind concern embryonic malformations, and may be found in his *Observationes medicae*, especially Bk. III, Chaps. 37-38, "Partus monstri bicipitis" (edit. nova, 1652, pp. 256-60).

95. Malebranche gave his theory of prenatal influence, to which La Mettrie here makes the mistake of subscribing, in the *Recherche de la vérité*, II, 1, 7 (éd. G. Lewis, 1946, 1, 118-33). It grew out of a long line of similar speculations by Kenelm Digby, Van Helmont, Boyle, Swammerdam, and others. Malebranche's belief in prenatal impressions was based on the assumption that the *esprits animaux* flowed from the maternal brain, via the umbilical cord, to the foetal brain. He hoped thus to explain not only the general inheritance of physical and mental traits (including, incidentally, original sin), but also the occasional production of abnormal embryos, which could be ascribed to the effect of violent emotions felt by the mother during pregnancy. Malebranche's theory had a great vogue, and as late as 1745 Maupertuis's *Vénus physique* was to utilize certain of its features in an effort to solve the problem of heredity. But it had already met with strong criticism in the work of James Blondel: *The Strength of Imagination in Pregnant Women examined: and the Opinion that Marks and Deformities in children arise from thence, demonstrated to be a vulgar error* (London, 1727, pp. 21-30). Blondel's objections were based on (1) the low incidence of congenital malformation as compared with the frequency of violent emotions experienced by pregnant women; (2) the anatomical and physiological unlikelihood of a passage of animal spirits from the mother's brain to that of the child; and (3) the inconsistency of prenatal influence with the established theory of preformation, to which Malebranche was no less committed than Blondel. Among the followers of Blondel, La Mettrie probably had in mind Isaac Bellet, who had recently published the *Lettres sur le pouvoir de l'imagination des femmes enceintes, où l'on combat le préjugé qui attribue à l'imagination des Meres le pouvoir d'imprimer sur le corps des enfans renfermés dans leur sein la figure des objets qui les ont frappées* (Paris, 1745). While the main weakness of Malebranche's theory was the lack of any observable communication between the maternal and foetal nervous systems, the possibility that

NOTES

such a link might exist, although generally doubted in La Mettrie's time, had not been entirely rejected.

96. Giovanni Alfonso Borelli (1608-79), famous Italian physicist and anatomist, was perhaps the first to apply the geometric method in a wholly consistent manner to general investigations of animal physiology, as seen by his principal work, *De motu animalium* (1680-81). Although the crudeness of scientific instrumentation in the seventeenth century caused his conclusions—particularly in the measurement of muscular force—to be often quite inaccurate, Borelli has nevertheless been accredited with the founding of the iatromechanist school. La Mettrie here believes that, by extending the iatromechanical method to the mind-body problem, it is possible to show that a "natural harmony" based on the "material unity of man" explains better the reciprocity of mental and organic functions than does Leibniz's metaphysical doctrine of the pre-established harmony.

97. Pierre Bayle died in 1706 at the age of 59. La Mettrie's psychosomatic diagnosis of his fatal malady is rather questionable. Though Bayle had fallen ill more than once because of excessive mental work, there is no reason to think that his final illness, which lasted over a year, had the same origin; and he himself was convinced that it did not. Bayle's own description of his symptoms suggests tuberculosis: "Mon mal ne vient point du travail de l'étude. Je . . . dis que c'étoit une toux fâcheuse, & une fluxion sur la poitrine qui affectoit déjà le poumon; & que c'est une maladie héréditaire, puisque ma mère & sa mère, quelques oncles & tantes, en sont morts. C'est en effet l'état où je me trouve; c'est un mal incurable" (*Oeuvres diverses de Pierre Bayle*, La Haye, 1731, IV, 883).

98. A complex system of dietary prohibitions was part of the quasimonastic life of the Pythagorean brotherhood. Owing to the esoteric nature of their teachings, it is not clear whether these rules had a literal, figurative, or symbolic sense, nor just how they applied to the various levels of initiation into the sect. The food taboos of the Pythagoreans applied mainly to all forms of meat, to beans, and wine.

Plato laid down a number of restrictions concerning the use of wine in *Laws*, II, 666, 673-74.

99. See above, p. 193.

100. Georg Ernst Stahl (1660-1734), German chemist and physician, was the founder of a school of animistic medicine which, toward the end of the eighteenth century, merged with the vitalism of Montpellier. From 1694 to 1716 he held the chair of medicine at Halle, and served thereafter as doctor to the King of Prussia. Stahl also played

a leading role in the early history of chemistry—he was, among other things, responsible for the phlogiston theory—and his extensive medical writings often reflected his interests in that field. His biological philosophy, coming as a reaction against the seventeenth century's oversimplified view of the mechanical basis of life, stressed the specifically vital processes of the body which had no clear counterparts in mechanics, and attributed these to the agency of an immaterial rational soul, although the organism itself continued to be regarded as structurally nothing but a machine. While differences of interpretation are possible regarding the exact sense of Stahl's animism, the opinion ascribed to him by La Mettrie is well illustrated by the following passage from the *Theoria medica vera* (1707): "Or, comme il est déjà suffisamment démontré que le corps existe de toute nécessité pour l'âme, nous pouvons encore fournir une autre preuve non moins capable de confirmer aussi, *a priori*, ce même fait, savoir: que ce qui conserve le corps dans son intégrité, ce qui favorise et accomplit en lui l'exercice de l'âme . . . est une chose réelle, bien différente du corps par son essence. . . . D'une part, en effet, cette chose, cette force est immatérielle comme l'âme elle-même; et, d'autre part, elle exerce comme l'âme, dans le corps et sur le corps, une puissance et une activité on ne peut plus réelles et positives. . . . Dans les actes les plus nobles, les plus éminents et de la plus grande activité, l'âme exerce évidemment un pouvoir absolu sur ce principe en question; à tel point que c'est toujours elle qui, en pareil cas, gouverne, dirige, accroît et diminue d'une manière absolue l'action de ce principe, qu'elle meut et maîtrise selon son libre arbitre. . . . Ce principe n'est autre en lui-même que le MOUVEMENT; car c'est par le mouvement seul que l'âme accomplit ses actes. . . . Je puis donc évidemment conclure ici, que c'est l'âme elle-même qui dispose habituellement le corps pour son propre usage, et qui le rend apte à un service auquel seul le corps est astreint, et qu'enfin c'est l'âme qui dirige, excite et meut directement et immédiatement ce même corps, sans l'intervention ni le concours d'un autre agent" (*Oeuvres médico-philosophiques*, III, 48-52).

101. Philippe Hecquet (1661-1737) had practised medicine for some years at Port-Royal-des-champs. Having subsequently obtained a doctor's degree from the Medical Faculty of Paris, he was appointed to teach there, and rose in 1712 to the position of *doyen*. It was Hecquet whom Le Sage portrayed in *Gil Blas* under the pseudonym of "docteur Sangrado," ridiculing his exaggerated claims about the curative virtues of alternately bleeding a patient and filling him with water. La Met-

trie respected him, however, for his *Brigandage de la médecine* and other works, in which the cupidity of doctors was aptly satirized. The remark attributed here to Hecquet, comes actually from Horace: "Non cuivis homini contingit adire Corinthum" (*Epistolae*, I, xvii, l. 36).

102. The *Institutiones rei medicae* gave, in Boerhaave's eclectic manner, a number of explanations for the heart beat. Having rejected the various chemical theories based on "ebullition, fermentation, or effervescence," and knowing nothing about the stimulus due to the inorganic salts in the blood, he was hard put to it to assign a purely mechanical cause in their stead, and in fact confessed at one point that "il y a dans la fabrique du coeur une disposition occulte, & merveilleuse, à continuer ces mouvemens réciproques de systole & de diastole, même après la mort, même dans un coeur coupé, & enfin, qui plus est, dans des morceaux d'un coeur coupé (*Institutions de médecine*, trad. par La Mettrie, II, 311, §187). Despite this passing mention of irritability as an occult power in the heart, Boerhaave resorted generally to the more common notion that muscular contraction was due to the agency of the animal spirits issuing from the cerebellum (§§189, 402-04, 406). In the special case of cardiac motion, he described three appropriate causes, without, however, explaining in any detail their respective spheres of action or modes of interaction: "Il y a trois causes qui concourent à la contraction du coeur. 1° Le sang veineux que le coeur reçoit dans ses cavités, des sinus & des oreillettes. On sçait en effet par expérience qu'on reveille le mouvement du coeur par le souffle, l'eau, & quelque liqueur que ce soit qu'on injecte dans le cadavre; & par conséquent on peut mettre cette irritation au nombre des causes de la systole du coeur. 2° Le sang artériel qui, repoussé en arriere, entre de l'aorte dans les artères coronaires. 3° L'action nerveuse qui vient au coeur par la huitième paire [read: vagus nerve], l'intercostal, & le récurrent" (*ibid.*, IV, 53, §409). Concerning the rhythmic transmittal of nervous impulses to the heart —a subject which at the time was hardly understood at all—Boerhaave had a curious explanation. He supposed that the cardiac nerves were compressed in their passage between the aorta and the pulmonary artery, as in the heart itself, by the contraction of the latter's musculature, so that they momentarily obstructed the flow of *esprits animaux* and brought about the relaxation of the heart in the diastole. But when this in turn decreased the pressure on the nerves, a passage was again opened to the *spiritus animalis*, which promptly entered the heart and made it contract in the systole; and so on with each new cycle.

103. Thomas Willis distinguished two souls in man: a higher soul that was rational, immaterial, immortal, and remained peculiar to him alone; and a lower soul, possessed in common with the beasts, which performed all involuntary acts of a sensory, motor, and vital nature. Describing this animal soul concretely as a "sulphureous, fiery component of the blood," Willis imagined it to be "généralement répandue par tout le corps." As such, it represented (except for its being restricted to a subintellectual level) a chemiatric version of the Epicurean "subtle atoms" theory: "The Brutal Soul doth consist of Particles of the same matter, out of which the organical Body is formed, but that they are choyce, most subtle, and highly active.... This heap of subtle Particles, or the Soul, which explicating itself more largely, and insinuating its Particles into others more thick, and weaving them together, frames the Body, is Co-extended with it, and, fitted exactly, actuates, inlivens, and inspires the whole, and all its parts" (*Dr. Willis's Practice of Physick: Two Discourses Concerning the Soul of Brutes*, p. 6). This definition of the animal soul drew criticism from theological quarters because of its affinity with Epicurean doctrine, despite the fact that Willis himself, who was of a pious turn of mind, had not intended in the least to abet materialism.

Claude Perrault (1613-88), an architect of the Louvre, was also a graduate of the Paris Medical Faculty. His publications in natural science covered a wide range of topics pertaining to physics, physiology, comparative anatomy, natural history, and plant biology. Perrault's opinion about the coextension of the soul with the organism was presented in his *Essais de physique, ou recueil de plusieurs traitez touchant les choses naturelles*, Tome II (1680), pp. 260-310. Doubting whether the brain was the central organ of sensory and motor activity, because of the difficulty of explaining mechanically its control over the body by means of the *esprits animaux*, he assumed instead that a soul, spread throughout the organism, directed its manifold operations: "L'ame qui est unie à toutes les parties du corps animé, n'a que faire d'aller contempler ces images dans le cerveau, puisqu'elle les peut contempler dans chaque organe où elles sont imprimées pendant la sensation" (*ibid.*, II, 266). Unlike Willis' *anima brutorum*, Perrault's "soul" was described, notwithstanding its extensible properties, as substantially distinct from the corporeal mechanism, so that it anticipated in large measure the animistic doctrine of Stahl: "l'ame se sert des organes du corps, qui sont de véritables machines, comme estant la principale cause de l'action de chacune des pieces de la machine," etc. (*ibid.*, III, 1). Moreover, to account for the difference between rational or voluntary behavior, on the one hand, and instinctive, involuntary or habitual behavior, on the other, Perrault distinguished between a conscious and an unconscious level of the soul: "Il y a une pensée expresse & distincte pour les choses auxquelles nous nous appliquons avec soin, & une pensée negligée & confuse pour les choses qu'un long exercice a rendu si faciles que la pensée expresse & exacte n'y est point necessaire" (*ibid.*, II, 283).

104. La Mettrie has in mind the *Aeneid*, VI, ll. 724-32:

> Principio caelum ac terras camposque liquentes
> Lucentemque globum lunae Titaniaque astra
> Spiritus intus alit, totamque infusa per artus
> Mens agitat molem et magno se corpore miscet.
> Inde hominum pecudumque genus vitaeque volantum
> Et quae marmoreo fert monstra sub aequore pontus.
> Igneus est ollis vigor et caelestis origo
> Seminibus, quantum non noxia corpora tardant
> Terrenique hebetant artus moribundaque membra.

The concept of the *anima mundi*, as it is expressed by Virgil in this passage, derived very likely from the physical doctrines of the Stoic school, which depicted the individual soul as a spark of the fiery substance said to permeate the material world and to generate the various forms of life in it. Though such a notion of the soul lent itself easily to Epicureanizing tendencies, it is probable that Virgil did not wish to present the *anima mundi* in that particular light, as indeed his choice of words would indicate: "spiritus intus"; "mens agitat molem." Despite this, La Mettrie's reference to Virgil is here colored by the materialist interpretations of the world-soul concept that were current in the eighteenth century, of which an example may be cited from the anonymous *Ame matérielle*: "Il y a dans le monde un esprit très subtile, très delié, toujours en mouvement, dont la plus grande partie ... et la source est dans le soleil.... C'est assurément l'ame du Monde ... c'est là ce qui fait l'ame de l'homme et des animaux," etc. (pp. 115-16).

105. The regeneration of Trembley's polyp from each of its severed portions into complete new polyps came as a blow to those who believed in the immateriality and indivisibility of the animal soul, and strongly favored the opposite claim that the vital and sensitive principle was coextensive with the organism and hence itself corporeal. Both Willis and Perrault had previously supported their theories of an extended soul with data concerning autonomic muscle action, even though they had interpreted these in accordance, not with the concept

of irritability, but with the particular brand of animism that characterized the biological thinking of each. Perrault, for instance, had offered as an empirical proof of the coextension of body and soul the case of "une Vipere qui fut dissequée à la Bibliotheque du Roy, laquelle après qu'on luy eut couppé la teste & osté le coeur avec tout le reste des entrailles, rampoit à son ordinaire, & passant d'une cour dans un jardin, y chercha un tas de pierres, où elle s'alla cacher" (*op.cit.*, II, 276). La Mettrie's use of the term "reste d'Ame" in relation to the type of hypothesis given by Perrault and Willis referred, very probably, to the latter's frequent mention of the "parts" or "portions" of the divisible animal soul. It calls to mind a passage in the *Anima brutorum*, where Willis had attributed various phenomena of a sort that La Mettrie would have classed under irritability to what was described in the original as the "animae extensae plures & distinctas portiones": "Wherefore, since there is no medium between the Body and the Soul, but that the members and parts of the Body are the Organs of the Soul; what can we think else, or affirm, but that many and distinct portions of the same Extended Soul, actuate the several members, and parts of this Body? Besides, it is seen in several living Creatures, whose Liquors, both the Vital and the Animal (in which the Soul as to all its parts immediately subsists) are viscous, and less dissipable, that the Soul is also divided with the Body, and exercises its Faculties, to wit, of Motion and Sense, in every one of the divided members, layd apart by themselves. So Worms, Eeles, and Vipers, being cut into pieces, move themselves for a time, and being pricked will wrinkle themselves together" (*op.cit., The Soul of Brutes*, p. 5).

106. Cf. above, pp. 63-64.

107. In "La Méchanique des animaux" (*Essais de physique*, Vol. III), Perrault explained contraction in a manner which, by endowing muscle tissues with a kind of inherent force, seems to La Mettrie to have foreshadowed the law of irritability. However, Perrault's opinion would appear, on closer examination, to refer more to the general notion of elasticity than to that of contractility in any true sense: "La conclusion que je tire de ces hypotheses est, que les esprits appellez vulgairement animaux, servent au mouvement des muscles en les relaschant & non en les tendant ou en les accourcissant; l'accourcissement qui leur arrive estant naturel & absolument involontaire, puisqu'il depend de la constitution elementaire qui est commune à tous les corps qui ont ressort" (*op.cit.*, III, 79-80). Likewise, with respect to the heartbeat he stated: "Je ne croy donc pas qu'il y ait d'autre puissance ni d'autre principe de cette dilatation du coeur, que celuy que j'ay déjà

proposé comme la cause generale de l'action de tous les autres muscles, sçavoir la vertu élastique que je suppose dans les muscles, de mesme que dans la pluspart des corps, par le moyen de laquelle chaque corps a une consistance naturelle, à laquelle il est capable de luy-mesme de se rétablir quand elle a esté changée" (*ibid.*, III, 229-30). The full meaning of these remarks is made clear by Perrault's special theory of contraction. He had assumed that in the inactive state the contractile fibers of the muscle, being elastic, were maintained in a tense or "outstretched" condition, so that when these were released by the relaxing influence of the *esprits animaux* on the antagonist fibers, the result was contraction, which thus represented the "springing back" of the muscle mass by virtue of its natural elasticity (*ressort*). Despite the strangeness of Perrault's theory, it may be said to have favored the development of the irritability principle to the extent that its notion of "ressort naturel" directed attention to a contractile property inherent in muscle fiber.

108. Concerning the changes which, on this point and others, La Mettrie's thought underwent from the *Histoire de l'âme* to *l'Homme machine*, see above, Chapter III.

109. Julien Leroy (1686-1759), French watchmaker and mechanist, improved the construction of repeater watches by increasing the solidity of their parts and the precision of their movements. He applied his superior methods to the manufacture of pendulum clocks as well, which he perfected in particular by the use of a compensation mechanism that nullified the effect of temperature variations on the pendulum. Leroy also made important contributions in the field of gnomonics. From 1739 on, he held the rank of *horloger du roi*.

The "pendule planétaire" of Christian Huygens, an object of much scientific curiosity in its day, was a mechanical model of the solar system, designed by him and executed by the clockmaker van Ceulen, which faithfully duplicated the movements of the planets. Huygens gave a technical account of it in his *Descriptio automati planetarii*, and in a letter to a friend described it briefly as follows: "elle a son mouvement d'elle-mesme, montrant tousjours l'heure, le jour du mois, et l'acroissement de la lune, outre le mouvement des autres planetes . . . [qui] se voient avec leurs satellites au dessus de la plaque. . . . Tous les cercles des planetes y sont dans leurs proportions veritables" (*Oeuvres complètes de Huygens*, La Haye; VIII, 343).

110. Jacques de Vaucanson (1709-82) presented in 1738 to the Académie des sciences his famous "joueur de flûte," of which he gave a description in his *Mécanisme d'un flûteur automate*. This automaton

was soon followed by others of such ingenious construction that Vaucanson's talents won universal admiration, and in 1748 he was elected to the Académie des sciences. His "canard" was a mechanical duck that could paddle itself about, partake of food, and even digest it after a fashion. Among the more remarkable of his creations there were also a "joueur de tambourin et de galoubet" and an "aspic sifflant et s'élançant sur le sein de Cléopâtre."

111. The portio mollis is the cochlear branch of the eighth (i.e. acoustic) pair of cranial nerves, and is the nerve immediately involved in hearing.

112. The *Histoire naturelle de l'âme* purported, on its title page, to be "traduite de l'Anglois de M. Charp"—a pseudonym that might have referred to Samuel Sharp, a noted London surgeon and disciple of Cheselden, who was a friend of La Mettrie's teacher, Hunauld, and the author of a widely read *Treatise on the operations of surgery* (1739). The *Histoire de l'âme* had dismissed Descartes's doctrine of the animal-machine with the scornful words: "Une opinion si risible n'a jamais eu d'accès chez les philosophes que comme un badinage d'esprit, ou un amusement philosophique. C'est pourquoi nous ne nous arrêterons pas à la réfuter." With respect to La Mettrie's change of view on this particular point, see above, Chapters III, IV.

113. Owing to the temporary persistence of life in decerebrated animals and in acephalous monsters it was realized in La Mettrie's time that, while the cerebrum was probably the seat of conscious motor activity, the medulla oblongata retained a large measure of independent control over the automatic vital functions. The allusion here to Haller concerns his memoir: "Observatio de Scirrho Cerebelli," *Philosophical Transactions*, Vol. 43, no. 474 (1744), pp. 100-01, which reported the case of a beggar girl who, despite the tumefaction of almost the whole of a cerebellar hemisphere, had until her death "gone on asking alms from door to door." Haller's observation, the value of which La Mettrie was quick to appreciate, helped in correcting Willis' erroneous belief (still accepted by Boerhaave) that the cerebellum served as the primary organ of involuntary activity.

114. In this paragraph La Mettrie takes the spermatist side of the ovist-spermatist controversy which, having begun in the previous century, was far from being finished in his period. The ovists maintained that the foetus, already pre-existing inertly and invisibly in the ovum, needed the male sperm only in order to acquire life and motion; the spermatists, on the other hand, who based their opinion on the microscopic observations of Leeuwenhoek and Hartsoeker, claimed that the

preformed organism was present in the spermatozoon, and that it developed as a result of the nourishment it found in the ovum. La Mettrie's sympathy for the latter viewpoint reflects, no doubt, the influence of Boerhaave, who was one of the leading spermatists of the time. Despite the experimental failure to perceive the outlines of the human embryo in either the ovum or the spermatozoon, the spermatists had an advantage over the ovists in that their theory started out at least with an observable living organism, thus avoiding the difficulty with which the ovists were faced, of having to explain the transition of the ovum from a vegetative to an animal state. Notwithstanding this, in 1748 and for some years thereafter, the ovist theory enjoyed, for various other reasons, the greater popularity; cf. Diderot, D'Alembert, *l'Encyclopédie*, article "Génération," VII (1757), 563.

115. Vide Boerhaave, *Institutiones rei medicae*, § 651.

116. Nicolas Hartsoeker (1656-1725), Dutch physicist, mathematician, and microscopist, who was among the first to observe spermatozoa, disputed with Leeuwenhoek the honor of that discovery.

117. The *punctum saliens* refers to the foetal heart. Its appearance in the chick forty hours after incubation was described in Malpighi's *Dissertatio de formatione pulli in ovo* (London, 1673; p. 10).

118. The *Spiritus rector* was a chemical notion that Boerhaave had done much to set in vogue, and which denoted the "essence" in which the smell of odoriferous substances was supposed to reside. La Mettrie draws here a rather dubious analogy between the relationship of the human head to the body, and that of the flower to the plant. The passage is interesting, however, because it suggests the train of thought that will be pursued before long in *l'Homme plante*.

119. By "semence de la femme" La Mettrie means, of course, not the ovum, but a seminal fluid. The idea that generation resulted from the mixture of seminal secretions by both the male and female was an ancient one, and its career was not yet finished in the time of *l'Homme machine*. Supported by the authority of Hippocrates and Galen, it had often been associated in antiquity with the Epicurean school. During the seventeenth century Descartes made the "mélange des deux liqueurs" the basis of the theory of generation outlined in his *Traité de la formation du foetus*. The belief in a female seminal fluid was soon discarded, however, with the discovery of the true functions of the ovaries and Fallopian tubes. While this led to the formulation of the ovist doctrine, the subsequent discovery of spermatozoa gave rise, in its turn, to the spermatist position. But because the ovist-spermatist controversy insisted on finding the preformed foetus in *either* the male

sperm or in the ovum, it could give little hope of ever explaining the frequent resemblance of offspring to both parents. Therefore, it was with the aim of clarifying the problem of bilateral heredity that Maupertuis, in his *Vénus physique* of 1745, discarded preformation in favor of epigenesis, and at the same time supposed that both the male and female parent furnish a seminal fluid which, mixed together, and gradually modified by the influence of the law of attraction, gives rise to the embryo. In the present paragraph and in the one that follows, La Mettrie is thinking of Maupertuis's hypothesis, which he rightly rejects on the ground that conception does not depend on any female secretion resulting from sexual excitement. (The same criticism will be given at greater length in *l'Ouvrage de Pénélope*, III, 201*-12*.) Just after *l'Homme machine*—in 1749—the idea of a "combinaison des deux semences" was to play a more ingenious, but no less erroneous role in Buffon's theory of generation, according to which the seminal fluids of both sexes swarmed with innumerable *molécules organiques* that coalesced to form the embryo.

120. The "reigns of nature" were the mineral, the vegetable, and the animal.

BIBLIOGRAPHY

I. EDITIONS OF *L'HOMME MACHINE*

L'Homme machine. A Leyde, De l'Imp. d'Elie Luzac, Fils, 1748. 108 pp. 18°

L'Homme machine. A Leyde, De l'Imp. d'Elie Luzac, Fils, 1748. 109 pp. 18°

L'Homme machine. A Leyde, De l'Imp. d'Elie Luzac, Fils, 1748. 148 pp. 12°

(Reprinted in the following editions of La Mettrie's collected works:)

Oeuvres philosophiques, Londres [Berlin], 1751. 4°
" " , Amsterdam, 1752. 2 vols. 18°
" " , Berlin, 1753. 2 vols.
" " , Amsterdam, 1753. 2 vols. 18°
" " , Amsterdam, 1764. 2 vols.
" " , Amsterdam, 1764. 3 vols. 18°
" " , Berlin, 1764. 2 vols. 18°
" " , Berlin, 1774. 2 vols. Sm. 8°
" " , Amsterdam, 1774. 3 vols. 18°
" " , Berlin, 1775. 3 vols. 16°
" " , Berlin & Paris, 1796. 3 vols. 8°

L'Homme-machine, avec une introduction et des notes de J. Assézat, F. Henry, Paris, 1865. (Tome II of *Singularités physiologiques.*)

L'Homme machine, suivi de l'Art de jouir. Introduction et notes de Maurice Solovine, Bossard, Paris, 1921.

L'Homme machine, Paris, Nord-Sud, 1948. (*Collection classique.*)

La Mettrie. Textes choisis. Préface, commentaires et notes explicatives par Marcelle Tisserand. Editions sociales, Paris, 1954.

TRANSLATIONS

Man a Machine. Translated from the French of the Marquiss D'Argens. London: Printed for W. Owen, 1749.

Man a Machine. Translated from the French of Mons. De la Mettrie. The second edition, London: printed for G. Smith, 1750.

Man a Machine. . . . Translated from the French of Mons. de la Mettrie, a celebrated Physician of the Faculty at Paris, and author of

Penelope, or the *Machiavel* in Physic. The Third Edition, London: printed for G. Smith, 1750.

Man a Machine; including Frederick the Great's "Eulogy" ... and extracts from "The Natural History of the Soul." Philosophical and historical notes by Gertrude C. Bussey. Chicago, The Open Court Publishing Co., 1912. (Has French and English texts.)

(Same as above) ... Chicago, London, The Open Court Publishing Co., 1927. (Has only English text.)

(Same as above) ... La Salle, Ill., The Open Court Publishing Co., 1943. (Has French and English texts.)

Der Mensch eine Maschine. Uebersetzt, erläutert und mit einer Einleitung über den Materialismus versehen von Dr. Adolf Ritter. Leipzig, 1875. (*Philosophische Bibliothek*, Bd. 67.)

Der Mensch eine Maschine. Uebersetzt, mit einer Vorrede und mit Anmerkungen versehen von Max Brahn. Leipzig, 1909.

L'Uomo macchina, versione dal francese, con prefazione et note di Luigi Stefanoni. Milano, 1866.

L'Uomo macchina. Roma (Soriano nel Cimino), tip. Sistina, 1885. (*Biblioteca d'un curioso*, Vol. 3.)

L'Uomo macchina. Roma, dagli eredi del Barbagrigia (Soriano nel Cimino), tip. Capaccini, 1889.

L'Uomo macchina e altri scritti. Traduzione dal francese a cura di Giulio Preti. Milano, G. Feltrinelli, 1955. (*Universale economica*, No. 203. *Serie storia e filosofia*, Vol. 63.)

Chelovek-mashina. Per. so vstupit. stat'ey "Zhizn' i uchenie De Lamettri" i prim. V. Konstansa. Sankt-peterburg, 1911. 140 str. (*Filosof. b-ka izd.* M. I. Semenova. *Filosofy-materialisty.*)

Lamettri. *Izbrannye Sochinienia*. Per. i predisl. A. Deborina. Moskva-Leningrad, 1925. LI, 370 str. (*In-t K. Marksa i F. Engel'sa. B-ka materializma.*)

Czlowiek-maszyna. Przelozyl Stefan Rudnianski. Warszawa, 1925. (*Biblioteka Filozoficzna, wydawana przez Warszawski Instytut Filozoficzny.*)

Czlowiek-maszyna. W przekladzie i z przedmowa Stefana Rudnianskiego. Wyd. nowe przejrzane i uzupelnione. Warszawa, 1953. (*Biblioteka Klasykow Filozofii.*)

II. REVIEWS, DISCUSSIONS, AND REFUTATIONS OF *L'HOMME MACHINE* IN THE EIGHTEENTH CENTURY

(Anon.). *Acta historico-ecclesiastica*, Weimar, XIII (1749), 467-72.

Clément, Pierre. *Les Cinq Années littéraires,* Berlin, 1756, I, 120-22.

BIBLIOGRAPHY

Denesle. *Les préjugés des anciens et nouveaux philosophes, sur la nature de l'âme humaine, ou Examen du matérialisme*, Paris, 1765, I, 210-412.

François, Laurent. *Défense de la religion contre les difficultés des incrédules*, Paris, 1755, Vol. I.

Franzen, Adam Wilhelm. *Widerlegung der französischen Schrift*: L'Homme Machine, *nebst dem Beweis der Gegensätze*, Leipzig, 1749.

Gauchat, Gabriel. *Lettres critiques, ou analyse et réfutation de divers écrits modernes contre la religion*, Paris, Vol. XVIII, 1763.

(Anon.) *Göttingische Philosophische Bibliothek* (Windheim), Hannover, I (1749), 197-98, and passim.

Haller, Albrecht von. *Göttingische Zeitungen von gelehrten Sachen*, Dezember 1747, pp. 905-07.

Hayer, Hubert. *La spiritualité et l'immortalité de l'âme, avec le sentiment de l'Antiquité tant sacrée que profane, par rapport à l'une & à l'autre*, Paris, 1757. 3 vols.

Hollmann, Samuel Christian. "Widerlegung des *homme machine*," in *Göttingische Zeitungen von gelehrten Sachen*, Mai 1748, pp. 409-12, 425-28. Published also in translation as: *Lettre d'un anonyme pour servir de critique ou de réfutation au livre intitulé: l'Homme machine*.

Krause, Karl Christian. *De homine non machina, disputatio physica*, Leipzig, 1752.

Lelarge de Lignac, abbé Joseph-Adrien. *Elémens de métaphysique tirés de l'expérience: ou Lettres à un matérialiste sur la nature de l'Ame*, Paris, 1753.

Luc, Jacques François de. *Observations sur les savans incrédules, et sur quelques-uns de leurs écrits*, Genève, 1762, pp. 373-92.

Luzac, Elie. *L'Homme plus que machine*, 1748, in *Oeuvres philosophiques de La Mettrie*, Amsterdam, 1774, Vol. III.

Luzac, Etienne. *Nouvelle bibliothèque germanique*, VI, 2e partie, Amsterdam, 1750, pp. 429-41.

(Anon.) *The Monthly Review*, I (1749), 123-31.

(Anon.) *Nachrichten von einer Hallischen Bibliothek*, I (1748), pp. 75-84.

(Anon.) *Neue Theologische Bibliothek*, Leipzig, Mai 1748, pp. 68-70.

(Anon.) *Neue Zeitungen von gelehrten Sachen*, February 1748, pp. 138-41.

Neumayr, Francisco. *Frag: Ob der Mensch weiter nichts seye als eine Maschine? Beantwortet wider die Freydenker und Materialisten* [Augsburg], 1761.

BIBLIOGRAPHY

Pichon, Th. *Cartel aux philosophes à quatre pattes, ou l'Immatérialisme opposé au Matérialisme* [1763].

Plouquet, Gottfried. *Dissertatio de materialismo, cum supplementis et confutatione libelli*: l'Homme machine: *inscripti*, Tübingen, 1751.

Pluquet, abbé François-André-Adrien. *Examen du fatalisme*, Paris, 1757, I, 432-46; II, 494-98, and passim.

Pury, Daniel. *Pensées pour et contre les écrivains mécréants, à l'occasion de deux écrits nouveaux, intitulés; l'un, l'Homme machine; l'autre, Discours sur le bonheur*, Neuchatel, 1752.

Roche, abbé Antoine-Martin. *Traité de la nature de l'âme, et de l'origine de ses connoissances, contre le système de M. Locke & de ses partisans*, Paris, 1759, I, 1-106.

Roques, Pierre. *Nouvelle bibliothèque germanique*, v, 2e partie (1748-49), Amsterdam, 1750, pp. 328-57.

Tralles, Balthasar Ludwig. *De machina et anima humana prorsus a se invicem distinctis commentatio, libello latere amantis auctoris gallico Homo Machina inscripto opposita, et ad illustrissimum virum Albertum Haller exarata*, Leipzig & Breslau, 1749.

Tressan, comte de. "Réponse à un de mes Amis, qui avait fait l'apologie de l'Homme-Machine de la Métrie," *Oeuvres*, Paris, 1823, x, 237-40.

Verini, J. G. *Gründ- und deutlicher Begriff von der natürlichen Freyheit ... etc. etc.; nebst einer Widerlegung des sogenannten Alethini Liberti, und kurzen Zugabe aus den im vorigen Jahre herausgekommenen französischen Tractat: L'Homme machine*. Frankfurt u. Leipzig, 1749.

III. GENERAL WORKS

(Anon.) *L'Ame matérielle*, MS Arsenal 2239.

Bastholm, Eyvind. *The History of Muscle Physiology, from the Natural Philosophers to Albrecht von Haller* (*Acta historica scientiarum naturalium et medicinalium*, Vol. VII), Copenhagen, 1950.

Bergmann, Ernst. *Die Satiren des Herrn Maschine*, Leipzig, 1913.

———. "The Significance of La Mettrie and Pertinent Materials," *The Open Court*, XXVII (1913), 411-32.

Berthier, Auguste-Georges. "Le mécanisme cartésien et la physiologie au XVIIe siècle," *Isis*, II (1914), 37-89, III (1920), 21-58.

Boerhaave, Hermann. *De usu ratiocinii mechanici in medicina* (1703), in *Opuscula selecta neerlandicorum in arte medica*, Amsterdam, 1907.

———. *Institutions de médecine*, trad. par M. de La Mettrie, 2e édn., Paris, 1743-50.

BIBLIOGRAPHY

Boerhaave, Hermann. *Praelectiones academicae in proprias institutiones rei medicae*, edidit, et notas addidit Albertus Haller, Naples, 1754-55. (Original edition, Göttingen, 1739-44.)

Boissier, Raymond. *La Mettrie, médecin, pamphlétaire et philosophe*, Paris, 1931.

Cabanis, Pierre-Jean-Georges. *Rapports du physique et du moral de l'homme*, in *Oeuvres philosophiques de Cabanis*, éd. C. Lehec et J. Cazeneuve, Paris, 1956.

Canguilhem, Georges. *La formation du concept de réflexe aux XVIIe et XVIIIe siècles*, Paris, 1955.

Delaunay, Paul. "L'évolution philosophique et médicale du biomécanisme: de Descartes à Boerhaave, de Leibnitz à Cabanis," *Le Progrès médical*, 1927, pp. 1289-93, 1337-42, 1347-52, 1369-84.

———. *La vie médicale aux XVIe, XVIIe et XVIIIe siècles*, Paris, 1935.

Du Bois-Reymond, Emil. "Rede: öffentliche Sitzung vom 28. Januar 1875," *Monatsberichte der königlich Preussischen Akademie der Wissenschaften zu Berlin*, 1875, pp. 85-112.

(Anon.) *Essai sur les facultés de l'âme*, MS Mazarine 1192.

Frederick II of Prussia. *Eloge de La Mettrie*, La Haye, 1752.

Gaubius, Hieronymus David. *Sermo academicus de regimine mentis quod medicorum est*, Leyden, 1747.

Haller, Albrecht von. *Mémoires sur la nature sensible et irritable des parties du corps animal*, Lausanne, 1756.

Hentig, Hans von. "La Mettrie als Kriminalanthropologe," *Archiv für Kriminalanthropologie und Kriminalistik*, LI (1913), 53-59.

Holbach, Paul Heinrich Dietrich, Baron d'. *Système de la nature, ou des Loix du monde Physique & du monde moral*, Londres [Amsterdam], 1770.

La Mettrie, Julien Offray de. *Abrége de la théorie Chymique.... Auquel on a joint le Traité du Vertige*, Paris, 1741.

———. *Histoire naturelle de l'âme*, La Haye, 1745.

———. *Histoire naturelle de l'âme, nouvelle édition . . . augmentée de la Lettre Critique à Madame la Marquise du Chattelet*, Oxford, 1747.

———. *Observations de médecine pratique*, Paris, 1743.

———. *Oeuvres philosophiques*, Amsterdam, 1774. 3 vols.: *Traité de l'âme. L'Abrégé des systèmes. L'Homme plante. Les Animaux plus que machines. Anti-Sénèque, ou Discours sur le bonheur. Système d'Epicure.*

———. *L'Ouvrage de Pénélope; ou Machiavel en médecine*, Berlin, 1748-50.

Lange, Frederick Albert. *The History of Materialism*, trans. E. C. Thomas, 3rd edn., New York, 1950.

Le Camus, Antoine. *Médecine de l'esprit; où l'on cherche 1º le méchanisme du corps qui influe sur les fonctions de l'âme. 2º Les causes physiques qui rendent ce méchanisme ou défectueux, ou plus parfait. 3º Les moyens qui peuvent l'entretenir dans son état libre, & le rectifier lorsqu'il est gêné*. 2e édn., Paris, 1769. (Original edition, 1753.)

Lemée, Pierre. *Julien Offray de La Mettrie, médecin, philosophe, polémiste; sa vie, son oeuvre*, 1954.

Luzac, Elie. *Essai sur la liberté de produire ses sentimens*, Au Pays libre, Pour le Bien Public, 1749.

Maître, Jean-Marie-Louis-Charles-Joseph. *Un médecin philosophe: De la Mettrie (1709-1751)*, Paris, 1919.

Malebranche, Nicolas. *De la recherche de la vérité*, éd. G. Lewis, Paris, 1946.

Meunier, L. *Histoire de la Médecine*, Paris, 1924.

Mirabaud, Jean-Baptiste de. *Le monde, son origine et son antiquité. De l'Ame, et de son immortalité*, 2e édn., Londres, 1778. (Original edition, 1751.)

Needham, Joseph. *Man a Machine, in Answer to a Romantical and Unscientific Treatise Written by Sig. Eugenio Rignano & Entitled "Man not a Machine,"* New York, 1928.

(Anon.) *Nouvelles libertés de penser*, in *Examen de la religion*, Trévoux, 1745.

Perkins, Jean E. "Diderot and La Mettrie," *Studies on Voltaire and the 18th Century*, Geneva, x (1959), 49-100.

———. "Voltaire and La Mettrie," *ibid.*, 101-11.

Pernetti, abbé Jacques. *Lettres philosophiques sur les physionomies*, La Haye, 1746.

Perrault, Claude. *Essais de physique, ou recueil de plusieurs traitez touchant les choses naturelles*, Paris, 1680-88.

Pflug, Günther. "Julien Offray de Lamettrie und die biologischen Theorien des 18. Jahrhunderts," *Deutsche Vierteljahrsschrift für Literaturwissenschaft und Geistesgeschichte*, XXVII (1953), pp. 509-27.

Picavet, François. *La Mettrie et la critique allemande*, Paris, 1889.

Poritzky, J. E. *Julien Offray de Lamettrie, sein Leben und seine Werke*, Berlin, 1900.

Quépat, Nérée [René Paquet]. *Essai sur La Mettrie, sa vie et ses oeuvres*, Paris, 1873.

BIBLIOGRAPHY

Rignano, Eugenio. *Man Not a Machine: A Study of the Finalistic Aspects of Life*, London, 1926.

Rosenfield, Leonora C. *From Beast-Machine to Man-Machine: Animal Soul in French Letters from Descartes to La Mettrie*, New York, 1941.

Sluckin, W. *Minds and Machines*, Penguin Books, 1954.

Stahl, Georg Ernst. *Theoria medica vera*, in *Oeuvres médico-philosophiques et pratiques*, Paris, 1859-64.

Tuloup, Guy-Francis. *Un précurseur méconnu: Offray de La Mettrie, médecin-philosophe (1709-1751)*, Dinard, 1938.

Valkhoff, P. "Elie Luzac," *Neophilologus*, IV (1918), pp. 10-21, 106-13.

Vartanian, Aram. *Diderot and Descartes: A Study of Scientific Naturalism in the Enlightenment*, Princeton, 1953.

———. "Elie Luzac's Refutation of La Mettrie," *Modern Language Notes*, LXIV (1949), 159-61.

———. "Trembley's Polyp, La Mettrie, and 18th-century French Materialism," *Journal of the History of Ideas*, XI, 3 (June 1950), 259-86.

Vernière, Paul. *Spinoza et la pensée française avant la révolution*, Paris, 1954.

Verworn, Max. *Irritability: a Physiological Analysis of the General Effect of Stimuli in Living Substance*, New Haven, 1913.

Vézeaux de Lavergne, Paulin. *Du caractère médical de l'oeuvre de La Mettrie*, Lyon, 1907.

Voltaire. *Lettres philosophiques*, éd. R. Naves, Garnier, Paris.

Wade, Ira O. *The Clandestine Organization and Diffusion of Philosophic Ideas in France from 1700 to 1750*, Princeton, 1938.

Wiener, Norbert. *Cybernetics; or Control and Communication in the Animal and the Machine*, New York, 1948.

Willis, Thomas. *Two Discourses concerning the Soul of Brutes*, in *Dr. Willis's Practice of Physick*, trans. S. Pordage, London, 1683-84.

Wolf, A. *A History of Science, Technology, and Philosophy in the XVIIIth Century*, 2nd edn., London, 1952.

INDEX

Abbadie, Jacques, 176, 226
Abrégé de la Théorie chimique, Boerhaave, 3, 40n, 78n
Abrégé des systèmes, La Mettrie, 65
Académie royale des sciences, 215; *Mémoires*, 210, 219
Acta historico-ecclesiastica, 110n
Adversus gentes, Arnobius, 221f
Aeneid, Virgil, 244
Albinus, Bernhard Siegfried, 87, 202
Algarotti, Francesco, 9
Ame matérielle, anon., 73f, 81, 244
Amman, Johann Conrad, 160f, 213f
anima mundi, 244
animal-automaton (*bête machine*), 19, 48, 57ff, 72, 93, 191, 214, 247
Animaux plus que machines, La Mettrie, 11, 21n, 29n, 54f, 59n, 105, 217, 220
animism, 18, 19, 47, 61, 87, 240f, 243, 245
anthropoid ape, 26f, 160ff, 213, 214ff, 218
Aphorismes sur la connaissance et la cure des maladies, Boerhaave, 3
Archimedes, 145, 203
Argens, Jean de Boyer, marquis d', 8, 9, 115, 142n, 199
Aristotle, Aristotelianism, 41, 46, 48, 49, 64, 168, 206
Arnobius, 169, 221f
Ashby, W. R., 134, 135
Assézat, Jules, 130, 199
Astruc, Jean, 236
atheism, atheist, 24, 64, 98, 99, 103, 110, 117, 120, 141, 176, 177ff, 227, 228, 230
Austrian Succession, War of the, 4
"Avertissement de l'Imprimeur," Luzac, 7, 8, 17, 98, 141f, 199

Bacon, Francis, 84, 181, 182, 232
Baglivi, Giorgio, 84, 235
Baker, John R., 218
Balzac, Honoré de, 130
Bastholm, Eyvind, 83n
Bayle, Pierre, 97, 102, 167, 185, 228, 240
Bellet, Isaac, 239
Bergmann, Ernst, 6n, 96, 102n, 131, 137, 199, 200
Bergson, Henri, 132

Bernard, Claude, 130
Berthier, Auguste-Georges, 57n
Biblia Naturae, Swammerdam, 232
Bibliotheca anatomica, 233
Bibliothèque raisonnée, 68f
Bichat, Marie François Xavier, 130
Blondel, James, 184, 239
Boece, Hector, 225
Boerhaave, Hermann, 3, 41, 75ff, 83, 85f, 87, 90, 157, 188, 192n, 200, 202, 232, 237, 242, 247, 248
Boindin, Nicolas, 177, 229
Boissier, Raymond, 12, 131
Bonnet, Charles, 91, 123n, 217
Borelli, Giovanni, 184, 240
Bouillier, David-Renaud, 59n
Boyle, Robert, 19, 84, 181, 232f, 239
Broussais, François-Joseph-Victor, 130
Büchner, Ludwig, 130
Buffon, Georges-Louis Leclerc, comte de, 55, 214, 215, 217, 224, 234, 249
Bugati, Gasparo, 225

Cabanis, Pierre-Jean-Georges, 114, 116, 123ff
Caen, collège de, 1
Cailliet, Emile, 129
Canguilhem, Georges, 237
Canus Julius, 153, 207
Cartel aux philosophes à quatre pattes, Pichon, 112
Cartesian, Cartesianism, 2, 17, 19, 48, 57ff, 62, 75, 76, 84, 102, 127, 167, 188, 214, 230. See also Descartes
Châtelet, Emilie de Breteuil, marquise du, 5, 63, 206
Chaudon, abbé, 115n
Chayla, vicomte du, 10
Chiverny, Philippe Hurault, comte de, 157, 210
Cicutae acquaticae historia et noxae, Wepfer, 235
Cinq Années littéraires, Clément, 97n, 111n
Clément, Pierre, 97n, 110
Comte, Auguste, 130
Condillac, Etienne Bonnot, abbé de, 62, 120ff, 127f, 129, 220

INDEX

Condorcet, Marie Jean Caritat, marquis de, 202
Connor, Bernard, 222
Corneille, Pierre, 29, 168
Cours de philosophie positive, Comte, 130
Coutances, collège de, 1
Cowper, William, 19, 84, 180, 231
cybernetics, 134ff
Czolbe, Heinrich, 130

Dacier, André, 203
Dacier, Anne-Lefèvre, 145, 203
De anima brutorum, Willis, 61, 158, 211, 243, 245
De Bar, Mlle, 144, 202
De cerebri anatome, Willis, 158, 211, 212f
De comparando certo in physicis, Boerhaave, 75
De corpore, Hobbes, 122n
"Dédicace à Haller," La Mettrie, 32, 95, 103, 104, 143ff, 199ff
Défense de la religion, François, 96, 108f
De fibra motrice, Baglivi, 235
De homine, Hobbes, 65, 122n
deism, 25, 79, 176ff, 227
De l'âme et de son immortalité, Mirabaud, 74
Delaunay, Paul, 119n
De l'Homme, Helvétius, 121n
De l'Homme, Marat, 117
De machina et anima humana, Tralles, 103
De motu animalium, Borelli, 240
De motu cordis, Harvey, 231f
De motu tonico vitali, Stahl, 235
De natura substantiae energetica, Glisson, 234
Denesle, 112
De partibus corporis sensibilibus et irritabilibus, Haller, 85, 111n, 202
De regimine mentis, Gaubius, 90f, 207, 224, 238
De rerum natura, Lucretius, 229f
Derham, William, 176, 226
Desbarreaux, Jacques Vallée, 177, 228f
Descartes, René, 2, 13, 14, 19, 44, 47, 48, 49, 57ff, 60, 64, 67, 75, 77, 81, 82, 83, 90, 107, 149, 152, 168, 176, 191, 203, 206f, 227, 238, 247, 248
Dettingen, battle of, 4
De usu ratiocinii mechanici in medicina, Boerhaave, 76f
De venae portae porta malorum, Stahl, 208

De ventriculo et intestinis, Glisson, 234
Dialogues des morts, Fontenelle, 159, 211, 221
Diderot, Denis, 2, 30, 54, 55, 109f, 114, 116, 117ff, 120, 128, 129, 177, 220, 227, 229
Digby, Kenelm, 239
Discours anatomiques, Lamy, 230
Discours de la méthode, Descartes, 90, 206f
"Discours préliminaire," La Mettrie, 97
Discours sur le bonheur (Anti-Sénèque), La Mettrie, 11, 50ff, 99, 115, 116, 224
Discours sur l'origine de l'inégalité, Rousseau, 218, 220
Dissertatio de materialismo, Plouquet, 100f
Dissertatio de sede cogitantis animae, Lancisi, 210
Dissertationes variae, Baglivi, 235
Donati, Marcello, 225
Driesch, Hans, 132
Droneau, Marie Louise, 3
dualism, 13, 31, 38, 39, 60, 93, 123n
Du Bois-Reymond, Emil, 131
Dumesnil, Mlle, 203

Elémens de métaphysique, Lelarge de Lignac, 96, 106f
Eléments de physiologie, Diderot, 118
Eloge de La Mettrie, Frederick II of Prussia, 1, 2, 12
enormon, 22, 183, 186, 237f
Epictetus, 185
Epicurus, Epicureanism, 25, 31, 32, 61, 74, 102, 103, 109, 110, 178, 188, 230, 248
Epinay, vicomte d', 223
"Epître à Mlle A C P," La Mettrie, 102n
"Epître à mon Esprit," La Mettrie, 59n, 102n
Erasmus, Desiderius, 159
esprit recteur, 193, 248
Esquirol, Jean-Etienne Dominique, 130
Essai analytique sur les facultés de l'âme, Bonnet, 91, 123n
Essai sur la liberté de produire ses sentimens, Luzac, 98
Essai sur les facultés de l'âme, anon, 74
Essai sur les règnes de Claude et de Néron, Diderot, 116n
Essai sur l'origine des connaissances humaines, Condillac, 120, 220
Essais de physique, Perrault, 61n, 243f, 245
Essais sur le raisonnement, anon, 41n

INDEX

Essay Concerning Human Understanding, Locke, 62, 66, 204f, 216f
Essay on Man, Pope, 146
Ethica, Spinoza, 63
Euripides, 168
Evangelium medici, Connor, 222
Examen du fatalisme, Pluquet, 111n
Examen du matérialisme, Denesle, 112
Exercitationes medicae quatuor, Gorter, 236

Faculté vengée, La Mettrie, 6
Fénelon, François de la Mothe, 176, 226
Feuerbach, Ludwig, 130
"fille sauvage de Châlons," 173, 222ff
Flourens, Pierre, 130
Fontenelle, Bernard Le Bovier de, 4, 159, 163, 167, 203, 211, 221
Fontenoy, battle of, 4
Fracastor, Hieronymus, 143, 202
François, Laurent, 96, 108ff
Franzen, Adam Wilhelm, 99, 101
Frederick II of Prussia, 1, 2, 4, 5, 7, 8, 9, 11, 12, 95, 131, 204
Freiburg, siege of, 4, 5

Galen, Galenic medicine, 90, 152, 206, 207, 248
Galileo, 206
Gardes, Françaises, 4, 5
Gaston d'Orléans, 173, 224
Gaubius, Hieronymus David, 90ff, 207, 224f, 232, 238
Gauchat, Gabriel, 112
Glisson, Francis, 84f, 88, 234
Gorter, Johann de, 84, 236
Gottingische Zeitungen v. gelehrten Sachen, 101n, 110n, 199, 200
Grammont, duc de, 4
Guise, Henri, duc de, 157, 209

Haeckel, Ernst, 131
Haller, Albrecht von, 80, 82, 85ff, 95, 103, 104, 105, 110, 111, 124, 143ff, 192n, 199ff, 203, 208, 209, 236, 237, 247
Harcourt, collège d', 2
Hartley, David, 122n, 123n
Hartsoeker, Nicolas, 192, 227, 247, 248
Harvey, William, 19, 84, 181, 231f, 234
Hayer, Hubert, 96, 102f
Hecquet, Philippe, 187, 241f
Helvétius, Claude-Adrien, 121, 127, 129
Henri III of France, 157, 210
Hentig, Hans von, 226
Herder, J G. von, 224

Hippocrates, Hippocratic medicine, 22, 152n, 183, 186, 206, 207, 237, 238, 248
Histoire de l'esprit humain, D'Argens, 115n
Histoire naturelle, Buffon, 55
Histoire naturelle de l'âme, La Mettrie, 5, 8, 40, 41ff, 55, 62, 64, 71, 79, 108, 118, 120, 122, 160n, 161n, 189, 200, 204, 206, 213, 214, 217, 219, 221, 222, 224, 226, 237, 246, 247
Histoire naturelle des animaux, Perrault, 215
Historia universale, Bugati, 225
Historia vitae et mortis, Bacon, 181, 232
History of Materialism, Lange, 95n, 130
Hobbes, Thomas, 65, 102, 110, 122n, 123n
Holbach, Paul Dietrich, baron d', 114, 116, 117, 120, 128, 129
Hollman, Samuel Christian, 101
Homme plante, La Mettrie, 11, 50, 55n, 248
Homme plus que machine, Luzac, 105
Hunauld, François-Joseph, 2, 3, 4, 247
Huygens, Christian, 190, 246

iatromechanism, 14, 19, 72, 75ff, 83, 240
idéologues, 125, 128, 129
Impetum faciens dictum Hippocrati, etc, Kaau-Boerhaave, 237
Institutiones rei medicae, Boerhaave, 3, 41, 79f, 85ff, 200, 237, 242, 248
Institutions de physique, Mme du Châtelet, 206
Interprétation de la nature, Diderot, 118
irritability, 18, 19ff, 25, 45, 65, 74, 82ff, 111, 119, 124f, 180ff, 186ff, 201f, 231ff, 234ff, 238, 242, 245f

James, Robert, 229
Jansenism, 2, 10
Jardin du Roi, 2
Journal Chrétien, 102n
Journal des savants, 201, 214
Jussieu, Bernard de, 217, 227

Kaau-Boerhaave, Abraham, 237f
Kraft und Materie, Buchner, 130

La Beaumelle, L. A de, 8n
Lachèvre, Frédéric, 229
La Condamine, Charles Marie de, 223
Lamy, Guillaume, 178, 230
Lancisi, Giovanni, 81, 158, 210
Lange, Friedrich Albert, 95, 96, 130
La Peyronie, François de, 81, 158, 210

· 261 ·

INDEX

Le Camus, Antoine, 92f
Leeuwenhoek, Antony van, 84, 247, 248
Leibniz, Leibnizianism, 13, 14, 59, 63ff, 149, 152, 162, 184, 188, 218f
Lelarge de Lignac, Joseph-Adrien, 96, 106ff
Lemée, Pierre, 1, 4, 102n, 132, 199
Leroy, Julien, 190, 246
Le Sage, Alain René, 241
"Lettre critique à Mme du Châtelet," La Mettrie, 5, 43ff
Lettre d'un anonyme, etc., Hollman, 101n
Lettre sur les aveugles, Diderot, 55, 110
Lettre sur les causes premières, Cabanis, 124
Lettre sur les sourds et muets, Diderot, 220
Lettres critiques, Gauchat, 112
Lettres persanes, Montesquieu, 218
Lettres philosophiques, Voltaire, 66, 206
Lettres sur les physionomies, Pernetti, 70f, 156, 209
Leyden, 6, 75, 87, 97, 137; Eglise Wallonne of, 7; Medical Faculty, 76, 87, 90
Linnaeus, Carl, 147, 203f, 227
Locke, Lockeanism, 13, 23, 28, 42, 48, 49, 62, 66, 93, 102, 121, 122, 127, 129, 149, 150, 157, 161, 167, 191, 204f, 216f, 222, 224
Lower, Richard, 84, 234
Luc, Jacques François de, 18n, 112
Lucretius, 102, 110, 178, 229
Luzac, Elie, 6f, 8, 17, 97f, 105f, 109, 199
Luzac, Etienne, 98f

Magendie, François, 130
Maillet, Benoît de, 55
Maine de Biran, F.-P.-G., 107
Maître, Jean-Marie-Louis, 132
Malebranche, Nicolas, 13, 14, 60f, 73, 107, 145, 149, 152, 167, 176, 184, 188, 203, 221, 227, 238, 239
Malpighi, Marcello, 176, 193, 227, 248
Man a Machine, Needham, 132, 134n
Man not a Machine, Rignano, 132, 133n
Marat, Jean Paul, 117
Maupertuis, Pierre Moreau de, 5, 7, 8, 9, 147, 157, 204, 217, 234, 239, 249
McCulloch, W. S., 135
Mechanique des animaux, Perrault, 61, 188, 245
Médecine de l'esprit, Le Camus, 92f
Mémoires pour servir à l'histoire d'un genre de polypes, Trembley, 217

Memoirs of what passed in Christendom, Temple, 216
Mérope, Voltaire, 203
Mirabaud, Jean-Baptiste de, 74
Moleschott, Jacob, 130
Montesquieu, Charles de Secondat, baron de, 129, 218
Monthly Review, 97
Moral Essays, Pope, 208
Muschenbroek, P. van, 227
Myotomia reformata, Cowper, 231

Napoleon I, 128
Natural History, Pliny, 206
natural law, 53f, 156, 170ff, 179f, 197
Needham, John Turberville, 217, 234
Needham, Joseph, 132, 133
Neumayr, Francisco, 99
Neveu de Rameau, Diderot, 54
Newton, Newtonianism, 17, 29, 61, 66, 147, 168, 191, 227
Nieuwentijd, Bernard, 176, 226, 227
Niklaus, Robert, 227
Nouveau Traité des maladies vénériennes, La Mettrie, 3
Nouvelle bibliothèque germanique, 98n, 110n
Nouvelles libertés de penser, anon., 72f, 82, 112

Ob der Mensch weiter nichts seye als eine Maschine, Neumayr, 99
"Observatio de Scirrho Cerebelli," Haller, 247
"Observationes anatomicae in avibus et cuniculis," Steno, 233
"Observationes circa motum cordis," etc., Steno, 233
Observationes medicae, Tulpius, 213, 239
Observations de médecine pratique, La Mettrie, 3, 40n
Observations on Man, Hartley, 122n
Observations sur les savans incrédules, Luc, 18n, 112
Observationum medicarum rariorum libri VII, Schenk, 224
Ocellus Lucanus, D'Argens, 115n
"Ode an Gessner," Haller, 200
Orang-outang, sive homo sylvestris, Tyson, 214
Ouvrage de Pénélope, La Mettrie, 4, 10, 12, 202, 216, 227, 229, 249

INDEX

Paquet, René, 130
Paracelsus, Theophrastus, 209
Parerga anatomica, Peyer, 235
Paris, Medical Faculty, 3, 230, 241, 243; Parlement de, 5
Pascal, Blaise, 66, 174, 226
Pensées philosophiques, Diderot, 177, 227, 229
Pensées pour et contre les écrivains mécréants, Pury, 99n
peristalsis, 86
Perkins, Jean, 118n
Pernetti, Jacques, 69ff, 209
Perrault, Claude, 61, 74, 188, 215, 243f, 245f
personalism, 107
Petit homme à longue queue, La Mettrie, 105
Petronius, 153, 207
Peyer, Johann Conrad, 84, 234f
Philosophie der Geschichte der Menschheit, Herder, 224
Picavet, François, 129, 131
Pichon, Th., 112
Pièces philosophiques et littéraires, Bouillier, 59n
Pinel, Philippe, 130
Piron, Alexis, 144, 202
Plato, 185, 221, 222, 240
Plessis, collège du, 2
Pliny, the elder, 150, 206
Plouquet, Gottfried, 100f
Pluche, Noël, 150f, 205f
Pluquet, François-André-Adrien, 111
"Poème sur la loi naturelle," Voltaire, 54, 224
Politique du médecin de Machiavel, La Mettrie, 6
polyp, 25, 45, 161, 177f, 181, 188, 194, 217f, 227, 234, 244
Pomponazzi, Pietro, 41
Pope, Alexander, 146, 155, 184, 208
Poritzky, J. E., 96, 131
preformation, 227, 233f, 249
Primae lineae physiologiae, Haller, 236
Prochaska, Georg, 236, 237
Protagoras, 129
Prussian Academy of Sciences, 8, 12, 131, 204
Psychologia empirica et rationalis, Wolff, 104
Pury, Daniel, 99
Pyrrhonism, 16, 167, 179
Pythagoras, Pythagoreans, 185, 221, 240

Rapports du physique et du moral, Cabanis, 123ff
Ray, John, 176, 227
Réaumur, René Antoine de, 201, 217
Rebel, François, 144, 202
Recherche de la vérité, Malebranche, 60, 73, 221, 239
Recherches philosophiques, Saint-Hyacinthe, 68
reflex action, 22, 133, 182f, 234, 236f
"Réflexions sur l'existence de l'âme," anon., 72f
Réfutation d'Helvétius, Diderot, 118, 121
"Réponse à l'auteur de la Machine terrassée," La Mettrie, 102n
Rêve de D'Alembert, Diderot, 117, 118, 119
Rheims, Medical Faculty, 3
Richardson, Jonathan, 144, 203
Rignano, Eugenio, 132
Roche, Antoine-Martin, 108
Roques, Pierre, 98, 110n
Rosenfield, Leonora C., 57n
Rousseau, Jean-Jacques, 129, 208, 218, 220

Saint-Hyacinthe, Thémiseul de, 68
Savioz, Raymond, 91n
Scaliger, Joseph-Juste, 145, 203
Schenk, Johann, 224
Scholasticism, 44, 63, 64, 84
Scotorum historiae, Boece, 225f
Seneca, 153, 207
sensationalism, sensationism, 62, 120ff, 127f, 222
sensorium commune, 80, 81, 210, 212
"Sentimens des philosophes sur la nature de l'âme," anon., 72
"Sermo alter de regimine mentis," Gaubius, 92
Shannon, C. E., 134
Sharp, Samuel, 247
siège de l'âme (sedes animae), 47, 81f, 158, 210
Socrates, 185
Sophocles, 168
sourd de Chartres, 163, 219f
Spectacle de la nature, Pluche, 150, 205
Spinoza, Spinozism, 14, 47, 48, 62f, 101, 109, 110, 177, 228
Spiritualité et immortalité de l'âme, Hayer, 96, 102f
Stahl, Georg Ernst, 18, 87, 133, 187f, 202, 208, 235, 240f, 243
Steele, Richard, 157

INDEX

Steiger, Hans Ludwig, 155, 208f
Steno, Nicholas, 19, 84, 181, 233
Strasbourg, Bibliothèque nationale et universitaire de, 137
Strength of Imagination in Pregnant Women, Blondel, 239
Stuart, Alexander, 84, 236
"Sur la liberté," anon , 73
Surdus loquens, Amman, 214
Swammerdam, Jan, 232, 239
Sydenham, Thomas, 76
Sylva Sylvarum, Bacon, 181n, 232
Système de Boerhaave sur les maladies vénériennes, 3
Système de la nature, D'Holbach, 117, 120
Système d'Epicure, La Mettrie, 11, 23, 50, 55f, 214, 220f

Taine, Hippolyte, 130
Telliamed, Maillet, 55
Témoignage du sens intime, Lelarge de Lignac, 107
Temple, William, 161, 216f
Theoria medica vera, Stahl, 208, 235, 241
Torricelli, Evangelista, 151, 206
Tractatus de corde, Lower, 234
Tracy, Destutt de, 129
Traité de la formation du foetus, Descartes, 248
Traité de la matière médicale, Boerhaave, 3
Traité de la nature de l'âme, Roche, 108
Traité de l'Asthme, La Mettrie, 12
Traité de l'homme, Descartes, 57, 203
Traité des passions de l'âme, Descartes, 57
Traité du Vertige, La Mettrie, 3, 40, 77, 174n, 226
Traité sur la Dyssenterie, La Mettrie, 11
Tralles, Balthasar, 54, 103ff, 113
Trembley, Abraham, 25, 161, 177, 217f, 227, 234, 244

Tressan, comte de, 110n
Trublet, abbé N C. J, 4, 102n
Tuloup, Guy-Francis, 132
Tulpius, Nicolas, 184, 213, 239
Tyrconnel, Lord, 12
Tyson, Edward, 214

Unzer, J. A , 236
Usefulness of Experimental Natural Philosophy, Boyle, 232f

Valkhoff, P , 7n, 199
Van Helmont, J. B., 87, 155, 209, 239
Vanini, Lucilio, 177, 228
Vartanian, Aram, 59n, 229
Vaucanson, Jacques de, 35, 47, 67, 134, 190, 246f
Vénus physique, Maupertuis, 239, 249
Vernière, Paul, 63n
Verworn, Max, 84n, 88n
Vézeaux de Lavergne, Paulin de, 132
Virgil, 188, 231, 244
vitalism, 36, 119, 132f, 134, 209, 240
Vogt, Carl, 130
Voltaire, 9, 11, 33, 54, 62, 66f, 77n, 129, 139, 144, 184, 199, 203, 204, 206, 209, 224, 228
Volupté, La Mettrie, 5, 202
Voyage de Bougainville, Diderot, 54

Wade, Ira, 73n
Walter, Grey, 134
Wepfer, Johann, 84, 87, 235
Whytt, Robert, 235
Widerlegung der französischen Schrift L'Homme Machine, Franzen, 99n
Wiener, Norbert, 135
Willis, Thomas, 61, 74, 83, 158, 159, 188, 210f, 212f, 236, 243, 244f, 247
Wolff, Christian, 64, 104, 152

GPSR Authorized Representative: Easy Access System Europe - Mustamäe tee
50, 10621 Tallinn, Estonia, gpsr.requests@easproject.com

www.ingramcontent.com/pod-product-compliance
Lightning Source LLC
Chambersburg PA
CBHW061438300426
44114CB00014B/1730